Packaged Plants

EMBODYING INEQUALITIES: PERSPECTIVES FROM
MEDICAL ANTHROPOLOGY

Series Editors
Sahra Gibbon, UCL Anthropology
Jennie Gamlin, UCL Institute for Global Health

This series charts diverse anthropological engagements with the changing dynamics of health and wellbeing in local and global contexts. It includes ethnographic and theoretical works that explore the different ways in which inequalities pervade our bodies. The series offers novel contributions often neglected by classical and contemporary publications that draw on public, applied, activist, cross-disciplinary and engaged anthropological methods, as well as in-depth writings from the field. It specifically seeks to showcase new and emerging health issues that are the products of unequal global development.

OTHER TITLES IN THE SERIES

Cancer and the Politics of Care
Edited by Linda Rae Bennett,
Lenore Manderson and Belinda
Spagnoletti
https://doi.org/10.14324/111.9781800080737

Managing Chronicity in Unequal States
Edited by Laura Montesi and
Melania Calestani
https://doi.org/10.14324/111.9781800080287

Viral Loads
Edited by Lenore Manderson,
Nancy J. Burke and Ayo Wahlberg
https://doi.org/10.14324/111.9781800080232

Critical Medical Anthropology
Edited by Jennie Gamlin, Sahra Gibbon,
Paola M. Sesia and Lina Berrío
https://doi.org/10.14324/111.9781787355828

Packaged Plants

*Seductive supplements and
metabolic precarity in the Philippines*

Anita Hardon and Michael Lim Tan

First published in 2024 by
UCL Press
University College London
Gower Street
London WC1E 6BT

Available to download free: www.uclpress.co.uk

Text © Authors, 2024
Images © Authors and copyright holders named in captions, 2024

The authors have asserted their rights under the Copyright, Designs and Patents Act 1988 to be identified as the authors of this work.

A CIP catalogue record for this book is available from The British Library.

Any third-party material in this book is not covered by the book's Creative Commons licence. Details of the copyright ownership and permitted use of third-party material is given in the image (or extract) credit lines. If you would like to reuse any third-party material not covered by the book's Creative Commons licence, you will need to obtain permission directly from the copyright owner.

This book is published under a Creative Commons Attribution-Non-Commercial 4.0 International licence (CC BY-NC 4.0), https://creativecommons.org/licenses/by-nc/4.0/. This licence allows you to share and adapt the work for non-commercial use providing attribution is made to the author and publisher (but not in any way that suggests that they endorse you or your use of the work) and any changes are indicated. Attribution should include the following information:

Hardon, A. and Tan, M. L. 2024. *Packaged Plants: Seductive supplements and metabolic precarity in the Philippines*. London: UCL Press. https://doi.org/10.14324/111.9781800087460

Further details about Creative Commons licences are available at https://creativecommons.org/licenses/

ISBN: 978-1-80008-742-2 (Hbk)
ISBN: 978-1-80008-745-3 (Pbk)
ISBN: 978-1-80008-746-0 (PDF)
ISBN: 978-1-80008-751-4 (epub)
DOI: https://doi.org/10.14324/111.9781800087460

We dedicate this book to the team of World Central Kitchen aid workers who were killed in Gaza, Palestine on 1 April 2024, after delivering food aid. Their philosophy was simple: food is a universal human right, and it is especially important for those displaced by war and natural disasters to have access to 'thoughtfully prepared fresh meals', preferably hot, using local resources and recipes.

We also dedicate this book to Leo Andrew B. Diego, one of our researchers in Puerto Princesa. A valued high school teacher, Leo worked tirelessly to augment his income by selling supplements – until his wife convinced him to stop this 'sideline'. He passed away from acute respiratory failure at the age of 34, leaving behind a wife and two preschool children. We miss him.

Contents

List of figures	viii
List of tables	x
List of abbreviations	xi
Notes on contributors	xiii
Preface	xiv
Acknowledgements	xvii

1 Introduction: Packaged plants and the loss of plant sovereignty in the Philippines 1

Part I: Socio-metabolic shifts and the loss of plant sovereignty

2 Post-colonial metabolic rifts 35

   Photo Essay 1: Living on the edge: food and precarity among Filipino urban poor 63

3 Attributing therapeutic efficacies to plant materials 71

4 Reading the scripts 95

Part II: Socio-metabolic precarity and work in a rural boomtown

5 'Be your product': metabolic precarities in Puerto Princesa 125

6 Endgame 153

Part III: Proposals for repair

7 Towards plant sovereignty: proposals for repair 179

   Photo Essay 2: Bringing plant sovereignty to town 211

References	227
Index	241

List of figures

1.1	The entrance to Palawan First Vita Plus product centre and a promotional poster.	2
1.2	Lyrics from 'Bahay Kubo', a popular children's song.	13
1.3	Lagundi (*Vitex negundo*).	16
1.4	Advertisements for Hemo drink and Blueband margarine, from the 10 July 1948 issue of *Philippines Free Press*.	22
2.1	Picture of a popular brand of noodles. Bulalo is a popular meat dish in the Philippines, considered to be *sustansiya* or nutrient-rich because it contains bone marrow. Lucky Me is a best-selling brand of Monde, a Philippine-Indonesian company.	41
2.2	Chow Mein noodles – natural flavours and no MSG added.	42
2.3	Left: Community 'sari-sari' store selling highly processed breakfast snacks for school children. Right: Nutritional content of Muncher Green Peas.	44
2.4	Indigenous cultivation of brown rice in the Northern Cordillera Region, where people prefer their own rice over the milled rice, the staple for lowland Filipinos.	45
2.5	Malunggay (Moringa) tree.	47
2.6	A billboard along a highway in Metro Manila.	49
2.7	Package of MNP food supplement, produced as 'Vita Meena'.	52
2.8	Unilever-sponsored conference bag, from the 2014 conference of the Philippine Society of Nutritionists and Dieticians.	53
2.9	Image from the Pinggang Pinoy campaign.	56
2.10	Image from the Pinggang Pinoy campaign.	56
2.11	Breakfast packaging waste found on roadside in Puerto Princesa.	58
3.1	Locally sourced lagundi syrup.	78
3.2	Lagundi Leaf, ASCOF Forte package (front and back).	80
3.3	A First Vita Plus sachet, designed to meet consumer preference for small packages of specialty goods.	84

3.4	Screenshots from promotional video 'First Vita Plus – Dr Jaime Galvez Tan' posted by a First Vita Plus distributor.	85
3.5	An information leaflet for Vida! supplement.	89
3.6	Image heading the DSM leaflet for resVida.	90
3.7	Graphs shown in DSM product information for resVida.	90
3.8	The *Tuklas Lunas* program framework, 2017–22.	93
4.1a & b	(Top) Front of Extra Joss Suplemen Makanan (food supplement) sachet, sold in Indonesia, Malaysia, the Philippines. (Bottom): Back of the same sachet.	99
4.2	Cobra advertisement.	100
4.3	Robust, a supplement for sexual stamina (product sample, front).	100
4.4	Robust, a supplement for sexual stamina (product sample packaging).	101
4.5a & b	Front and back of a First Vita Plus sachet, in dalandan flavour.	103
4.6	Malunggay capsules.	104
4.7	Watsons Mangosteen + Malunggay capsules, with the image of a mangosteen fruit.	105
4.8	Manna Plus with moringa, online advertisement.	105
4.9	Manna Plus supports farmers and plants malunggay trees.	106
4.10	Promotional leaflet for C24/7 including information on its metabolic action, contents and benefits.	107
4.11	GDetoxPlus product information.	109
4.12	Black seed capsules and seeds used to prevent COVID-19.	112
4.13	Lola Remedios.	112
4.14	Tolak Angin, repackaged for the Philippines, including a front image of the package, and one side panel.	113
4.15	Text provided inside the packaging of Lola Remedios.	114
4.16	FDA warning about unregistered food supplements.	116
5.1	First Vita Plus promotional poster, from the First Vita Plus product centre in Puerto Princesa.	126
5.2	Nurse Pam explaining the potentials of the herbs in First Vita Plus.	133
5.3	Detoxification leaflet, featuring Dr Rolan Mendiola, given to attendees during the seminar.	134
5.4	Poster advertising Power Pack discount (left) and attendees buying boxes of First Vita Plus (right).	135

5.5	The benefits of the five power herbs, presented in a YouTube video of a 2020 First Vita Plus Health Symposium, led by Dr Roland Mendiola.	137
5.6	The front cover of the booklet of testimonials that Ms Venhoff had collected (left) and one of the testimonials (right).	138
5.7	Example of a testimonial compiled by Ms Venhoff.	138
5.8	AIM Global Business Center in downtown Puerto Princesa.	140
5.9	Guapa Rich Health Center, in a residential Puerto Princesa neighbourhood.	141
5.10	C24/7 content, as listed on the production information in the C24/7 welcome pack, bought in 2014 at the AIM Global business Center.	143
5.11	C24/7 product information.	143
5.12	The promise of C24/7.	144
5.13	The AIM Global welcome pack.	146
5.14	Anita Hardon's CardioPulseR test result.	147
6.1	The business opportunities offered by AIM Global and First Vita Plus.	154
6.2	A local trainer explaining how distributors can earn money by recruiting down-lines.	161
6.3	Leo talking to Flor in her backyard (left), where she grows chillies (right).	164
6.4	Earning by recruiting.	166

List of tables

2.1	Percentage of stunted infants in the Philippines (2008–15).	39
2.2	The top-ranking countries for servings of noodles per year (unit: million servings).	40
5.1	Puerto Princesa statistics for infectious and cardiovascular disease.	131

List of abbreviations

AIM	Alliance in Motion
AMWAY	American Way
CBHP	Community-based health programme
CBMS	Community-based monitoring system
CGF	Chlorella Growth Factor
CHW	Community health workers
DDB	Dangerous Drugs Board
DoE	Department of Education
DoH	Department of Health
DoST	Department of Science and Technology
DSAP	Direct Selling Association of the Philippines
FDA	Food and Drug Administration
FNRI	Food and Nutrition Research Institute
FTC	Federal Trade Commission
GRAS	Generally recognized as safe
HOMA	Homeostasis Model Assessment
IPCC	Intergovernmental Panel on Climate Change
IU	International Unit
LTO	License to Operate
MIMAROPA	Mindoro Oriental & Occidental, Marinduque, Romblon, and Palawan
MIMS	Monthly Index of Medical Specialties
MLM	Multilevel marketing
MNP	Micronutrient powder
MSG	Monosodium glutamate
NAST	National Academy of Science and Technology
NFWC	The National Federation of Women's Clubs
NGO	Non-governmental organization
NIRPROMP	National Integrated Research Program on Medicinal Plants
PIMS	Philippine Index of Medical Specialties
PITAHC	Philippine Institute of Traditional and Alternative Health Care
PPAN	Philippines Plan of Action for Nutrition
SPHC	Selective primary health care

TAMA	Traditional and Alternative Medicines Act
TB	Tuberculosis
TCM	Traditional Chinese medicine
TPN	Total Parenteral Nutrition
UNESCO	United Nations Educational, Scientific and Cultural Organization
UNICEF	United Nations Children's Fund
UTI	Urinary tract infection
WHO	World Health Organization
WINA	World Instant Noodles Association

Notes on contributors

Anita Hardon is a medical anthropologist. She is Department Chair of the Knowledge, Technology and Innovation group at Wageningen University and Professor of Anthropology at the University of Amsterdam. She was co-author (with Susan Reynolds Whyte and Sjaak van der Geest) of *Social Lives of Medicines* (University of Chicago Press, 2002) and (with Emilia Sanabria) of 'Fluid drugs: Revisiting the anthropology of pharmaceuticals' for the *Annual Review of Anthropology* (2017). In 2016, Hardon was elected Fellow of the Royal Netherlands Academy of Arts and Sciences. She was a fellow at the Centre for Advanced Study in the Behavioural Sciences (CASBS) at Stanford University in 2019–20.

Michael Lim Tan is Emeritus Professor of Anthropology at the University of the Philippines, where he served as Chancellor from 2014 to 2020. In 2012, he was elected to the Philippines' National Academy of Science and Technology as National Academician. Since 1997, he has been writing an op-ed column for the *Philippine Daily Inquirer*, the country's largest English newspaper.

Francesca Mauricio* is an early-career researcher with an interest in the applications of anthropological thought in environmental, health, and urban development. She completed her bachelor's degree in Anthropology from the University of the Philippines Diliman in 2024.

Denice Salvacion* is a researcher for the Embodied Ecologies Project and senior lecturer in the School of Fine Arts and Design at the Philippine Women's University. She graduated with a BFA in Visual Communication at the University of the Philippines Diliman and is currently finishing her master's thesis in anthropology, focusing on the intersections between art, anthropology and urban studies.

*Co-writers for Photo Essay 2.

Preface

One early morning when I (Michael) was busy working at home on the final edits for this book, I decided to check our kitchen to see what our housekeeper was preparing for breakfast. I did this with some trepidation because I could guess, from the smell, what she was cooking. Indeed, she was frying several hot dogs and at her feet were three of our dogs – one a dachshund – doing their puppy eyes routine in anticipation of getting their share of the loot.

'Giatay!', I exclaimed, the term is from Cebuano, a southern Philippine language, and it roughly means 'Oh my liver!' to express surprise, shock, dismay. I reminded her that we had already talked about dietary norms in my household – my being vegetarian, and my wanting my children to grow up healthy even if they are not vegetarian, so the instructions were to minimize ultra-processed foods (UPF) like instant noodles, fast food, 'forever foods' (don't they ever perish?) and of course, hot dogs.

The real dogs were still sitting listening to our conversation, probably hopeful that my lecture would force our cook to throw away the hot dogs.

This time I told her that I'd been so busy working on a book about food and had come across so many studies about the danger of hot dogs and other UPFs. I didn't want to bandy terms like metabolic syndrome, so I chose something more familiar: cancer.

She was apologetic, but defensive: 'But the hot dogs were not for you or for your children. It was for me and the driver.'

I quickly retorted, 'But I don't want you or the driver to be put at risk for cancer!'

She had the final say, an enthusiastic 'thank you' for my concern, but I couldn't help but feel there was a tinge of cynicism, if not sarcasm, in her thanks.

That incident reminded me I had to finish the preface for this book, where I started by referring to a *British Medical Journal* (*BMJ*) article featuring a massive umbrella study of previously published meta-analyses that involved, in total, 9.9 million people. I was alerted to the *BMJ* article by a feature in the British newspaper *The Guardian*, headlined 'Ultra-processed food linked to 32 harmful effects to health, review finds' (Gregory 2024).

The title and tone of the *BMJ* article was more sedate but still alarming. In a summary of their findings, the authors of the article said that a 'direct association (was) found between exposure to UPF and 32 health parameters covering mortality, cancer, mental, respiratory, cardiovascular, gastrointestinal and metabolic health outcomes'. Furthermore, the authors pointed to other studies suggesting other linkages between UPF and ill health, especially in terms of chronic inflammatory diseases (Lane et al. 2024).

The article made Anita and me pause: should we further delay the book and add more materials on UPF as found in the *BMJ* article?

Anita and I decided not to delay. UPF did figure prominently in our book, but as part of a spectrum of metabolic rifts or ways through which plant-based food and medicines have, through new forms of production, processing, marketing and consumption, created numerous problems not just around nutrition and health but also in exacerbating social inequities.

But the 'hot dogs incident' reminded me of the real world out there and the difficult tasks that lie ahead. How can the *BMJ* article's findings be disseminated and spur people to take action? How do we translate terms like 'danger' and 'risk'?

The odds are tremendous given the way science is eclipsed by advertising and promotions, including multilevel marketing that pushes vitamin-minerals, supplements and UPFs. Alternative information and education on healthy eating have few platforms available, especially since even scientists and professionals are often captives of the metabolic rifts we describe in our book, the loss of plant sovereignty or control over our food and medicines.

The poor are put at greatest risk in the way their food sources are now limited to the packaged UPFs, including beverages like soft drinks. Our packaged plants theme took on more urgency as we found a growing body of literature describing how the packaging themselves are problematic, plastics especially endangering the health of people, of non-human animals, and the planet itself. Solutions to malnutrition, a paradox of underweight and stunting on one hand and of overweight on the other, take on the character of UPFs with fortification programmes, with an emphasis on micro-nutrient deficiencies that further expand the market for vitamins and minerals.

Going through voluminous research reports reminded us about how we are lagging behind in the race for better nutrition and health and why we need more foresight, anticipating other problems on the horizon. An article by Wickramasinghe et al., published in 2021, warns that even plant-based nutrition is being co-opted, and urges greater regulation of the many plant-based products that have appeared on the market, riding on the search for 'organic' and 'natural' foods, preferably packaged. Wickramasinghe and his associates note that many of these new plant-based products are in fact UPFs, with the same problems of high salt, sugar and fats found in meat-based UPFs (Wickramasinghe et al. 2021).

Even nutritionists and health professionals are still unfamiliar with the term 'UPF' despite its having been introduced and defined several years ago (Monteiro et al. 2019). So much advocacy work will involve translation, and not necessarily from one language to another but in terms of demystifying the jargon. Advocacy will also involve dissemination of good practices in the many fields related to nutrition and health.

As we finalized our preface, local newspapers featured still another relevant article, this time about scams in the Philippines involving supplements claiming unsubstantiated anti-cancer properties for their products. One patient diagnosed with breast cancer said that she spent some $909 US per month for the supplements and agreed to chemotherapy only after her cancer metastasized.

We were touched by the valiant efforts of individuals to counteract the scams. A Filipino oncologist working in a government hospital said, 'five out of 10 patients I see ask me about something they have seen or read on the internet – 90 percent of the time the information is incorrect'.

When Adam, a Melbourne-based Australian doctor, began to post YouTube videos countering the misleading claims of supplement manufacturers, he was threatened with lawsuits by the companies. He has since quit his advocacy.

Agence France Presse (AFP) has been conducting investigations of online promotions of supplements and reporting the deceitful promotions to Meta, the parent company of Facebook, which is widely used by the unethical supplements producers. Even when flagged for their false claims, the companies will take down their promotions temporarily and then bring them back.

The Philippines Food and Drug Administration says it is helpless, with one official saying that it still does not have implementing guidelines on online advertising to accompany the law that created (actually, reorganized) the FDA in 2006.

Both of us (Anita and Michael) became grandparents as we finished writing this book, feeling a greater sense of urgency than when we began to write it, realizing that we will face even tougher questions from future generations who will assess what we did, and didn't do, in these times of metabolic rifts.

Acknowledgements

Many people helped make this book possible. We would like to name those who made the most crucial contributions:

Our interlocutors who over the years have patiently shared their experiences, stories and views with us, as well as our families who put up with us spending long hours in the early mornings, evening and weekends writing it all up.

Michael Doblado, Alvie Timbancaya, Ian Anthony Davatos, Leo Diego, Floralice Josol, Ralph Pulanco of the Palawan Studies Center and Gideon Lasco and Madel Landicho of the Anthropology department of the University of the Philippines, for participating in collaborative inquiry on MLM in Puerto Princesa.

Takeo David Hymans for incisive editing of earlier versions of book chapters, and Helen Faller for carefully editing the full manuscript to the point that it could be submitted to UCL Press, and for giving such valuable suggestions on the book's core concepts and arguments.

The anonymous peer reviewers, the series editors Sahra Gibbon and Jennie Gamlin and, at UCL Press, the commissioning editor Chris Penfold for encouraging and constructive feedback; assistant editor Elliot Beck and copy editor Katharine Norman for efficient work on the final submission.

In the Philippines, we also received valuable advice on legal aspects from Fides Cordero-Tan, attorney, former Dean of the University of the Philippines (UP) College of Law, and Dr. Lee Edson Yarcia (MD, JD), Senior Lecturer at the UP College of Law.

Special thanks go to two researchers, Hayley Murray in the Netherlands and Denice Alyssa Salvacion in the Philippines, helping with what the Dutch call 'monks' work', digging up all the minute bits and pieces of information that allowed us to stitch the book together. We also thank Denice for her creative design used on the cover.

The European Research Council funded research for this book within the Chemical Youth (ERC-2012-AdvG-323646) and Embodied Ecologies (ERC-2021-AdvG-101054300) projects, and the UP System extended an Enhanced Creative Work and Research Grant (ECWRG) to Michael to work on a cultural history of vitamins and supplements in the Philippines.

1
Introduction: Packaged plants and the loss of plant sovereignty in the Philippines

In 2014 we started conducting fieldwork in Puerto Princesa, the rapidly growing capital city on the remote, rainforest-covered island of Palawan in the Philippines. The plan was to conduct fieldwork with a team of researchers from Palawan State University on the chemicals that young people use to boost pleasure, mood, vitality, appearance and health. On one of our first walks around the city to take stock of the chemicals on sale in the town, we stumbled upon the First Vita Plus product centre.

We were surprised. We had heard about First Vita Plus a decade earlier, when colleagues told us that Dr Jaime Galvez Tan, with whom we had worked in community-based health programmes (CBHPs) in the 1980s, was developing a 'blockbuster' herbal supplement through a local multilevel marketing company. The CBHPs encouraged villagers to use nutritious and medicinal plants from forests, community gardens and their own backyards to decrease their reliance on packaged herbal supplements. Consequently, Tan's partnership with the multilevel marketing company raised eyebrows among some of our former colleagues. We were collectively opposed to packaging plants into commodities to be sold as part of profit-driven, mass consumption schemes. We had not expected his invention to gain much traction.

Mounting the stairs of the product centre, we encountered a receptionist in what appeared to be a seminar hall, selling boxes of First Vita Plus in a wide variety of flavours. The walls were covered with pictures of plants. Posters proclaimed First Vita Plus as an 'outstanding natural health drink' that protects a person against 28 diseases, including asthma, diabetes, cancer and psoriasis (see Figure 1.1).

Figure 1.1 The entrance to Palawan First Vita Plus product centre and a promotional poster. Source: Author (Hardon), 2013.

Our co-researchers in Puerto Princesa, working as young lecturers and researchers at Palawan State University, told us that many young people in the town had become invested in selling First Vita Plus, and that many trusted the health value of the product because it was made from five Filipino herbs and developed by a (now-famous) Filipino doctor. We were shocked to find First Vita Plus, which cost $0.80 US per sachet, so popular in Puerto Princesa, where people had little disposable income – the minimum wage being only $6 US per day.

Why would people with easy access to abundant natural resources turn to a supplement like First Vita Plus to shore up their health? Why would they invest scarce resources in seemingly superfluous substances? Why would they engage with a multilevel marketing company to sell a product to prevent a plethora of health conditions when the product has no proven efficacy?

The reasons are complex. Answering them requires a fine-grained ethnography that looks deeply into changing modes of living in Puerto Princesa and the Philippines as a whole. In the analysis this ethnography engenders, we use a socio-metabolic framework (Hardon et al. 2019) to examine changing relations between people and their environments, particularly people's relationships with the plants they use for various purposes, including food and medicine (Chen 2009).

The concept of metabolism as a framework for analysing socio-ecological change emerged in the mid-nineteenth century, when Karl Marx used it to refer to the material and energetic exchanges between humans and nature. Marx's analysis in *Capital* (Marx 1977) focuses on the metabolic nature of labour and the ecological depletion caused by the emergence of capitalist modes of agricultural production and urbanization. Inspired by the influential soil chemist Justus von Liebig (1863), who in the mid-nineteenth century used *stoffwechsel* (metabolism) to refer to nutrient loss in agricultural systems, Marx (1977, 637) pointed out how capitalist production collects the population in urban centres, disturbing 'the circulation of matter between man and the soil'.

Marx's metabolic framework has inspired generations of social scientists to examine the way capitalist accumulation changes relations between agriculture and food provisioning and creates ecological crises. Foster (2000) was the first to introduce the term 'metabolic rift' to refer to the separation between humans and natural conditions. In particular, he wrote about the antagonistic division between town and country (urban and rural) as an alternative frame for looking at the climate crisis. Food production and consumption is seen as being oriented mainly towards cities, using industrial processes that are mainly extractive and disrupt the renewal of resources (Moore 2015; Foster 2000).

Moore (2015, 178) moves on from Foster and writes about how the agricultural revolution increased the number of calories specific amounts of labour produced and led to a 'shake-out of uncompetitive farmers' and the expulsion of 'superfluous' populations from the land but goes further to critique Foster and the 'Green Marxists' for separating nature and humans, preferring to use the term 'web of life', which includes nature and humans together, as being disrupted. The rift, he says, consists of reconfigurations and shifts (Moore 2017).

Moore defines metabolic shifts as the way science is practised, for example imperial projects to map and catalogue natural products of every kind for the benefit of colonialism, including field expeditions to catalogue the economic use of plants for food and medicine, in particular.

The simplest way of differentiating our usage of the two terms: metabolic rift is the over-all change, the separation or alienation of humans from natural conditions, while metabolic shifts are changes in ideas and practices – in this book, as they relate to nutrition and health.

We continue the discourse on socio-metabolic rifts and shifts by showing how, in the Philippines, the resulting processes of urbanization and the emergence of surplus service-sector labour resulting from the agricultural revolution combine to fuel the demand for packaged plants, by which we mean plants and plant by-products that have been processed, through various technologies, into products with claims as food, supplements and medicines. Our particular concern would be vitamins, supplements and ultra-processed foods. We concur with

Moore's analysis of metabolic shifts as epistemic shifts that have great impact on research, on capitalist production and commodification and the very practice of medicine and nutrition. The language of metabolic shifts is therefore used to facilitate the flows of power and capital in the metabolic rifts, with far-reaching impacts on social life such as between colonizing powers and the colonized, as well as metabolic precarities or exposure to risks, financially and health-wise.

González de Molina and Toledo (2014) take stock of empirical studies and conceptual work that most English-language researchers miss, calling on scholars to broaden their socio-metabolic frameworks to incorporate understandings of how information flows, institutional dynamics and technology shape socio-metabolic transformations. Their theoretical approach inspires our analysis of the influence of global exchanges of plants (transplantation) and the accompanying transformations of social relations around food, nutrition and health that government policies enact. Their approach likewise helps us examine what brought packaged plants into existence: changes in science and technology – the industrial revolution that began in the nineteenth century – with their far-reaching impact on the production, distribution and consumption of food and medicines.

In what follows, we focus on the complex pathways through which socio-metabolic transformations culminate in a loss of both plant sovereignty and control over valuable natural resources, including knowledge of how to use those resources. In this introductory chapter, we present our analysis of the erosion of plant sovereignty. In Part I (Chapters 2–4), we describe in detail how nutritional policies created a demand for packaged plants in the Philippines. We also outline how well-meaning efforts to reappropriate plants in community healthcare projects initially shaped plants' emergence as health commodities, which subsequent ethnopharmacological research seeking to determine their medicinal properties intensified, before the industry capture of packaged plants commodified them as a health panacea for metabolic precarity.

Part II focuses on our ethnographic case study exploring the popularity and marketing of packaged plants in Puerto Princesa (Chapters 5–6). We develop the approaches of urban political ecologists who call for learning from the perspectives of people from the Global South (Tzaninis et al. 2020), as well as the ecological knowledge local actors produce, including their embodied experiences and metabolic practices (Heynen 2006; Loftus 2012). We illustrate the particularities of the rapidly changing urban environment in Puerto Princesa. These include a loss of plant sovereignty caused by diminished access to land, worries about the nutritional deficiencies of processed foods, the changing rhythms of everyday life (Lefebvre 2004), increased access to smartphones and social media, and environmental pollution (Moore 2015), all of which fuel the demand for supplements. In these chapters, we build on a powerful example of metabolic shifts in the insightful analytical work of Hannah Landecker (2013), who points out that, in the new millennium, scientific understandings of the body have moved away from the (Marxist) conceptualization of it as a motor in need of calories, to one that depicts the body as a complex set of biochemical interactions which, if disturbed, cause metabolic health conditions, such as obesity and diabetes. Her work is based on what is happening in the United States, where post-industrial capitalism goes through a shift in explaining diabetes and obesity (so-called fat information) and which translates into new directions in research and development activities for pharmaceuticals, as we are seeing with the drug semaglutide, so new on the market and yet already with two best-selling brands: Ozempic and Wegovy.

We also refer to the work of Harris Solomon (2016), who, in his seminal book, *Metabolic Living*, depicts the processes of metabolic absorption in Mumbai, providing a thick description of how people experience the city as a stressor. Stress can itself contribute to metabolic syndromes and, like metabolic disorders such as type 2 diabetes, may be exacerbated by factors such as nutritionally deficient diets or heat and air pollution in dense urban centres. Our ethnographic work looks at metabolic shifts in terms of popular discourse around stress, coming from consumers as well as from multilevel companies capitalizing on the anxieties around stress and a perception that these are connected to illnesses.

We also critique nutritionism as another example of a metabolic shift, where nutritional health is reduced to identifying specific deficiencies, especially of vitamins and minerals, to be solved through fortification, which created niches for supplements and vitamin/mineral preparations. Ultraprocessed foods are, likewise, products of the metabolic shifts, using industrial technology to produce cheap food to maintain cheap labour, but at great costs in terms of health risks (Lane et al. 2024).

Long-term ethnographic engagements

We write this book based on our long-term engagement with medicinal plants, nutrition, pharmaceuticals and health in the Philippines. Having both received our first degrees in the natural sciences, we continued to graduate degrees in anthropology. Our approach favours ethnographic conversations, which entail constantly engaging people in discussions of contemporary social issues and their social contexts. We use the term 'interlocutors' (Gay and Wardle 2019) rather than 'informants', to emphasize the dynamic exchanges that comprise our ethnography.

Initially trained as a veterinarian, after his graduation from the University of the Philippines in 1977, Michael was working on medicinal plants when he was offered a research project looking into their efficacy for CBHPs. Having grown up in the city, he had to learn about plants from libraries, researchers of natural products and traditional healers. Reflecting on this process now, he recognizes the importance of learning from the vendors in Quiapo, a district in central Manila and a hub for public transportation connecting to points all over the National Capital Region. Quiapo's Basilica of the Black Nazarene attracts thousands of devotees each day, who come to pray and touch the statue, and to visit the market outside the church. There, in addition to crucifixes, rosaries and prayer books, many vendors sell items used in witchcraft and healing: candles, amulets, love charms and an array of plant medicines. During fieldwork in the late 1970s, Michael observed vendors' willingness to dispense advice, not just about health but also on life's many uncertainties. For example, unfaithful husbands, the vendors told him, made for a brisk trade not only in love charms to bring back the unfaithful partners but also in a plant-derived powder to sprinkle in their underwear, causing itching and pain. When all else failed, vendors would sell the women black candles in the form of a human body, euphemistically referred to as *pang-konsensiya*, to prick the conscience of unfaithful partners. Michael subsequently conducted research on medicinal plants in Mindanao and in the Cordillera Region in the northern Philippines, producing self-care manuals that aimed to reconnect people with the therapeutic potential of plants.

Anita, trained as a medical biologist, turned to medical anthropology in graduate school. In the 1980s, conducting fieldwork on a coconut plantation in the Philippines to research malnutrition and children's health, she noticed that the everyday meals of families in this poor community mostly consisted of plants from their backyards. People generally lacked cash, but they did have bananas, papayas, *kalamansi* (local limes), cassava, bitter gourd, eggplant, okra, red peppers, tamarind, string beans, tomatoes and multiple kinds of green leafy vegetables, all foods that have long comprised the Filipino diet. Living for a year among agricultural workers on the coconut plantation, Anita became aware of the popularity of Western pharmaceuticals in self-care. Local sari-sari, (informal) stores, sold a range of cough, cold and anti-diarrheal medicines, and antibiotics. An article she published exploring these self-medication practices led to an invitation from Jaime Galvez Tan to work with the CBHPs to examine why, despite their emphasis on using herbal medicines in self-care, people in the Philippines were still so attracted to Western pharmaceuticals.

Anita and Michael first met at a CBHP gathering, in 1984, when Anita presented her new project on how people in communities where CBHP programmes were active were responding to the promotion of herbal medicines for self-care. We return to our early experiences with the CBHPs in Chapter 3.

Without fail, we both combined engagement in critical medical anthropology with health advocacy, collaborating closely with community organizations and always working with teams of young researchers. We were active members of Health Action International in the 1980s and 1990s (of which Anita was chair for many years), lobbying for drug policies to promote the use of essential drugs – safe, effective, affordable and needed – and empowering communities with education about health and nutrition. Our work often entailed tackling Big Pharma. In the 1990s, we acquired funds from the European Union to do further studies on the use of medicines in communities, which involved grounded ethnographic research, observing and talking with people to understand how they confronted common illnesses (Hardon 1991; Tan 1999).

Straddling our role as ethnographers (we are both academic medical anthropologists) and advocates, we found ourselves continuously dealing with ambiguities and counter-currents. When the movements in which we participated called for banning cough syrups that only provide symptomatic relief and were easily replaced by ginger root concoctions, we pointed out that cough syrups don't require the use of scarce firewood to prepare, and take less time to acquire, and this made them more convenient for the urban poor. We also pointed out that people needed the quick symptomatic relief that cough syrups provided, because they could not afford to lose even one day's work.

Over the past 40 years, we have continued to conduct fieldwork in the Philippines, in a series of multi-sited ethnographic inquiries, while also teaching at our respective universities in the Philippines (Michael) and Amsterdam (Anita). We are both heavily involved in mentoring, to pass on and innovate skills in social research and inquiry. Michael's doctoral dissertation published as *Good Medicines: Pharmaceuticals and the construction of power and knowledge in the Philippines* (Tan 1999) analyses how the commodification of health occurs during the making and marketing of pharmaceuticals. Anita co-authored *Social Lives of Medicines* with Susan Whyte-Reynolds and Sjaak van der Geest (Whyte et al. 2002). Over the years, we increasingly became interested in material cultures, and analysing how the advertising and packaging of medicines and vitamins reflect key societal concerns (Hardon et al. 2008; Pordié and Hardon 2015).

This book applies our theoretical understandings of pharmaceutical anthropology to the booming field of food supplements. It was our encounter with First Vita Plus in Puerto Princesa in 2014 that alerted both of us to the importance of food supplements in people's everyday heath-seeking practices – an area we had somewhat neglected in our scholarly work. Chapters 5 and 6 present ethnographic findings from the Chemical Youth project. This project was funded by a European Research Grant (2013–18), which provided resources for Anita's fieldwork with a research team from Palawan State University on the multilevel marketing of food supplements in Puerto Princesa, and a University of the Philippines grant received by Michael, to fund research on the cultural history of vitamins.

The pandemic lockdowns in 2020–2 gave us the time to update our knowledge of ethnobotany and familiarize ourselves with the emerging historical accounts of socio-metabolic shifts and rifts – sharing notes during regular Zoom meetings. This engagement helped us better understand how food supplements could become so popular in a region of the Philippines where people have such easy access to abundant natural resources.

Erosion of plant sovereignty in the Philippines

Ethnobotanical studies in the Philippines provide insights into what gets lost when people turn to packaged plants to supplement their diets and promote health. Ethnobotanists have documented the abundance of fruits, vegetables, root crops and mushroom varieties that people in the Philippines collect and cultivate as food, especially among indigenous communities that live in or near forests. They note that such communities have both a practical understanding of plants and an affective engagement with them, knowing where to find them and how to tell when they are ripe, through appearance, scent and touch. Traditionally, mothers and grandmothers taught young people how to prepare plants as food or as medicine. As a result, Filipinos ate a large variety of backyard fruits and vegetables as well as wild plants, which together comprised a healthy and diverse diet for adults and children (Laderman 1983).

The Philippines is one of 18 extremely biodiverse countries in the world, which together contain two-thirds of the earth's biodiversity and 70–80 per cent of the world's plant and animal species.[1] This biodiversity includes a large variety of plants and fungi that provide both food security and access to medicines in various Filipino ecosystems, reflected in the breadth of traditional dietary and herbal medicinal practices. As noted elsewhere (Etkin and Ross 1983; McNamara and Prasad 2013; Chen 2009), Filipinos use both cultivated and wild plants as food and to promote health.

Abe and Ohtani's (2013) study on Batan Island in the northernmost part of the Philippines found that *Carica papaya* (papaya), *Musa sapientum* (bananas), *Moringa oleifera* (*malunggay*, or moringa), and *Cocos nucifera* (coconuts) are all consumed as part of people's everyday diets, while also being used as medicinal plants. In Kalinga in northern Luzon, where the recipe for First Vita Plus allegedly originated, researchers found that of six popular medicines, three were also eaten as food: *bawang* (garlic), *bayabas* (guava), and *ampalaya* (bitter gourd) (Ammakiw and Odiem 2014). Chua-Barcelo (2014) notes that their interlocutors used 36 different wild and cultivated fruit species as ingredients for cooking, condiments, and snacks, as well as in brewing alcohol and treating common ailments. Many studies indicate that the fruits and vegetables collected in forests and cultivated in backyards are sold in local markets as a source of extra income.

Gayao et al. (2018) note that people rely on 20 different kinds of roots and tubers (including arrowroot, now in global demand as a 'superfood') as vegetables and staple foods, and sometimes sell or barter them at local markets or on the roadside to bus passengers. Corazon and Licyayo (2018) examine the gathering of wild edible mushrooms, which have recently become a delicacy in the region's tourist spots, in the mountainous Cordillera Region. They identified 23 genera of wild edible fungi, typically gathered by men and boys as they walk to and from their swidden farms or collect firewood in the forest.

Many of these studies demonstrate that food and medicinal practices have other social implications. Corazon and Licyayo (2018) describe how gathering mushrooms is sometimes a family activity, especially during the rainy season, when mushrooms are abundant. They recount how elderly family members are consulted to confirm whether the mushrooms are edible, while mothers prepare them for family meals and take the surpluses to the local market along with a variety of root crops, such as ginger, to generate income. A study in Guimaras, a rural island in the Visayas Region, found that families use 69 wild edible plants and that children are not just fed but also forage for fruits on their own (Ong and Kim 2016), a practice that nutritional studies of food intake tend to overlook (Fleuret 1986).[2] On Guimaras, people attested to the importance of root crops in times of crisis, praising them for being 'bulky, heavy and fill[ing] the stomach', in contrast to rice (Ong and Kim 2016, 15).

These ethnobotanical observations in the Philippines are remarkably like those made by Tsing (2004) while conducting research on neighbouring Borneo, an island to which the Philippines is linked through the ecological bridge of Palawan. Tsing observes that people living in the Meratus Mountains use a wide range of different plants as food and medicines, distinguishing less between species of plants and more between 'planted plants' (*tanaman*) and plants that 'grow themselves', similar to the distinction between annual and perennial plants. The boundaries are fluid, though, as wild plants can be 'planted' by deliberately burying seeds. Tsing (2004, 155) writes:

> The most amazing thing about a Meratus swidden field is the extraordinary numbers of plants growing together in the same small spot. There may be trees saved from the forest that was cut to make the field: fruit trees, honey trees, sugar palms. Fallen trunks and stumps, sometimes resprouting, litter the ground. Between them grow an exuberance of plants: not only grains, such as rice, corn, millet and job's tears, but root crops, such as taro, cassava, and sweet potatoes, as well as beans crawling up the stumps, eggplant bushes five feet high, dense clumps of sugar cane, spreading squashes, gangling banana and papaya trees, gingers and basils and medicinal plants, and on and on.

People cherish this diversity, the multiple varieties of bananas and mangos, each with their own flavours and properties that inform harvesting practices and consumption. For instance, small chilli peppers are harvested for sale in nearby markets, where they are in high demand. Tsing (2004, 155) concludes: 'Meratus grow many kinds of crops because they value variety for its taste, for the sociability it allows, for its sheer exuberance, and because it increases the chances of a bountiful harvest.'

Taste acquires particular importance when plants are used medicinally. Gollin (2004), working among the Kenyah Leppo'ke of Borneo, elicited people's criteria for evaluating the uses of medicinal plants and found they included a long list of sensory attributes, each correlating with what the plant could do. Bitter (*pait*) plants, for example, 'chased illness out of the body' and were used to treat stomach aches, skin infections and dental caries. *Pait* plants also worked by 'shrinking and compressing' and were employed to facilitate childbirth. Traditional knowledge of plants and their uses may thus be extensive, including an awareness of plants' natural habitats and a multisensory approach, including smell and taste, to identifying plants and their uses.

What gets lost when people are seduced to use packaged plants such as First Vita Plus for nutrition and health? We concur with Yates-Doerr (2012, 304), who states that 'taste, pleasure and awareness of all the social relations inherent in the production and consumption of any meal' are lost. But there is more. When people resort to supplements, they lose knowledge of how ordinary vegetables and fruits taste and the work they do. But they also lose access to and local control over the medicinal plants that grow in their immediate environments, and practical understanding of how these can be used in self-care. They lose plant sovereignty.

We use 'plant sovereignty' to refer to the embedding of plants in everyday relations of care, including as ingredients in (cooked) food and drinks, and their preparation as remedies for health problems such as common colds, diarrhoea and wounds – domains of application which are intertwined. Plant sovereignty also includes practical knowledge of how to use plants, which is passed down, often along gendered lines – in the Philippines, this knowledge used to descend from grandmothers to mothers and daughters – and maintained by specialized healers, to whom people turn when they cannot resolve poor health with self-care. Such practical knowledge involves cultivating plants as food and for medicinal purposes in backyards and foraging for them in forests, as well as understanding how to dry, salt or ferment plants to make them last longer (without refrigeration). Crucially, it involves a multisensory appreciation of plants, linked to a lay understanding of their efficacy and appreciating them as ingredients in food. Finally, it involves the social relations through which knowledge about how to use plants flows and in which the plants are used as food and medicine.

The concept of food sovereignty inspires our use of 'plant sovereignty'. First coined in the 1970s (Wittman et al. 2010), food sovereignty was subsequently adopted by Via Campesina, an international movement of peasants challenging industrial, profit-oriented models of agriculture that marginalize small-scale farmers and reduce access to land.[3] At a conference in Nyéléni, Mali in 2007, Via Campesina activists employed food sovereignty as a mobilizing device to call for the right to culturally appropriate food, produced through ecologically sound, sustainable methods and for the right of local people to variously define their own food and agricultural systems (Nyéléni Forum 2007; Edelman et al. 2014; Coté 2016). Having inspired multitudes of food movements worldwide (Canfield 2022), food sovereignty refers to local control over the plants in one's environment, along with the local knowledge systems that inform their use. We chose to use the term plant sovereignty to acknowledge the ways in which local plants are not just food, but equally important as medicines.

Historical sources reveal that the remote communities on which ethnobotanists focus are often participants in global trade, enriching the diversity of plant resources in everyday life everywhere. Spengler (2019), building on Watson's (1983) classic work *Agricultural Innovation*, describes how botanical exchanges and plant diffusion have occurred for millennia, intensifying during the early centuries of Islamic expansion and predating the Western 'Age of Discovery'. Trade routes were often by sea, with ships carrying spices, cereal grains, fruits and vegetables, as well as medicines. King (2015) traces the global routes of the Sasanian Empire from the third to seventh centuries, which stretched from present-day Iran to Southeast Asia. Several Southeast Asian polities were active in the increasingly lucrative trade in spices, aromatics and medicines. Anthropologists document how indigenous communities participate in global trade by selling valuable plant materials that they collect from their surroundings. These insights inform our analysis of the changing relations between people and plants.

When taking a walking tour with some of his students and botanist David Ple, Michael was struck by the long history and multiple vectors of exchange reflected in the foreign roots of many 'Filipino' vegetables and fruits. The tour passed through several mini-forest systems that the Institute of Biology had created on the campus of the University of the Philippines with support from the Lopez Foundation. It was a spectacular experience, and the students ooh-ed and ahh-ed their way through it, fascinated especially by the edible plants. At one point, the guide asked a surprising question: 'Did you know that none of the vegetables named

Bahay kubo, kahit munti,	Our cottage, albeit small
Ang halaman doon ay sari-sari	The plants there are varied
Singkamas at talong	Turnip and eggplant
Sigarilyas at mani	String beans and nuts
Sitaw, bataw, patani	Beans, lentils, peas
Kundol, patola, upo't kalabasa	Kundol, patola, upo and pumpkin
At tsaka mayro'n pang	And there is more
Labanos, mustasa	Radish, mustard
Sibuyas, kamatis, bawang at luya	Onion, tomato, garlic and ginger
Sa paligid-ligid ay puno ng linga	And all around on the side are sesame

Figure 1.2 Lyrics from 'Bahay Kubo', a popular children's song.

in "Bahay Kubo" [a popular song, see Figure 1.2] are indigenous to the Philippines?'

The students on the tour were all stunned. Some began singing the song, which they had learnt as children. With his background in economic botany, Michael realized the plants had originally come from China and Latin America. The guide prodded the group further, saying that the Philippines' most popular fruit, the mango, was introduced from abroad, as was the star apple (*kaimito*). The guide was making the point that, through the centuries, Filipinos have lost knowledge of plants, both indigenous and imported.

The popularity in the Philippines of vegetables that originated in China reflects the influence of Chinese immigrants. Starting in the fourteenth century as periodic visiting traders, growing numbers of Chinese began to settle on the islands, taking on the role of middlemen, buying goods from remote regions of the Philippines and transporting them to Manila and other urban centres for sale to large traders (Kian 2013). In cities, too, the Chinese grew vegetables of Chinese origin and, together with itinerant street vendors called *panciteros* (*pancit* is the Hokkien Chinese word for ready-made meals), influenced the Filipino diet, including both cooking methods and the names of common foods. It is not surprising that the mostly male Chinese settlers married local women; many of their offspring came to engage in trade, in rice in particular, and to enter politics as well (Li 1969). The Philippines was thus already integrated into a global trade system long before the Spanish arrived in the sixteenth century (Henley 2015; Reid 1995).

Along with 'transplantation' (the transport of packaged plants and seeds), intense transculturation, and the exchange of knowledge and views, occurred – not just about the traded and consumed plants but also about philosophies and religions, the arts and humanities, and health and illness.

By the time the Spaniards arrived in the Philippines, the islands were already exchanging plants with faraway places and had developed knowledge systems integrating ideas from many different cultures. After Spanish colonization (1565–1815), the Manila galleons made trans-Pacific trips once or twice a year, bringing Chinese goods and local items from the islands to Acapulco in Mexico, a hub for goods from throughout Latin America. The return voyage to Manila brought goods from Europe and Latin America to the Philippines and, from there, to other parts of Asia. This trade system fuelled the circulation of medicinal plants, which, as early as the seventeenth century, were packaged and sold as branded tonics and powdered teas, and whose foreign nature added to their perceived potency.

These global exchanges marked the beginnings of plant packaging – needed to maintain plants on long voyages. It also led to the planting of new varieties, new ways of cooking meals and new ways of treating common ailments. People's relations to plants are never static because they regularly appropriate new plants into their everyday lives. Filipino ecosystems provided fertile ground for numerous plants that had been transplanted via pre-colonial trading routes.

In the rest of this chapter, we highlight how colonizers' devaluations of local knowledge of the value and uses of plants along with industrialization and the commodification of food provisioning and health maintenance further changed the relations between people and plants in the Philippines. The Philippines' national hero, Jose Rizal, wrote about the drastic changes to the islands caused by forced labour and loss of land. Responding to a Spanish colonial administrator's description of 'Filipino indolence', Rizal bitterly notes that colonial policies created abominable working conditions on the haciendas and a loss of knowledge about farming and other traditional skills, with many 'left to die of hunger' and some surviving on 'poisonous herbs' (Rizal 1890, 7).

Rizal's nineteenth-century observations provide a context for our detailed analysis of what was yet to come in the twentieth century: neoliberal policies enabled market forces *that led to disruptions in food production and nutrition and metabolic rifts*, and these included the popularity of dietary supplements.

Devaluing indigenous plant knowledge

Filipinos' relations to plants and each other changed dramatically under Spanish colonialism. The Spaniards treated indigenous healing practices with suspicion, thus reducing locals' trust in home remedies. They appropriated plant medicines for inclusion in Galenic medical systems and introduced plantation agriculture, which limited locals' access to land.

Spanish friars were wary of the use of plants by widely respected traditional healers, whom they rightly recognized as potential threats to the authority of the Catholic Church. The Jesuit missionary Ignacio Alcina wrote a series of monographs compiled in 1668, which have been translated and published as *History of the Bisayan People in the Philippine Islands* (Alcina 2005). Reflecting the general mistrust among friars, he suggested local people practised sorcery, based on their knowledge of poisons and the antidotes to them.

Although Spanish friars denigrated traditional uses of plants in healing practices, they simultaneously documented the plants in the Philippines' diverse eco-systems, appropriating them for their own use and integrating them into Galenic medicine. Alcina's writings contain 24 chapters of detailed economic botany, mainly describing plants' uses as foods and beverages, but also as medicine, and as timber for ships and buildings. With such an abundance of wild edible plants to explore, cultivated vegetables (*hortalezas*) were relegated to just one chapter that listed several varieties of squashes and melons, cucumbers, cabbages, and beans.

The Spanish Jesuit Francisco Colin's (1592–1660) botanical manuscript (Colin 2018) outlined the many ways in which Filipinos used *lagundi* (*Vitex negundo*, see Figure 1.3): the leaves of the plant for headaches and ulcers, its seeds for skin diseases, its flowers for numerous diseases including diarrhoea and cholera. Its black fruit was dried and eaten to alleviate intestinal discomfort, while its roots were used as a remedy for rheumatism and dysentery.[4]

Lavishly illustrated with coloured prints that accompany its descriptions of plants as foods and medicines, Father Manuel Blanco's (1837) *Flora de Filipinas* reads like an update to Alcina's monographs. It likewise details local knowledge of an astonishing variety of edible plants – twenty different kinds of plantains or bananas, nine varieties of rice, four kinds of ginger, and so on.

Father Blanco also produced a self-help health manual adapted from the eighteenth-century homecare manual that Swiss physician Samuel Tissot first published in 1761,[5] which was part of a popularization

Figure 1.3 Lagundi (*Vitex negundo*). Source: FLPA/Alamy Stock Photo.

of medicine in Europe in the eighteenth century (Singy 2010). Father Blanco's manual was reprinted multiple times, most recently in 1916, several years after American colonial rule replaced Spanish occupation of the Philippines.[6]

The Spaniards' manuals introduced Galenic medicine to the Philippines. At the same time, the Spaniards recognized that many of the medicinal plants used in Spain were unavailable in their colonies. In both Latin America and the Philippines, they sought out local substitutes among the plants that Spanish economic botanists had extensively documented. In the process, Filipino people (apart from the isolated groups referenced in the ethnobotanical studies noted above) lost indigenous knowledge of plant medicines and were pressured to adopt Spanish appropriations of local plants into Galenic diagnostic and treatment schemes. Huguet-Termes (2001), tracing the impact of Latin American plants on Spanish medicine, emphasizes that besides the system of physicians, catering mainly to the rich, another system developed in households among women, in particular, practising self-medication and modifying the uses of medicines. This applied equally to the Philippines, Spain's far-flung colony, where friars tended to bodies as well as souls, using Spanish Galenic medicine manuals that highlighted the medicinal qualities of local plants.

Sadly, Spanish colonization, with the appropriation of agricultural lands for sugar plantations in the nineteenth century, left the islands with widespread hunger and declining populations.

The plantations, run by friars and Spanish laymen, diminished Filipinos' access to agricultural land and forced them into conscripted labour (Newson 2011). Sugar became one of the country's main agricultural export commodities, serving European and, later, US markets (Aguilar 2017).

United States colonization

The United States formally acquired the Philippines in 1898. Sta. Maria (2020, 57–9) cites information from various health booklets and materials from a (now-defunct) Office of Adult Education that produced several important publications on kitchen gardening as a means to address the food insecurity that was the Spaniards' legacy, a project that involved several government agencies: the Bureau of Education, the Bureau of Science, the Bureau of Plant Industries, the Bureau of Labor, as well as private civic groups, such as the National Federation of Women's Clubs. With titles such as *Ang Gulay at Pangpahaba ng Buhay* (Vegetables and lengthening of life, 1937), *Ang Pagpapaunlad ng Gawain ng Isang Magsasaka* (Improving farming practices, 1937) and *Mga Pagkain sa Ikalulusog ng Katawan* (Healthy foods for the body, 1938), the booklets promoted cultivation and consumption of vegetables and fruits. In 1939, there was even one entitled *Mga Halamang Pangbakod* (Hedge plants) that promoted growing certain vegetables as hedges or living fences: *malunggay* (Moringa oleifera), *katuray* (Sesbania grandifloria) and *kamatsili* (Pithecellobium dulce), with bougainvillea and *gumamela* (hibiscus) recommended as flowers to adorn them. The National Federation of Women's Clubs (NFWC) seems to have played an important role in popularizing these manuals in the 1940s by setting up diet kitchens in communities (Sta. Maria 2020). The NFWC made a good case for keeping vegetable gardens, explaining that the plants grown were not just high in nutritional value, but also provided inexpensive food, made homes beautiful, were convenient because one did not have to go to the market, and served as a source of national pride, since they decreased dependence on imports (Sta. Maria 2020).

While mandating kitchen gardening and school gardens (and thereby supporting plant sovereignty), the Americans' educational system also introduced highly processed foods into school lunches which profoundly changed people's dietary practices. They fed Filipino schoolchildren key components of a standard American diet

(DuPuis 2015): 'soup and stew, buttered sandwiches and ice cream', while school canteens sold 'fritters, tarts, cookies, pies, hot biscuits and muffins ... donuts, chicken pie' (Hollnsteiner and Ick 2001, 81). Note the inclusion of stew and chicken, indicating that the designers of these school health programmes considered meat beneficial to good health (DuPuis 2015), while there is also a complete lack of fresh vegetables and fruits.

As to the use of plants as medicines, the Americans, like the Spanish colonizers denigrated traditional plant-based healing practices, while simultaneously documenting the potential uses of plants that grew in the archipelago. They sponsored studies to inventory those plants useful as sources of food, fibre, shelter and medicine (Kian 2013), as reflected in Brown's (1950) three-volume *Useful Plants of the Philippines*. American research in the field of ethnopharmacology was oriented towards screening medicinal plants for their therapeutic value in treating non-communicable diseases, including cancer and cardio-vascular diseases – conditions that were not yet prominent causes of morbidity in the Philippines.

American colonization set the stage for several more subsequent metabolic rifts in terms of food and diet: the consumption of highly processed foods, sugar-laced breakfast cereals and drinks, and the introduction of American-style fast-food hamburger establishments. Even after the restoration of Philippine independence in 1946, American influence remained strong, especially with the mass migration of Filipinos to the United States. Filipino-Americans sent packages of canned goods and processed food back to the Philippines as representations of affluence and the good life.

Western food processing methods (mainly canning) caused people to abandon fresh vegetables and fruits. Canning represented modernity, displacing traditional preservation methods of fermentation that enhance nutrition and produce probiotics as opposed to depleting nutrients. The presence of US military bases further promoted the colonization of Filipino food culture; goods smuggled out of the bases were like the cargo cults of the South Pacific, representing the bounty of Westerners. Michael's childhood memories of growing up in the Philippines include sweet breakfast cereals, chocolate bars, Spam and other canned foods, and sweetened drinks such as Tang. 'Stateside' entered his vocabulary, representing food perceived as safe, convenient and nutritionally superior. Tang was not only associated with America; it was marketed as the drink of astronauts. In relation to villagers' incomes, canned goods were astronomically priced, and considered exceptional food for special occasions and visitors. Michael would ask rural communities not to use expensive canned goods to feed us.

Sugar

Sidney Mintz's (1985) seminal study describing the pivotal role sugar plays in the global political economy of food has relevance here. Mintz demonstrates the metabolic rifts caused by industrializing sugar production. Initially an exotic ingredient consumed by the rich in Europe and the United States, sugar entered mass consumption after import trade tariffs lifted. Sugar fuelled industrialization, both in terms of meeting a growing demand and by fuelling labourers' bodies. Sweet tea and bread with sweetened marmalade became part of working-class diets in the early industrial period, providing nutrients and functioning as stimulants to sustain people during long working hours. In the Philippines, industrializing sugar plantations left many landless agricultural workers un- and underemployed, driving migration to cities and rural areas such as Mindanao and Palawan, where the government parcelled out land to small farmers as part of agricultural reforms (Aguilar 2017; Rutten 2010).

Mintz (1985) notes the embodied effects of increased sugar consumption. Not only does calorie intake increase; people also replace complex carbohydrates with simple ones that lead to increased rates of obesity. Citing an American study (Cantor and Cantor 1977), Mintz reports that between the early twentieth century and the 1970s, sugar as a proportion of consumed carbohydrates rose from 31.5 per cent to 52.6 per cent, while the per capita consumption of complex carbohydrates fell from about 350 g to 180 g per day. Increased consumption of industrially prepared foods, which often contain sugar to augment taste, not only affects metabolisms. It profoundly changes the social and temporal aspects of eating. Individuals can consume prepared foods at any time, while home-cooked meals encourage people to gather and share food while it is hot.

Sugar production in the Philippines caused dramatic metabolic rifts. By the mid-twentieth century, just three Filipino families had accumulated massive wealth and political power from sugar capitalism. In Pampanga and Tarlac, in Central Luzon, there were the Cojuangco and Aquino families, the latter producing two presidents. In Negros, sugar generated wealth for the Lopez family, who expanded into various businesses, including mass media. While sugar became the Philippines' leading export crop, sugar workers were among the country's most exploited, underpaid and living in conditions of servitude from one generation to another. Not surprisingly, the sugar-producing provinces were among the earliest strongholds of the communist insurgency that began in 1969, now considered Asia's longest.

In August 1983, Benigno Aquino Jr, an opposition leader in exile and a critic of the Marcos regime, flew back to the Philippines, but was detained by government soldiers and assassinated at Manila airport. The economic crisis worsened, together with political ferment, as protest rallies grew in intensity. The sugar industry suffered greatly, from both the domestic crisis and the plummeting world prices for sugar.

The Philippines was going through its worst economic crisis since World War II, brought about by years of plunder by the Marcos regime. In 1985, Filipinos slowly discovered through the alternative press (martial law had been lifted, but the press remained muzzled) that there were children starving to death in Negros. The photographs of emaciated and dying children, such as Joel Abiong, child of a family of sugar workers, shocked Filipinos, who thought deaths from malnutrition happened only in the famine-struck countries (see Espina-Varona 2020).

Better than nature

Industrial processing of foods and marketing them as better than nature is a socio-metabolic shift that fundamentally altered Filipinos relations with plants. Burnby and Bierman (1996) point out that, throughout the nineteenth century, natural scientists introduced scientific experiments to understand how various foods could improve health. At the end of the nineteenth century, John Kellogg introduced the idea that 'science could make better foods than nature' (Bauch 2017, 16). While perhaps not evident at the time, this idea has caused dramatic metabolic shifts in the United States, and the Philippines.

We concur with González de Molina and Toledo (2014, 314–15), who call for theorizing the interchange of energy and matter between society and nature, along with 'the existence of another dimension that is immaterial, symbolic or cultural, and which expresses as flows of information'. One of our core themes in this book is the mobilization of modern scientific knowledge to market supplements. We examine information flows from scientific studies to the promotional texts on packages of plant-based supplements, showing how the latter both reflect and reinforce people's concerns about nutritional deficiencies and their seemingly faulty metabolisms.

John Kellogg's nutritional experiments in the Battle Creek Sanatorium in the United States took as their foundation the idea that technological intervention could improve the body's capacity to digest food and be healthy. Ironically, these experiments also gave rise to the idea, likewise underlying the promotion of food supplements, that the meals that people prepare themselves from local produce are not good enough. Analysing these experiments and the evolution of the popular breakfast cereal, Kellogg's Corn Flakes, Bauch (2017) suggests that the spread of American diets to the rest of the world should be understood less in terms of the global flow of commodities and more as a relationship to nutrition characterized by mistrust in the body's capacity to manage ordinary food.

Kellogg and his contemporaries in Battle Creek spearheaded the industrial manufacturing of foods, initially with the goal of easing digestion and prolonging their viability. This soon evolved into a project to create food products that could be stored and used in different forms. Kellogg's Corn Flakes, margarine, and fruit juices are prime examples of plant-based products promoted not only for their nutritional value but also for their purity, with the idea that modern food processing would ensure foods were free of bacteria (DuPuis 2015). Promoted initially as 'better than nature', over time it became apparent that these highly processed foods can in fact cause or contribute to metabolic disturbances.

DuPuis (2015) gives the example of margarine, which nutritionists promoted as being healthy because of its high levels of unsaturated fats. The industrial process by which margarine is made involves hydrogenating vegetable oils to make the fats easy to spread. Making margarine also involves bleaching the oil and adding colourants to make the product look like butter. Other chemicals that emulsify water and fat are added to create the desired consistency, and vitamins A and D are added to increase the spread's nutritional value. Margarine was advertised as good for health – better than butter, the food item it mimics. By the early 1990s, margarine's disadvantages had become clear: the manufacturing process produces trans fats, which were now shown to negatively affect blood cholesterol and increase the risk of heart disease (Scrinis 2013).

This trend to promote processed food as 'healthy' intensified in post-World War II America, manifested in 'vitamin-fortified peanut butter, vitamin gum, even vitamin doughnuts – and far from expressing scepticism over these products, the public clamored for more' (Price 2016, xi). The Philippines followed suit. The 10 July 1948 issue of the popular weekly magazine, *Philippines Free Press* (Figure 1.4) shows several advertisements that embrace 'nutritionism', an approach to food that breaks it down into the nutritional value of its components, which are mainly vitamins and minerals (Scrinis 2013; Jacobs, Gross and Tapsell 2009).[7]

The advertisement for Blueband margarine (Figure 1.4), calls it an 'extra energy food' and touts its high vitamin A and D content: 'The doctors say that these vitamins are essential for good health'. The image of the girl playing with a ball states, 'Always active … never tired'. In a

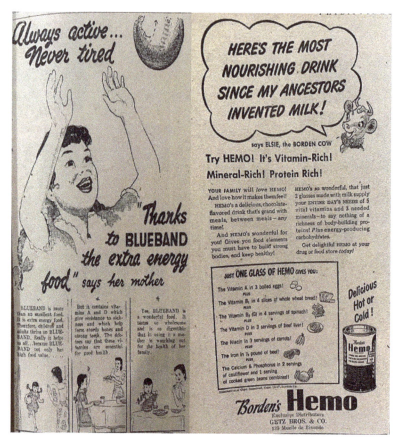

Figure 1.4 Advertisements for Hemo drink and Blueband margarine, from the 10 July 1948 issue of *Philippines Free Press*. Source: Author (Tan), 2021.

similar vein, the advertisement for Borden's Hemo drink proclaims: 'It's Vitamin-Rich! Mineral-Rich! Protein Rich!' The vitamins in one glass of Hemo are listed, equated as the amount of vitamin A in three boiled eggs, the vitamin B1 of four slices of whole-wheat bread, as much vitamin B2 as four servings of spinach and so forth.

Other advertisements in the magazine transmit the same overall message. An advertisement for Ovaltine, 'the protecting food-drink', urges mothers to give it to their children for its calcium, iron, vitamins A, B1, C, D and G, and warns that these 'food elements' are usually insufficient in average diets. An advertisement for a preparation called D-C Calcium is graced with a photograph of a young boy captioned 'Tarzan' and a testimonial from his father:

> After giving him D-C Calcium for five months he became the healthiest and most robust among his four brothers. Thanks to D-C Calcium, the right medicine for sickly nervous and anaemic persons.

The advertisement claims that the combination of calcium, vitamin C and tiki-tiki (thiamine)

> … enriches the blood, builds up health, prevents and cures beri-beri, nervousness, malnutrition, anaemia, rickets, jaundice and scurvy. It's excellent for expecting and nursing mothers, promotes growth in children and is indispensable to hastening convalescence from malaria, dysentery and tuberculosis.

Marketing for these products echoes the 'better than nature' slogan introduced by Kellogg in the first half of the twentieth century: providing 'extra' energy, being 'rich' in minerals and vitamins, and bolstering the health of modern consumers.

Vitamin deficiencies were recognized long before the chemicals were isolated in laboratories. Scurvy is the best example, with ships carrying citrus fruits to prevent the disease during long voyages. Combs and McClung (2019) devote two chapters in their much-used textbook to a history of vitamins that includes an empirical phase followed by the twentieth century where the term vitamin became popularized and researchers began to try to isolate specific vitamins, still without names, elucidating their structures, and synthesizing them. The last vitamin to be isolated and named was vitamin B12 or cobalamin, its date of 'discovery' given as 1948. In total, there are 13 of these internationally recognized vitamins. The nutritionist trend made possible by the discovery and subsequent isolation of vitamins gave rise to a growing fixation on vitamin deficiencies (Price 2016), which required correction through the industrial reconstitution of foods and plants and, later, the production and packaging of supplements. Nobel laureate (Chemistry and, later, Peace) Linus Pauling's *Vitamin C and the Common Cold* (published in 1970) reinforced the trend. Pauling prescribed mega-doses of vitamin C to prevent common colds (claiming that he took doses as high as 18 g per day), significantly exceeding the recommended daily dose at that time of 60 mg. This led to the flooding of drug stores with vitamin C preparations in strengths of 500 mg and 1,000 mg – available as capsules, powders and effervescent tablets, often orange flavoured to promote an association with fruit – and vitamin C-fortified processed foods and drinks. Pauling's *How to Live Longer and Feel Better* (1986), along with a myriad of self-help nutrition books, exemplifies how vitamins became panaceas for the stressors of modern living.

Metabolic drawbacks

For all the enthusiasm for the nutritional value of vitamin-enriched, processed foods as part of the 'modern' diet, twenty-first century knowledge raises concerns about the metabolic disturbances that such a diet with significant processed foods can cause or worsen. A longitudinal study in Australia of 10,000 women over 15 years, found that women with the highest proportion of ultra-processed foods in their diets were 39 per cent more likely to develop high blood pressure, increasing their risk for strokes and heart attacks (Pant et al. 2023). Aside from cardio-vascular morbidity, a growing number of studies associates consuming ultra-processed foods with metabolic disturbances such as obesity and gastrointestinal disorders, and with depression (Lane et al. 2021; Pagliai et al. 2021). Carlos Monteiro, among the first to raise concerns about the health impacts of processing food (2009), defines ultra-processed foods in a team-written policy guide written for the UN Food and Agricultural Organization as 'formulations of ingredients, mostly of exclusive industrial use, typically created by series of industrial techniques and processes' (Monteiro et al. 2015, 8). Ready to eat or heat up or consume immediately, such foods generally contain little to no whole foods, are low in fibre, high in fat, salt and/or sugar and contain multiple synthetic additives, including stabilizers, emulsifiers, sweeteners and flavourings that give the foods taste and texture and make them easy to eat. Commonly consumed ultra-processed foods in the Philippines include instant noodles, white breads, cookies, breakfast cereals, chips, nuggets and meat products – now part of people's everyday diet. Chris van Tulleken (2023), an infectious disease doctor at the Hospital for Tropical Diseases in London points out in his prize-winning book, *Ultra-Processed People*, that ultra-processed foods are designed for overconsumption, explaining that they are intentionally 'addictive'. He further notes that we are only starting to understand how the mismatch between the mouth's taste signals and nutritional content alter our metabolisms and appetites. Ironically, it is the metabolic disturbances caused by ultra-processed diets that fuel the market for food supplements, which themselves also tend to be ultra-processed.

Summary

This short political-ecological analysis of intersecting metabolic rifts and shifts helps us understand the seductive attraction of food supplements in the Philippines' green, biodiverse environment. In their appropriation of medicinal plants, their distrust of traditional healing methods and their introduction of plantation agriculture, Spanish friars disrupted plant sovereignty. The industrialization of foods and their fortification with vitamins, promoted heavily as being 'better than nature', left people believing that the ordinary fruits and vegetables that grew abundantly in their neighbourhoods and backyards did not constitute sufficient nutrition.

These metabolic shifts are not isolated events. They overlap in time and reinforce each other. The pre-colonial trade in exotic plants created health cultures that were open to new plant-based remedies. The negative evaluation of indigenous healing by Spanish and American colonizers made people insecure about the nutritional and health value of the plants in their own backyards. The industrialization of foods was detrimental to people's diets, creating a demand for vitamins and supplements. Plants were increasingly broken down into isolated chemicals and then reconstituted and packaged. The process removed them from their natural environment, with far-reaching consequences for plant sovereignty.

Challenges to plant sovereignty are various. Colonizers stigmatize traditional healers who use plants collected in their environments, at the same time appropriating plants for inclusion in their own health systems. Local people lose access to land due to plantation agriculture, small farmers become agricultural workers and herbicides reduce the biodiversity of natural surroundings. Industrially produced fast foods are promoted as 'better', often fortified with vitamins, although sometimes to compensate for their nutritional deficiency; people are left thinking that natural foods are not good enough. Finally, manufacturers package plants with misleading images of 'naturalness', simultaneously overemphasizing their products' efficacy as prevent-alls and cure-alls – but the prime aim is to generate profits for marketeers and industrial entrepreneurs. All these activities challenge plant sovereignty.

What follows

This introductory chapter has taken a longue-durée perspective. The rest of the book is structured in three Parts. There are also two photo essays that relate to consuming and growing food. We hope these will help our readers visualize the ethnographic context in which we conducted our research. The first photo essay, which depicts how poor people in Manila eat, immediately follows Chapter 2. The second, illustrating community projects aimed at reinstating plant sovereignty, follows Chapter 7. Part I (Chapters 2–4) of this book examines how, in post-independence Philippines, nutritional policies, scientific research and marketing shape the popularity of supplements like First Vita Plus. Part II (Chapters 5 and 6) is an ethnographical examination of the popularity of supplements in Puerto Princesa, the rural boomtown where we conducted fieldwork from 2014–20. Part III (Chapter 7) focuses on efforts to repair the loss of plant sovereignty.

Part I begins with Chapter 2, which describes the nutritional transitions that took place in the Philippines in the post-independence period. These transitions involved increased processing of ordinary foods into conveniently packaged commodities, such as noodles, breakfast cereals and vitamin-fortified juices, which are sold in local variety stores at affordable prices. These highly processed foods tend to contain a lot of saturated fats, sugar and salt, and have low nutritional value. National nutrition surveys in the Philippines over the past 40 years reveal a dramatic decline in the consumption of fresh vegetables and fruits, due to the widespread availability of cheap convenience foods and their aura of modernity. In consequence, the statistics reveal a shocking trend. Despite increases in GDP, malnutrition rates among preschool children in the Philippines have remained the same – the growth of around one-third of children nationwide is stunted. Government-sponsored nutrition programmes have addressed this embarrassing fact by promoting community gardens and nutrition supplementation. They encourage parents to help their children 'grow and glow' both by getting them to eat more vegetables and fruits and by adding micronutrient powders to preschool children's meals. This dual message reinforces the common understanding (promoted by industrial food manufacturers like Kellogg's) that ordinary food does not provide enough nutrients, fuelling the popularity of food supplements such as First Vita Plus.

Chapter 3 examines the revival of herbal medicines in the 1970s as part of health movements for increased plant sovereignty and how, subsequently, herbal remedies were commodified – having acquired the stamp of efficacy in scientific research. Michael's fieldwork in the 1970s had examined plants used in remote communities in the Philippines and generated published guides that outlined their pharmacological principles and also proposed mixtures of medicinal plants for treating common health problems. We trace the evolution of the government-sponsored research programmes in the Philippines that led to the reformulation of herbal medicines into modern medicines and their formal approval by the Philippines Food and Drug Administration – a period in which supplements began to proliferate. We also illustrate how a booming global market in supplements evolved in the wake of the US Dietary Supplement and Health Education Act of 1994, which eased the regulation of supplements. A similar regulatory stance was adopted in the Philippines.

Chapter 4 describes what happens when plants that have been traditionally valued for their taste, texture and medicinal properties are reconstituted and put into sachets and capsules. Researchers in the now global discipline of food science conduct animal studies and clinical research to identify the health properties of plants, with their findings often used in marketing.

Manufacturers of plant-based supplements in the Philippines compete in a rapidly expanding health market. Consumers view supplements as attractive health commodities with promises of natural-based potency, attractively encased in modern packaging. Our close readings of the packaging and promotional claims of a range of supplements reveal that these both reflect and reinforce consumers' concerns about nutritional deficiencies and health, and their changing understandings of metabolic processes.

We analyse packaged plants not as unchanging objects but as products articulated and re-articulated across time and space (Hardon and Sanabria 2017). Examining the state–market nexus for supplements, we contrast these dynamics with those of pharmaceuticals, building on anthropological analyses of pharmaceutical flows and value-making (Biehl 2006; Whyte, Hardon and Van der Geest 2002; Hardon and Sanabria 2017; Dumit 2012; Oldani 2004) while indicating what is specific to the rapidly expanding market for packaged plants that are presented as better than ordinary food.

In Part II, Chapter 5 examines multilevel marketing (MLM), a form of direct sales that has recently become popular for selling plant-based supplements in the Philippines (Euromonitor International 2016). MLM company representatives use persuasive methods to entice people that may be struggling to make ends meet to become food supplement distributors, with promises that they can attain desirable middle-class lifestyles and enjoy good health, too. After joining a company and selling memberships, distributors receive access to supplements at discounted rates for themselves and their family members. Our encounters with supplement-selling companies in Puerto Princesa reveal that multilevel marketers articulate the potencies of the packaged plants in response to the health concerns of their clients, often inspired by doctors who assign value to the supplements online in YouTube videos.

Our analysis locates the capacity of packaged plants to protect health within a web of interactions between their sellers and their consumers. Distributors are trained to capitalize upon people's worries about changing diets, polluted environments and the catastrophic costs of ill health. Like the government programmes set up to fight hidden hunger, these commercial firms fuel the belief that ordinary foodstuffs cannot meet dietary needs. We contrast the valuation of two supplement companies' products: Vita Plus, and one of its competitors, C24/7, which claims to contain a blend of 12 whole fruits, 12 whole vegetables, and 12 different kinds of mushrooms. We show how supplement distributors are encouraged to 'be their products' – that is, to consume them to be able to testify to their efficacy (Hardon et al. 2019).

Chapter 6 turns to the embodied labour that distributors in MLM schemes perform to sell supplements. We argue that the unchecked positive health imagery when promoting food supplements disguises corporations' exploitation of low-level sellers. Distributors higher up in the schemes benefit from the sales generated through the intense, multifaceted work of people lower down in the hierarchy.

MLM of packaged plants mobilizes poor people to expand the markets and maximize profits. The work they are pressured to perform is socio-metabolic. It involves consumption of products, tailoring selling pitches to potential clients' dietary and metabolic health concerns, and establishing, negotiating and maintaining emotional and interpersonal relations with customers (Hardon et al. 2019). These relations may appear caring, but they are not. Low-level distributors rarely earn back their initial investments, which perpetuates inequalities in socio-economic metabolic health. Moreover, they strain their kin relationships. Customers would be better off spending their scarce resources on ordinary vegetables and fruits. The higher-ups pressure MLM workers to negotiate and redraw boundaries between the intimate and economic spheres of their lives by using their family members and peers to make sales and generate profits for the MLM companies. This situation involves a socio-metabolic shift constituting a radical move away from the relations of care that exist under conditions of plant sovereignty, that is, when people have the knowledge and skills to prepare plants themselves to feed families or treat conditions of ill health.

Chapter 7 concludes with recommendations for how to create a balanced relationship between people and plants. The dynamics between people and plants become especially notable in times of crisis, when people feel driven to return to nature. We observed this during the COVID-19 pandemic, a period in which sales of supplements surged, while people simultaneously revalued kitchen gardening as a source of food sovereignty and health. Does this revaluation signal a new metabolic shift towards reappropriating plants that may lead toward achieving plant sovereignty? We likewise indicate other positive developments that point to a renewed scientific interest in fresh vegetables and fruits. These include a global trend that values food synergies – that is, an understanding of how ingredients in natural foods and plants can work together, particularly in positive ways – and a revived interest in the value of fresh plant-based diets, including those that help to maintain a beneficial gut microbiome (David et al. 2014; Thursby and Juge 2017). We examine these new configurations of plants and people in the Philippines, where agroecology is gaining traction and people are embracing kitchen or 'backyard' gardening.

We call for an amplification of these health efforts, so that future generations will value vegetables and fruits that grow in their environments and acquire knowledge of how to prepare them for their families and friends. We are inspired by visionary government agencies, such as the Ministry of Health in Brazil, whose alternative approaches to dietary guidelines 'attend to circumstances – time, focus, place, and company – which influence how foods are metabolized by the body and also the pleasure afforded by eating' (Secretariat of Health Care 2015). We take further cues from the Food and Agriculture Organization of the United Nations, which calls for eating a range of fruits and vegetables to protect biodiversity and aid the sustainability of our planet (Burlingame and Dernini 2010). Finally, we call upon the government of the Philippines to reappraise its nutritionist tendencies and on corporations to embrace integrity when manufacturing foods, vitamins and supplements and promoting their benefits. We hope the Filipino diet can become known for its positive effects on people's wellbeing, in terms of enabling a healthy symbiosis and sustainable relationship between humans and their environments.

Notes

1 Convention on Biological Diversity, *Philippines – Country profile*. https://www.cbd.int/countries/profile?country=ph (Accessed 6 June 2024).
2 In her study on how children supplemented their diets in Kenyan Taita communities, Fleuret (1986) followed children as they foraged along footpaths and roadways, in farm plots and pastures, on their way to school and back. The children she observed regularly consumed 97 species of fruits (of which 77 were wild and 20 cultivated) as part of this supplemental eating. None were found deficient in vitamin A or C.
3 See viacampesina.org (Accessed 6 June 2024). Food sovereignty is not to be equated with food security (a term much heard these days in relation to disruptions in global food provisioning). Food security refers to adequate nutrition for all, regardless of the food's origin (Gartaula et al. 2018).
4 The plant is now one of 10 medicinal plants endorsed by the Philippine Department of Health as having scientifically proven efficacy for asthma, flu, coughs, and common colds (see Chapter 3).
5 The full title was *Ang mahusay na paraan nang pag-gamot sa manga may saquit ayon sa aral ni Tissot* (Effective Medical Techniques to Cure the Sick, according to Tissot's teachings). See also Blanco, Manuel Romas. 1837. *Flora de Filipinas. Según el sistema sexual de Linneo*, Manila; and Tissot, Samuel. 1761. 'Avis au people sur sa sante'. Lausanne: J. Zimmerly.
6 Another Spanish manual (*A Manual of Various Medicines for the Consolation of the Poor in the Provinces and Pueblos without a Medic or Pharmacy*), first published in the eighteenth century, continued to be reprinted, with the last edition produced in 1905 by the Colegio de Santo Tomas in Manila.
7 Taking a different ontological perspective, we might say vitamins were 'suspected' much earlier, perhaps appropriately, during the Western 'Age of Discovery', which, since the fifteenth century, had entailed long sea voyages, during which sailors developed scurvy, a disease that could be fatal. Bown (2003, 3) writes that 'scurvy was responsible for more deaths at sea than storms, shipwreck, combat, and all other diseases combined', and estimates that two million sailors perished at sea from the disease. The most dramatic example was Ferdinand Magellan's circumnavigation of the world from 1519 to 1521, during which 208 out of the 230 men died, mostly from this disease, which was characterized by weakness, sore gums, painful joints and multiple hemorrhages (Price 2017). History books credit James Lind's achievement when, in a

small experiment in 1747 on the HMS *Salisbury* he divided 12 sailors into groups, each of which took a different preparation, to see which could tackle scurvy. The group consuming oranges and lemons did best. Lind published his findings in a *Treatise on the Scurvy* (1757), but it was not until the 1790s that the British Navy finally required rations of limes to be provided to sailors. However, long before Lind's study, the British, Dutch and Spaniards had observed a connection between the consumption of citrus fruits and leafy vegetables, and the prevention of scurvy (Price 2017).

Part I
Socio-metabolic shifts and the loss of plant sovereignty

2
Post-colonial metabolic rifts

Our introductory chapter traced how globalization and capitalism have dramatically changed people's relations to plants in the Philippines. These transitions have reduced people's practical knowledge of how to cultivate, prepare and use plants with the result that they lost plant sovereignty. In this chapter, we describe in detail the dietary transitions that took place in the post-independence period, which produced metabolic rifts. We show how these transitions reinforced the ideology that ordinary foods do not provide sufficient nutrition and inspired ambivalent government-sponsored nutrition programmes that responded to malnutrition by promoting both community gardens and nutritional supplementation.

Double burden

In the Philippines, as in some other middle-income countries in the Global South, high rates of obesity and persistent malnutrition co-occur, leading to a double burden in nutrition-related ill health (Dixon 2009). Nutritionists and public health experts in the country point to the health consequences of the shift from high-fibre diets that are low in sugar, salt and fat – cooked and consumed together at home – to low-fibre diets containing significant amounts of fat, sugar and salt – often consumed individually and on the go. The latter are associated with obesity and a multitude of 'non-communicable' diseases, such as hypertension and diabetes (Kraft et al. 2018; Popkin 2003; Sobreira et al. 2018).

Government national nutrition surveys document the increasing double burden, providing evidence on anthropometry (body measurements, including height and weight), biochemical test results (for anaemia and deficiencies in vitamin A, iodine and other micronutrients), other clinical health data (blood pressure, fasting blood glucose and lipids), as well as behavioural risk indicators like smoking, alcohol consumption and lack of physical activity, and diet or food consumption data based on 24-hour food recalls (structured interviews intended to capture information on what a person has eaten in a 24-hour period). Government surveys also collect household data, including family composition and the age, sex and occupation of the head of the household, and employ a 'wealth index' based on a household's ownership of selected assets, housing materials, and access to water and sanitation.

The Philippines Food and Nutrition Research Institute (FNRI) has a mandate to conduct a National Nutrition Survey (NNS) every five years, with expanded and updated surveys during the interim periods. It takes time before results are released. For example, in July 2023, a meeting was held to present 'the initial results of the 8th National Nutrition Survey', the 'latest'– which was conducted in 2013.

The COVID-19 pandemic further delayed survey administration and data-processing. Fortunately, 'rolling surveys' were conducted in 2018, 2019 and 2021 in specific provinces and cities, with results released relatively quickly (for example, the 2021 survey results were disseminated in 2022). The surveys attest to the growing double burden of overnutrition (and its metabolic conditions of cardiovascular disease and diabetes) and malnutrition. Overweight children were found across all 'wealth groups'. The 2018 rolling survey included data from Makati City, the country's financial centre, populated by many middle- and upper-class citizens. Significantly, even there, 10.5 per cent of children aged 5 to 10 years were underweight while 24.5 per cent were overweight.

These statistics expose the existence of food insecurity, defined by the Philippines Food and Nutrition Research Institute (FNRI) as

> … the state in which people are at risk or actually suffering from inadequate consumption to meet nutritional requirements as a result of the physical unavailability of food, their lack of social or economic access to adequate food and/or inadequate food utilization.

The FNRI notes that 50 per cent of respondents report that they regularly worry about not having sufficient food. When they lack enough income to buy food, they eat smaller meals than usual or skip meals altogether (Malabad 2019).

The 2018 survey also revealed inequities in malnutrition-related health indices by gender. Among adults, 11.5 per cent overall were found to be anaemic, while anaemia affected 17.7 per cent of women. Hypertension affected 15.6 per cent of adults, but more men than women, at 18.8 per cent. Rates of physical inactivity, which aggravates health problems, were also high, accounting for 75 per cent of adolescent males and 84 per cent of adolescent females.

To better understand both under- and overnutrition and the adverse health consequences of each, we need to disaggregate food consumption figures. Angeles-Agdeppa et al. (2019) in their analysis of the National Nutrition Survey of 2013 present disaggregated data for children and adolescents by income quintiles, something rarely seen in Philippine publications and scientific presentations. The report indicates a relatively high consumption of meat. Low-income children average 87.7 g per day, middle-income children 86.4 g per day, and wealthy children 106.2 g. When they can afford it, Filipino families eat meat or fish with their meals, tending to view vegetables as the food of poor people (Briones et al. 2017).

Rich children seem to be disadvantaged regarding consuming food from plants. Low-, middle- and high-income children consume daily 62.5 g, 48.3 g and 50.1 g of vegetables and 90 g, 89.8 g and 70.7 g of fruits, respectively. The figures for 'savoury snacks', a euphemism for junk foods (including noodles), are 22.5 g, 20.7 g and 30.9 g respectively, and for soft drinks are 95.9 g, 108.3 g and a staggering 161.8 g per day.

Filipinos overall are very heavy consumers of soft drinks, a factor which contributes to malnutrition (Baker and Friel 2014). Having a 'sweet tooth' can be influenced by all kinds of childhood experiences, including whether a child is breastfed or not and for how long (Muller et al. 2023). Infant formulas are notoriously high in sugar. Parents who pride themselves on being modern may say they no longer use candies and sweets as rewards for their children but forget that the snacks and drinks that they and school canteens provide are also packed with sugar, the sodas in particular. It is not surprising to hear diabetics in the Philippines complaining that the most difficult aspect of the dietary restrictions they live with is giving up soda.

Overconsumption of highly processed foods, including sugar, salt and fat, as well as a lack of physical activity, manifests in high rates of obesity and high blood pressure. But under-consumption of nutritious foods contributes to anaemia and the remarkably low average height of Filipinos.

The Non-Communicable Disease Risk Factor Collaboration (NCD-RisC), led by Imperial College London, has conducted studies on height, comparing different countries over time. The Philippines fares poorly in these studies, for example, females ranking second to the lowest and males ranking 192nd among 200 countries as of 1996, which is the subject of a journal article 'A century of trends in adult human height' (NCD-RisC 2016). More granular statistics are available, broken down by age from 5 years to 19 years, from 1985 to 2019, for the countries studied. A comparison of the figures for the Philippines and South Korea is instructive, given that both countries are in Asia and had about the same level of economic underdevelopment up to the 1970s, and both had periods of dictatorships, sometimes described as 'authoritarian development' (Ang 2017). Yet, thanks to a dedicated development of health and nutrition programmes (Kim, Moon and Popkin 2000) South Korea was among the countries showing the most progress in terms of height of children and adolescents over the last few decades, a trend that is, however, threatened now by overnutrition.[1]

In 2019, the average height of Filipino 19-year-old girls was 154.14 cm, equivalent to the average for 12-year-old South Korean girls. For that same year, the average height of Filipino 19-year-old boys was 165.23 cm, equivalent to the average for 13-year-old South Korean boys (NCD-RisC 2016).[2]

Persistent stunting

Unsurprisingly, in the face of food insecurity, one-third of Filipino children were found to be stunted in statistics the Philippines' Department of Health provided in 2017, with the figure reaching 50 per cent in some areas such as the Autonomous Region of Muslim Mindanao (Department of Health 2017). Moreover, stunting has increased among infants over the past decade, as the findings of national nutrition surveys conducted from 2008 to 2015 demonstrate (Table 2.1). In 2013, 31.5 per cent of one-year-olds were stunted. This figure rose to 36.2 per cent in 2015, a 15 per cent increase over a two-year period.

The World Health Organization (2014) warns that stunting has far-reaching developmental effects. Among these are negative indications for cognitive development that affect intelligence and performance in school, with well-documented scholastic underachievement and high

Table 2.1 Percentage of stunted infants in the Philippines (2008–15).

Year of National Nutrition Survey	0–5 months old	6–11 months old	12–23 months old
2008	11.6	14.3	27.7
2011	14.1	16.2	33.6
2013	13.1	16.2	31.5
2015	12.7	17.3	36.2

Source: National Nutrition Surveys (FNRI 2016).

dropout rates. All these factors increase the risk of poverty, which is often the core, initial contributing factor to stunting. In the Philippines, the Cebu Longitudinal Health and Nutrition Survey noted that early supplemental feeding increased the likelihood of stunting, while breastfeeding tended to prevent it (Adair and Popkin 2001). Another study also found that stunted children scored substantially lower on cognitive tests, were more likely to repeat years of school and had higher absenteeism than children who were not stunted (Mendez and Adair 1999).

Moreover, adults whose growth was stunted during childhood have a higher risk of developing degenerative diseases such as diabetes than those with normal growth (Sartika et al. 2021); women who are stunted are at higher risk for difficult pregnancies and labour; and children who have rapid weight gain after the age of two (a trend in the Philippines) have a greater risk of becoming overweight later in life, with increased risks for coronary heart disease, stroke, hypertension and type 2 diabetes.

To prevent stunting, nutritionists recommend eating fruits, vegetables, eggs and nuts, which are in the food groups consumed less and less by Filipino children (Daniels et al. 2009; Department of Science and Technology, Food and Nutrition Research Institute 2013; Kennedy et al. 2007; Wright et al. 2015). As Filipino nutritionists have pointed out, the dietary transition to processed carbohydrates (in biscuits, breads and noodles), oils and refined sugar, and increasingly to meat and milk (not to mention the heavy marketing of vitamins) has led to significant decreases in the consumption of ordinary fruits and vegetables (Department of Science and Technology, Food and Nutrition Research Institute 2013; Pedro, Benavides and Barba 2006). In 2013, the Food and Nutrition Research Institute reported a dramatic decline in per capita fresh fruit and vegetable intake since the late 1970s, when Filipinos consumed approximately 145 g of vegetables and 104 g of fruits daily. By 2003, these amounts had dropped to 111 g of vegetables (a reduction of 25 per cent) and 54 g of fruits per individual per day (a reduction of 50 per cent), and the trend continues (Department of Science and Technology, Food and Nutrition Research Institute 2013; Pedro, Benavides and Barba 2006).

The cultivation practices of farmers reflect Filipinos' changing dietary practices. A study by Eder (1999) in San Jose, a town eight kilometres north of Puerto Princesa, followed farmers from 1971 to 1988 and found a sharp decrease in the diversity of vegetables they cultivated. Whereas farmers grew around 12 different vegetables per garden in 1971, by 1988 this had dropped to around five commercially valuable cultigens (during which period the use of chemical fertilizers on farms increased fivefold). The farmers chose to cultivate what was most profitable, eliminating traditional vegetables like *alugabati*, a local variety of spinach, and *sigadilyas*, a variety of beans, for which there was limited demand. Another study in a vegetable-growing region in Samar (Briones et al. 2017) indicates that people ate fewer vegetables than before; household members saw the consumption of the same vegetables as monotonous and preferred to monetize their produce to buy less nutrient-dense, processed foods like noodles, which are easily accessible in neighbourhood stores.

Noodlemania

Presenting perhaps the most dramatic example of a metabolic rift are instant noodles. The World Instant Noodles Association or WINA (instantnoodles.org) monitors demand for their products. The data in Table 2.2, from WINA, demonstrates that instant noodles have become a global food, with the Philippines among the highest in consumption, taking seventh place among the top 10 countries, China and Hong Kong, several East and Southeast Asian countries and India, the US and Brazil.

Table 2.2 The top-ranking countries for servings of noodles per year (unit: million servings).

	Country/Region	2018	2019	2020	2021	2022
1	China/Hong Kong	40,250	41,450	46,360	43,990	45,070
2	Indonesia	12,540	12,520	12,640	13,270	14,260
3	Viet Nam	5,200	5,440	7,030	8,560	8,480
4	India	6,060	6,730	6,730	7,560	7,580
5	Japan	5,780	5,630	5,970	5,850	5,980
6	USA	4,520	4,630	5,050	4,980	5,150
7	Philippines	3,980	3,850	4,470	4,440	4,290

Source: World Instant Noodles Association.

Noodle manufacturers conduct market studies that include analyses of cultural tastes. The WINA website notes, for example, that people in China favour beef-based soups with 5-spice powder (fennel, cinnamon, cloves, *unshui* citrus peel and star anise) that use flour noodles, rice vermicelli or cellophane noodles, served in tub containers.

People in the Philippines, by contrast, favour *pancit canton* (noodles introduced by Cantonese itinerant food vendors, beginning in the Spanish colonial period) flavoured with *calamondin* (a local citrus fruit, *kalamansi* in Tagalog) and hot chilli peppers. The WINA website describes Filipinos as people who like to snack, so instant noodles are sold in smaller 'mini-sized cups'.

A large variety of instant noodles are sold in the Philippines, reflecting their popularity. They cater to every Filipinos' taste, paying attention to capacity and notions of food adequacy. The packaging suggests they contain a full meal (including, in addition to the noodles, meat, green vegetables, and corn), to make the products attractive to poor consumers. See Figure 2.1 for an example of a popular noodle brand, which we chose because of the chunk of meat portrayed on the package.

When we turn the package over, its low nutritional value and high salt content become apparent. The package has zero vitamin A and C, and 4 g of protein.

We spoke with people all over the Philippines about their noodle consumption and observed two trends. For poor people in towns, who

Figure 2.1 Picture of a popular brand of noodles. Bulalo is a popular meat dish in the Philippines, considered to be *sustansiya* or nutrient-rich because it contains bone marrow. Lucky Me is a best-selling brand of Monde, a Philippine-Indonesian company. Source: Author (Tan), 2021.

work long hours and do not have enough time to cook, noodles are convenient fast foods consumed as replacements for home-cooked meals. By contrast, middle- and upper-class families still cherish home-cooked meals (and, increasingly, meals in restaurants). For them, noodles are just snacks that fill the gaps in between meals. For the poor, the low nutrient value of instant noodles perpetuates malnutrition, while for the middle and upper classes, frequent consumption of them contributes to obesity.

To illustrate the way in which manufacturers tailor noodles to diverse market segments, let us present the variety of tastes Nissin, a market leader based in Japan, produces. In one afternoon, we purchased Nissin noodles of various provenances, easily obtaining a wide variety. These included Nissin products licensed to a local company, Universal Robina Corporation, that cost an average of 10 pesos ($0.18 US) per 55 g packet. There were also imported Nissin products, but not necessarily from Japan (one version was manufactured in Nissin's plant in Hong Kong with flavours like 'Tonkotsu with Black Garlic Oil' and priced at 33 pesos for a 100 g packet; another was Nissin Chow Mein Noodles Chicken Flavor with Other Natural Flavors, imported from Nissin's factory in Gardena, California, which prominently proclaimed 'No Added MSG' – it sold at 95 pesos for a 113 g package ready for the microwave, clearly catering to high-end consumers, as seen in Figure 2.2.

Figure 2.2 Chow Mein noodles – natural flavours and no MSG added. Source: Author (Tan), 2021.

The Philippine noodle market has many other players. A Chinese grocery sells popular Chinese brands, including one called Supreme, which features flavours like Lobster and Cheese. The packaging indicates (in both English and Chinese) a Hong Kong distribution address, but that the noodles are a 'Product of Vietnam'. South Korean products have a growing presence in the Philippines, advertised on large billboards. Formerly limited to Korean groceries, they are today sold widely in supermarkets and convenience stores. An example is Nongshim, produced in Seoul. A 75 g cup of chicken flavoured instant oolongmen noodles costs 69 pesos.

Historically, noodles may have been the original fast food, introduced originally by Chinese settlers (as noted in Chapter 1) and served in restaurants and by hawkers on sidewalks. In Japan, instant noodles had been invented as a response to a noodle shortage among the working class, who had previously been able to buy them from low-cost outlets. Momofuku Ando, a Japanese entrepreneur and the founder of Nissin, noted long queues of Japanese waiting to buy cooked noodles. In 1958, he developed, in his home, a technology that made use of the large volumes of wheat flour the US had donated to Japan to produce quick-cooking noodles that could be prepared at home. Instant ramen (derived from the Chinese *lamien*, 'hand-pulled noodles') took off not just in Japan but also worldwide, including in the Philippines.

In *The Noodle Narratives*, Errington et al. (2013) examine the popularity of noodles in Papua New Guinea. They discuss the 'satiety factor' that the ingredients in noodles induce, leaving eaters feeling full, and their value as cheap sustenance for the 'bottom of the pyramid' which, the authors argue, can give them a key role in the prevention of food shortages. Writing before Russia's full-scale invasion of Ukraine in 2022, they could not imagine that global conflicts would severely affect access to wheat – the main ingredient of noodles.

In the Philippines, noodles serve as cheap sustenance for the poor and simultaneously serve as a source for culinary experimentation among people from the middle and upper classes, who consume them as snacks. Additionally, the simple fact that a bowl of instant noodles is comforting and delightful to slurp – warm, salty and delicious – explains their prominence in Filipino diets.

Urbanization

Urbanization accelerates the spread of nutritionally compromised diets because the space available for backyard gardening diminishes in the dense living conditions of cities. Increasing numbers of women and men taking jobs in the emerging service sector affects diets because working long hours outside the home leaves little time for cooking full meals. In cities, community sari-sari stores do not stock fresh fruits and vegetables but instead offer foods and drinks with limited nutritional value that are highly processed and contain high levels of fat, sugar and salt (such as noodles, chips, candies, meats, sugary soft drinks and energy drinks, and alcohol), contributing to obesity (Vargas 2017). Urban families, increasingly reliant on these cheap, ready-made, high-calorie foods, are living in what the FNRI calls an 'obesogenic food environment' due to decreased consumption of fruits and vegetables.

Like noodles, many ready-made foods are unhealthy because they generally contain too much fat and sugar. A bag of Muncher Green Peas (Figure 2.3) may at first glance seem relatively healthy. It contains 14 g of protein, 24 per cent of the recommended daily intake of vitamin C, and 17 per cent of the recommended daily iron. But it also contains 13 g of (mostly saturated) fats and 5 g of sugar.

Figure 2.3 Left: Community 'sari-sari' store selling highly processed breakfast snacks for school children. Right: Nutritional content of Muncher Green Peas. Source: Author (Hardon), 2014.

Fighting hidden hunger

The Philippines government has responded to the cumulative deterioration of the quality of Filipinos' diets in various ways. In an early example of a deficiency-oriented policy, it promoted the production of fortified white rice. The apparent need to fortify rice is ironic. The country has a long history of planting and consuming diverse brown rice varieties as primary staple foods, with each region producing its own ecologically adapted strains, cherished for their distinct flavours and celebrated by nutritionists for their diverse nutritional values. However, because of wide-spread adoption of rice milling, the country's main staple food today is processed white rice (see Figure 2.4).

Figure 2.4 Indigenous cultivation of brown rice in the Northern Cordillera Region, where people prefer their own rice over the milled rice, the staple for lowland Filipinos. Source: *Stasis and Mobility* exhibition (part of Anita Hardon's project ChemicalYouth), University of the Philippines, 2018, https://www.chemicalyouth.org/#/projects/stasis-and-mobility (Accessed 6 June 2024). Used by permission.

Mapping the consequences of rice milling in the Philippines, Chiang (2020) demonstrates the association between increased consumption of white rice and malnutrition and an epidemic of beriberi (caused by thiamine deficiency) at the end of the nineteenth century. The epidemic particularly affected poor households, where people's diets relied heavily on rice, and was particularly severe in the lowlands, where large-scale production of rice took place. In response, a US chemist developed a technique for supplementing milled rice with thiamine; this supplementation process became mandatory in 1952, when the government of the Philippines adopted the Rice Enrichment Act (Chiang 2020).[3]

Fifty years later, Emil Javier, the president of the University of the Philippines and a plant geneticist and agronomist, advocated for a return to brown rice. In *Rice Today*, a trade publication, he declared:

> Now we must overcome the 'hidden hunger' of the poor for essential vitamins and minerals. As cereals constitute the bulk of the diet of those who cannot afford micronutrient-rich foods such as meat, milk, fruits and vegetables, any increase in the vitamin and mineral content of staple grains helps combat this insidious form of malnutrition. (Javier 2004, 38)

The Philippines has also started a programme with Golden Rice, which is rice bioengineered to have a high vitamin A content (a vitamin that people can obtain naturally from eating fresh fruits and vegetables). The strategy failed. Consumers did not like the taste of the new rice variety and farmers in poor regions of the country lacked access to land to grow the fortified crops (Brooks 2012; Glover and Stone 2020).

When Anita discussed this plant-breeding intervention with her father (Jaap Hardon, then a board member of the International Rice Research Institute in the Philippines) he said: 'Well, it was a proof of concept. Plant breeders could contribute by developing varieties high in vitamin A, but I never understood why the supplementation should be done through this staple food. Why not promote the eating of carrots or papaya?' This would have made good sense, since carrots and papaya not only contain vitamin A but also a host of additional phytochemicals and vitamins. As one Indian analyst commented regarding his own country's nutrition problems, 'We must look to our farms, not to our pharmacies, for the durable solution of our nutritional problems' (Gopalan 2001, 6).

Combating 'hidden hunger' with micronutrients, rather than ordinary foods, to reduce deficiencies in iron, iodine and vitamin A was the aim of a joint Philippine health ministry and UNICEF child health programme since the early 1990s. In 1993, Secretary of Health Juan Flavier declared 17 October to be Micronutrients Day or *Araw ng Sangkap Pinoy* (literally, Day of Filipino Ingredients). The campaign urged mothers to visit health centres and receive vitamin A capsules to prevent their children from becoming blind, iodized oil to prevent growth delays and *malunggay* seedlings to provide iron. Flavier also introduced *malunggay* cooking contests in schools. While well-intended, these campaigns 'charged mothers with the responsibility for correcting problems in diet for their children' (Gálvez 2018, 157) without tackling the underlying problems of capitalist provisioning in the Philippines. The campaigns were furthermore performative, given that *malunggay* trees are common in the Philippines (they grow on farmlands and in cities) and the tree's leaves are usually an essential ingredient in traditional soups (see Figure 2.5).

Figure 2.5 Malunggay (Moringa) tree. Source: Jessel Dela Torre. Used by permission.

Embracing the idea that collaborating with the private sector could help to address micronutrient deficiencies, Javier called on the food industry to fortify its products. The Philippines Health Department's *Araw ng Sangkap Pinoy* programme endorsed over 100 processed food items, including instant noodles, based on fortification with vitamin A and/or iron.[4] Swift Mighty Meaty Hotdogs likewise received endorsement for containing the daily allowances for vitamins A, B1 and D3. Swift company representatives declared: 'It's our way of helping see to it that blindness will soon disappear' (Tan 1999, 69). Lucky Me noodles was another blockbuster food product that received the *Sangkap Pinoy* seal of approval: its manufacturer, Monde, reported that each serving contained at least one-third of the daily requirements for vitamin A and iron.

Aya Hirata Kimura's (2013) feminist analysis of Indonesia's fortification programme reveals that it was developed by the World Bank and other global actors in tandem with the private sector. The model takes inspiration from neoliberal economic assumptions that fortifying staple foods is cost-effective because behavioural change through health promotion is hard to achieve. Relying on the private sector to fix the problem of micronutrient deficiencies, fortification programmes circumvent government investments in health promotion to motivate parents to feed their children more vegetables and fruit. Kimura argues against economizing nutrition in this way, stating that fortification programmes reduce people's abilities to feed themselves and their children well – rendering them 'passive recipients of fortified foods' (Kimura 2013, 40). She points out that corporate television advertisements and package labels convince mothers that they need fortified foods to feed their children well.

In 1995, Del Monte started featuring advertisements on TV and in newspapers trumpeting the presence of phytochemicals in fruit juice. Dr Galvez Tan (the inventor of First Vita Plus), who later became secretary of health, lent credence to Del Monte's health claims by speaking publicly about how phytochemicals can prevent cancer. Other juice companies followed suit, promoting their products' 'antioxidant' properties and suggesting that increasing levels of pollution required antioxidants for protection (Tan 1999, 70–1). In these cases, the food industry not only targeted nutritional deficiencies, but also made broad health claims, using scientific terms. This method continues in the contemporary marketing of packaged plants as food supplements, which we examine in detail in Chapter 4.

Vitamania

Meanwhile, the market for vitamins exploded. The Philippine Index of Medical Specialties (PIMS) is a catalogue of pharmacological products and their ingredients, formulations and indications, originally produced as a prescribing guide for health professionals. Studying successive editions reveals the increasing range of vitamins sold in the country since the 1970s.

With time, the PIMS came to include lay people as part of its readership and it is now sold in bookstores. Its lists of multivitamins and minerals have grown longer over the years, reflecting marketing changes following the 'more is better' paradigm: more products, more vitamins, more minerals, more claims. There is also an increase in demographic 'niches', with preparations specific to children, adolescents, women and the elderly. Targeting people's concerns about stunting, the PIMS lists combinations of multivitamins and antihistamines marketed as appetite stimulants. The campaign to counter this claim goes back to the 1980s, when Health Action International launched a campaign against problem drugs, including these multivitamin-antihistamine combinations (Health Action International 1986). The PIMS' paediatric section also includes multivitamins combined with 'growth factors'. These products come with promises of 'reaching your growth potential' and *tangkad-sagad* (height to the fullest), which capture the attention of parents and children alike, similar to the way Star margarine had captured the attention of the previous generation. Cherifer, the most popular growth supplement, is promoted using images of young celebrity basketball players (Lasco 2017), see Figure 2.6. Its key ingredient is 'Chlorella Growth Factor' (CGF), which has no proven efficacy.

Figure 2.6 A billboard along a highway in Metro Manila, July 2017. Cherifer is endorsed by basketball players. Source: Gideon Lasco. Used by permission.

In the 1990s, anti-stress preparations combining vitamin C and B-complex vitamins began to appear on the market. In 1997, at the height of the Asian economic crisis, the multinational pharmaceutical firm, Pfizer, launched Clusivol, a preparation containing vitamins B and C. Its promotional campaign, *Bawal ang magkasakit* (It is forbidden to fall ill), employed a 'no-work–no-pay' slogan that resounded with the millions of Filipinos whose salaries were based on daily wages. It was so successful that the slogan continues to be used today; Ritemed, a Filipino company, adopted a variation of the same approach, *Bawal magkasakit* (Don't get sick), for its entire line of medicines (Pozon 2019). During this same period, the Philippines Department of Health seized upon fortification as the solution. Vitamins and minerals were added to milk, breakfast cereals and even instant noodles, as during the government's *Sangkap Pinoy* programme.

We need to critically examine the continuing insistence on supplementation, especially as it frames nutrition in terms of deficiencies of individual vitamins or minerals – even as medical and nutrition textbooks describe their vital interactions. For example, vitamin D enables the body to tap calcium in food and vitamin C aids the absorption of iron, yet too much vitamin C can block the body's ability to assimilate copper.

Price (2016) uses 'vitamania' to describe the people's demand for vitamins, whether or not they have deficiencies. We add our concerns that people with this 'vitamania' fail to recognize that fresh vegetables and fruits are full of healthy vitamins, along with substances such as dietary fibre that helps maintain healthy gut flora. The heavy marketing of vitamins as vital elements of everyday life deepens the loss of plant sovereignty.

In the 1990s, while conducting fieldwork for his thesis, Michael found that Filipinos still knew that they could obtain vitamin C from the local citrus fruits *dalandan* and *kalamansi*, vitamin A from leafy green vegetables, and iron (for anaemia) from *malunggay* (moringa), *ampalaya* (bitter melon) and *kamote* (sweet potato). But, he noted, insecurities about whether one was getting 'enough' nutrients were increasing, especially in urban areas (Tan 1999). He quotes a 25-year-old office worker: 'I'm so busy. That's why sometimes I eat irregularly, so I need vitamins', and an 18-year-old student: 'My diet is not balanced. I don't have time to prepare a complete meal, so I need to take vitamins' (Tan 1999, 133).

Such worries have not abated. In recent years, zinc has become widely promoted, not only by UNICEF's micronutrient supplementation programme for children with diarrhoea, but also by drug companies that state in their advertisements that zinc improves immunity. When the COVID-19 pandemic first broke out in March 2020, a large supermarket chain in the Philippines put up large tarps at the entrances of their stores, with images and text promoting the use of masks, handwashing and physical distancing, alongside a sign stating: 'Take vitamins, especially those rich in vitamin C and zinc'.[5] Drugstores quickly ran out of multivitamin and mineral preparations during the first few weeks of the pandemic.

Nutri-Foods

At the start of the twenty-first century the Philippine Plan of Action for Nutrition (PPAN) had continued to set its sights on reducing malnutrition among preschool children by promoting micronutrient supplementation. The Department of Health subsidized the Philippines Nutri-Foods Corporation to develop and manufacture food supplements for national feeding programmes. Nutri-Foods formulates multiple supplements containing vitamins and minerals (A, D, C, B, folic acid, iron, zinc, copper, selenium and iodine) that may be added to or used as foods.

In 2016 we met a Nutri-Foods representative at the Annual Convention of the Philippine Society of Nutritionists and Dieticians in Puerto Princesa, where we were conducting fieldwork on the multilevel marketing of First Vita Plus (see Chapters 5 and 6), and at which Michael had been invited to present. The Nutri-Foods representative enthusiastically told us about a micronutrient powder (MNP) that could be added to children's food (see Figure 2.7). The powder contains 15 vitamins and minerals, and he assured us that children tolerated it well because it had no taste or smell.

The Nutri-Foods representative gave us a promotional leaflet that included nutritional 'findings' that helped make the case for giving MNP to children:

> *39 per cent of children age 6–24 months are malnourished!*
> *Malnutrition has a lifelong impact!*
> *Children are more prone to diseases.*
> *Children score up to 9 points lower on IQ tests!*
> *This affects their own productivity and also the country's economy!*
> *Let's save the next generation from this preventable situation!*

Give them Micronutrient Powder (MNP) in their first 1,000 days of life!

This is their critical development period – for brain function, muscle growth and tissue formation.

Let's invest in their future!

Figure 2.7 Package of MNP food supplement, produced as 'Vita Meena'. Note that MNP is presented as only a food supplement, with the disclaimer 'NO APPROVED THERAPEUTIC CLAIMS'. This phrase is required by the Philippines Food and Drug Administration, which only allows therapeutic claims if clinical trials have proven specific health outcomes (see also Chapter 4). Source: Author (Hardon), 2020.

The Nutri-Foods leaflet referred to the first 1,000 days of life. This was a nod to the Philippines Department of Health's latest nutrition programme, which relied on an assumption that the ill effects of persistent malnutrition could be prevented if health policymakers ensured that children were fed well in the first 1,000 days of their lives – starting from conception (Municipality of Mina 2016).

The Nutri-Foods representative informed us that community nutritionists and health workers were distributing the supplement as an income-generating project. They were able to buy the sachets at the wholesale price of two pesos per packet and sell them for three pesos, the same price they cost in pharmacies. If they sold a box of 30 packets each day, they would earn 30 pesos, a nice addition to their daily income of 260 pesos.

As attendees at the conference, we received Unilever-sponsored conference bags filled with unhealthy food items that were high in sugar and salt. The bags were emblazoned with the slogans 'Ingenious Nutrition: Rediscovering what Filipinos have and can do for sustainable nutrition', and 'I'M ON A LOW CARBON DIET' (see Figure 2.8), the punning carb/carbon reference troping climate change as a 'trendy' theme – one we had not previously seen food companies exploiting when promoting their products. To our surprise, the conference bag contained a sachet of grape-flavoured Tang, not only unhealthy (a 5 g sachet contains 4 g of sugar) but also grapes do not grow in the Philippines. The conference catering was equally surprising, given the context, offering white-bread sandwiches with copious amounts of mayonnaise, and very sweet fruit juice.

Michael had been invited to speak on the theme of 'resilience, food values and heritage'. The conference organizers had asked him to motivate the nutritionists present to appreciate the resourcefulness of Filipino people in the face of food insecurity, and also to showcase Filipino food cultures. Michael, however, began by gently criticizing the contents of the conference bag as an example of the ubiquity of unhealthy foods and then went on to decry Filipino companies selling small, low-cost packages of noodles containing empty calories along with high levels of sodium that made people thirsty for the sugary soft drinks sold

Figure 2.8 Unilever-sponsored conference bag, from the 2014 conference of the Philippine Society of Nutritionists and Dieticians. Source: Author (Hardon), 2014.

next to the noodles in local stores. Noting that people concerned about such imbalanced diets are advised to turn to vitamins and supplements, Michael suggested that people's scarce resources would be better spent on fresh food instead. He pointed out that fast food restaurants (increasingly popular among the burgeoning middle classes in the Philippines) also contribute to poor diets, by creating the desire to eat out in places where the budget meals have only slightly more nutritional value than instant noodles and soft drinks. To make his point, he pulled out the menu from his budget short flight from Manila to Puerto Princesa, which had offered the choice of beef or chicken instant noodles, along with instant coffee and chips.

Michael also shared his frustrations when observing both his students and his children, telling the audience, 'We offer them vegetables and fruits, but they crave fast food.' When Michael asked his students about their choices, they cited the low cost of fast food. Trying to convince them that they could eat tastier, healthier foods, even on tight budgets, he learned that they did not know recipes or even where to buy fresh food. Even his food science students did not know the names of local vegetables. He called on the audience to convince people that 'old-fashioned' foods (such as *tinolang manok*, a traditional recipe of chicken, green papaya, spinach and ginger) and 'retro' eating styles are key to health. He closed his presentation with a definition of healthy eating – slow-paced consumption of home-cooked food – and noted that the health impact of the Mediterranean diet comes not just from the use of olive oil, but from how people eat – more slowly, and with family or friends.

The next speaker at the convention was culinary expert Amy Besa, a well-known chef who at that time had well-rated restaurants in New York and Manila, both promoting traditional Filipino cuisine, with fresh ingredients, made to order food and using no chemicals or additives. Besa recounted her surprise when a major portion of the Filipino community in New York rejected the culinary art of Purple Yam, her restaurant there. They did not like the flavours. She did not understand why, she said, until she realized that her customers, just like Michael's children and students, had also grown up on fast food.

Besa lauded the value of fresh food markets where she goes to learn about Filipinos' diverse cuisine, asserting that such markets should become prime tourist destinations and invested in as such. Her presentation noted that the typical flavours of the archipelago can be traced to pre-refrigeration foodways, especially the use of fermentation in preservation. Encouraging her audience to value the diversity of flavours in the Philippines, she explained that even the micro-organisms of fermentation differ from one location to the other, making for different tastes. Besides this, different varieties of fruits and vegetables have different flavours. Besa told her audience of nutritionists and dietitians that traditional Philippine tastes need to be cultivated and implored them to start trying raw ingredients, saying: 'Reawaken your imagination. Taste the flavours and the textures ... You process everything through your own palate.' She called on her audience to become 'food warriors' and mentioned her work setting up community kitchens to teach people how to use local foods as but one example of what can be done. Besa ended her presentation by giving the attendees samples of a delicious nougat made from local honey and cashews.

You might have wondered, as did we, about Unilever's sponsorship of this conference. We learned more about this connection at the 2017 conference of the Philippine Association of Nutrition (a different association from the one mentioned above) in Quezon City, where we were invited to speak on the 'seduction of supplements'. In May 2016, Unilever entered into an agreement with the government-sponsored FNRI at the Department of Science and Technology. For Unilever, 'sustainable nutrition' entailed incorporating improved products into healthy recipes, with limited waste. The goal of the public–private partnership was promoting this sustainable approach to cooking through the government's *Pinggang Pinoy Go, Grow, Glow* campaign, first adopted in the 1960s. 'Go' indicates foods providing carbohydrates (mainly rice and cereals), 'grow' signifies proteins (primarily meats and dairy products) and 'glow' stands for fruits and vegetables. Pinggang Pinoy, can be translated as 'the Filipino plate' – the slogan uses a plate to indicate healthy meals (see Figures 2.9 and 2.10).

The categorization of food into three 'purposes' (go, grow and glow) was borrowed from campaigns implemented by the US Department of Agriculture. At the same conference, we learned about 'nutrition month', during which the government called on nutritionists to promote growing vegetables and fruit trees, home cooking and the provision of healthy meals in office canteens.

In the most recent Philippine Plan of Action for Nutrition 2017–22, the mixed strategy and confusing messages of encouragement to both grow community gardens and supplement the diet with packaged plants continues. However, there is now also an emphasis on sustainable nutrition (Department of Health 2017). Local health supplementation programmes are encouraged to use locally sourced foods, as was the case in the nutrition cooperative Yates-Doerr (2015) observed in

Figure 2.9 Image from the Pinggang Pinoy campaign. Source: https://doh.gov.ph/node/223 (public domain, Accessed 6 June 2024).

Figure 2.10 Image from the Pinggang Pinoy campaign. Source: https://doh.gov.ph/node/223 (public domain, Accessed 6 June 2024).

Guatemala, while simultaneously promoting the use of micronutrient powders. There is also an emphasis on the first 1,000 days of a child's life (from conception until the child reaches 24 months), in line with global attention to this important stage in life, when the child's brain, body and immune system are most sensitive to external environmental influences.[6]

None of these nutrition interventions address the root problem: ordinary vegetables and fruits are consumed much less than they were in the past, and children are fed ultra-processed foods such as Muncher Green Peas (green pea snacks), instant noodles, juices and sugary cereals that are not a healthy option. The Philippine government is making no attempt to reduce the population's reliance on industrial diets, which perpetuate malnutrition, but instead is calling on manufacturers to fortify their products with vitamins and minerals. As a result, recent generations of children and young adults think they need processed, fortified foods in order to be healthy. They no longer know how to prepare vegetable-based dishes from their backyards; nor are they able to source healthy vegetables from markets. They are not likely to cook meals at home or eat them with other members of their households – a nutritional strategy the Ministry of Health of Brazil proposed in 2014 (which, alas, subsequent regimes abandoned, see Monteiro et al. 2015). The Philippine government instead reinforces the consumption of convenience foods and then seeks to address the negative consequences through food supplements, buying into what Scrinis (2013) refers to as the 'nutritionism paradigm'. This fuels demand for food supplements, which deplete the already-meagre resources of people facing food insecurity.

During the course of our fieldwork in Palawan, we would find food wrappers strewn along the footpaths to schools, perhaps best illustrating the problem that confronts the next generation of Filipinos. In this region, families still have backyards and people grow at least some vegetables and fruits. However, children are given fast-food breakfasts and snacks, the brand names of which reflect the 'jungle' of the past (Figure 2.11).

Nutrition and nature

The Philippine government's embracing of nutritionism reinforces anxieties and generates a demand for food supplements in a country where people experience persistent malnutrition. This is due to a confluence of two factors. First, the government's tendency to address nutritional deficiencies through supplements and 'fortification' gives

Figure 2.11 Breakfast packaging waste found on roadside in Puerto Princesa, including Muncher Green Peas, Jungle Bites Biscuits, and cheese and chicharron (pork rinds) flavoured crackers. Source: Author (Hardon), 2016.

consumers the impression that ordinary food is not good enough; second, the collaboration between the Philippines government and big food corporations in food-fortification projects encourages people to continue to eat noodles and other highly processed foods and amplifies uncertainty among consumers about the nutritional value of fresh vegetables and fruits available for purchase in markets. The government embraces cooperation with big food corporations, without curtailing their aggressive marketing of hyper-processed convenience foods that cause diet-related health problems (Gálvez 2018; Guthman 2009).

Tofoya (2023), a Mexican economist who conducted research fieldwork in poor urban areas of Metro Manila, calls these products 'corporate food', and notes they are marketed with the government's endorsement. Heeding governmental advice, mothers, themselves stunted, adopt diets that leave them malnourished, which itself is a risk factor for raising another generation of stunted children. They spend scarce resources on vitamins and supplements, which means they have fewer resources for and are less inclined to invest in fresh vegetables and fruits. With each generation, vitamins, supplements, and hyper-processed foods account for a greater percentage of the population's total diet. Consumption of hyper-processed foods, vitamins, and supplements are not tangential, but indeed the very core reason for stunted growth in Filipino infants and children (Monteiro 2009).

Packaged problems

We chose *Packaged Plants* as the title of this book to emphasize that the issues of poor food and nutrition, and the effects of metabolic rifts, include the packaging itself. Metabolic rifts caused by increasing food processing displace knowledge and practices of traditional and unprocessed food production. Packaging itself aggravates this displacement because of the material from which it is made, and because it serves as a medium for marketing and misinformation.

With regard to packaging material, Filipinos previously stored processed foods in tins (canned food) and glass. This included home preservation methods to extend the shelf life for products, mainly vegetables and fruits. Since the turn of the millennium, packaging material has shifted toward various types of plastics, several of which have since been banned due to health risks. One example is bisphenol-A (BPA), an industrial chemical used to manufacture plastics for food containers, baby bottles and plastic water bottles. BPA is linked to infertility, obesity, type 2 diabetes, heart disease and cancers, and is an endocrine disruptor that mimics oestrogen.

Despite awareness of their dangers, many plastics are still used for packaging water and beverages. Most of these containers are single use, which creates further issues in terms of environmental pollution, since the plastics are not biodegradable and can remain in the environment for centuries. 'Shrinking' food packages (selling very small quantities, packaged) in countries like the Philippines to fit low-income budgets exacerbates environmental pollution. The renowned, late Filipino writer Nick Joacquin describes this context:

> Enterprise for the Filipino is small stall: the *sari-sari* … Commerce for the Filipino is the smallest degree of retail: the *tingi*. What most astonishes foreigners in the Philippines is that this is a country, perhaps the only one in the world, where people buy and sell one stick of cigarette, half a head of garlic, a dab of pomade, parts of the content of a can or bottle, one single egg, one single banana. (Benosa 2020, 2)

A Filipino environmental activist, Benosa (2020) describes how large companies have cashed in on *tingi* culture by creating a new niche market for retail sales. Benosa warns against the 'pro-poor narrative' of food manufacturers, who argue that single sachets make their products affordable for the poor. Benosa notes that *tingi* retail sales were originally tied to recycling. For example, to buy a small amount of vinegar, a consumer brought an old bottle to the sari-sari shop to be filled with the *tingi* amount. Today, Benosa laments, *tingi* is built on pre-packaged, plastic sachets.

In addition to plastics, there are per- and polyfluoroalkyl substances (PFASs) called 'forever chemicals' because, like plastics, they do not break down in the environment easily. In consumer food packaging in the United States and Canada, these chemicals are used for their water- and oil-repelling properties, for example, for microwaveable bags of popcorn (Minet et al. 2022). Non-stick cooking utensils likewise contain PFASs. There is even 'eco-friendly', plant-fibre-based food packaging, such as cups and plates, made with PFASs. In the United States, seven states have banned PFASs from materials that make contact with food.

Although studies are conducted in industrialized countries, countries in the Global South, like the Philippines, face these same problems. Moreover, in the Philippines, unsafe packaging is manufactured in unregulated, uninformed environments, with government regulatory authorities themselves among the uninformed. Moreover, imported food products with fancy packaging are considered high-prestige and desirable, and even perceived as safer and healthier than old-fashioned glass jars.

Packaging also markets products. Food packaging, whether for *tingi* sales or in large volumes to restaurants, is a powerful form of marketing. Above, we described our informal investigation of the many different types of instant noodles available, and their deceptive packaging, suggesting they constitute a balanced meal with all kinds of ingredients and flavourings. The packaging of processed foods is a vehicle for a massive advertising and promotions industry, with strategies based on extensive consumer research (often using social science methods such as focus groups) to inundate the market with advertisements in print, on radio and television and, in recent years, through social media and online celebrity influencers.

Packaging is branded as part of massive advertising campaigns aimed at specific demographic groups. Kelly et al. (2015) found the density of outdoor food and beverage advertising within a range of 250 m from schools in Manila was twice as high (6.5 per 100 sq. m) as areas between 250 and 500 m from schools. Billboards were mainly for unhealthy foods and drinks. Tofoya (2023, 266) points out that, in addition to these outdoor advertisements, potential consumers are exposed to advertisements on tricycles and on sari-sari storefronts. Manufacturers of food, beverages, cigarettes and alcoholic drinks offer free signs to owners that display their names (for example, 'Lita's Store'), alongside promoted products, for example Cobra (an energy drink). School canteens and sporting events also provide venues for advertising, especially for high-caffeine tonic drinks.

Big food blocking change

We have both been involved in consumer campaigns to ban dangerous medicines and introduce rational uses of medications and in the drawn-out, global battle for an International Code for Breastfeeding Substitutes, to pressure formula manufacturers to stop promoting their products for infants. As seasoned veterans, we're familiar with the numerous backhanded tactics large corporations can employ. Despite this, in our research on metabolic rifts, we still found ourselves shocked by the methods some food companies use, particularly producers of ultra-processed food, to avoid undercutting their profits, despite the increasing number of issues around food safety and nutrition itself. A comprehensive study (Huse et al. 2023, 2) found that ultra-processed food companies in the Philippines sought:

> … to delay, prevent, water-down and circumvent implementation of globally recommended food and nutrition policies by engaging in a range of strategies that includes discrediting proponents of proposed reforms, engaging policymakers with gifts, perks and incentives as well as 'scientific' data generated by the industry itself.

In the next chapter, we outline how communities, in particular community-based health programmes (CBHPs), responded to the metabolic rifts in Filipinos' diets. We focus on their efforts to revive plant sovereignty in the Philippines by promoting the use of plants grown in people's backyards to treat common disorders such as diarrhoea, skin infections and respiratory disorders. But first we present the photo essay that depicts how poor people in Manila eat.

Notes

1 For more information on South Korea (Republic of Korea) see 'The burden of nutrition at a glance: Republic of Korea'. *Global Nutrition Report.* https://globalnutritionreport.org/resources/nutrition-profiles/asia/eastern-asia/republic-korea/ (Accessed 6 June 2024).
2 Although the article publication date is 2016, the website on which the journal article is posted has additional granular data up to 2019.

3 In the mid-1970s, President Marcos sought to reduce malnutrition by improving the nutritional value of ordinary foods. He prohibited the production of 'over-milled' rice (with all the bran removed), thereby increasing the nutritional value of rice, which was seen as a good source of vitamin B1 and protein. This policy had little success, as demand for white rice had increased and mill owners found ways to circumvent it.
4 See 'Sangkap Pinoy program: The food fortification in the Philippines' Rice Bowl Asia, http://www.ricebowlasia.com/sangkap-pinoy-seal-program-the-food-fortification-in-philippines (Accessed 26 October 2020).
5 Zinc is not a vitamin, but a mineral.
6 See https://thousanddays.org (Accessed 6 June 2024).

Photo Essay 1:
Living on the edge: food and precarity among Filipino urban poor

The Filipino food described in coffee table books and glossy magazines is generally what the middle class and rich eat. The poor may eat some of these dishes, with cheaper ingredients, on special occasions like birthdays, Christmas and the New Year.

When attending a party celebration thrown by someone more well-to-do, the poor will warn each other not to binge or take too large servings, lest they be accused of *patay gutom* (dying of hunger).

This photo essay focuses on food that the urban poor in Metro Manila consume. There, the preponderance of ultra-processed food – quick to prepare and cheap but problematic because of high salt and fat content – is all too visible. Photo 1 shows typical food stock found in an urban poor home, mostly instant noodles and flavourings.

The instant noodles, whether for breakfast, lunch or dinner, will often be the meal itself and repeated for lunch and dinner and combinations thereof like *altanghap*, which is a combination of the Tagalog words *almusal* (breakfast), *tanghalian* (lunch) and *hapunan* (dinner), usually connoting a single meal the poor eat around midday.

Rice is a staple, with the noodles sometimes ending up as the viand. The flavourings sold with the instant noodles create 'variety', or sometimes people use packaged flavourings with names like Magic Sarap (magic good taste), consisting of salt, monosodium glutamate and specks of powdered spices.

We also find more low-cost prepared meals at *carinderias* (small restaurants), operated by urban poor residents and sidewalk vendors (see Photo 2). Instant noodles crop up again; some vendors make a living simply selling packaged instant noodles and supplying the hot water to pour over them.

Photo 1. 'Food' stocks in a home, mainly instant noodles and food flavourings. Source: Francesca Mauricio, Marikina, May 2023.

In areas near schools or offices, vendors may offer somewhat healthy snack foods, like turon (fried banana rolls) or lumpia (rolls with vegetables and/or bits of meat), hard-boiled chicken eggs or *kwek kwek* (fried quail eggs) (see Photo 3). The quail eggs, however, are high in cholesterol.

For others, especially students, there are many packaged snacks available from sidewalk vendors as well as from the ubiquitous variety stores called sari-sari stores.

Photo 4 shows one such variety store, operated out of a home in a slum tenement (see bottom row of apartments). These sari-sari stores provide livelihood – *hanap-buhay* (looking for life) – for the women who run them. The commodities they sell are mainly small packaged foods, but even these may cost too much for some urban poor. So the women repackage them in smaller amounts. The plastic generated from packaging and repackaging foods and beverages is a major contributor to a growing garbage problem, choking rivers and creeks.

Photo 2. Food stall owner preparing flavourings (usually a mix of vinegar, chopped tomatoes, onion and chilli peppers) for the meals they serve.
Source: Sheila Mae Pagurayan, Marikina, May 2023.

Drinks are a scarce commodity, which, like food items, are packaged and repackaged. While soft drinks are popular in the Philippines, they have become expensive and are now resold in smaller quantities. Cheaper than soft drinks are those made from flavoured powders (see Photo 5). They mimic expensive brands like Tang, which comes in artificial flavours like grape and orange.

PHOTO ESSAY 1: LIVING ON THE EDGE

Photo 3. Woman selling home-cooked healthier snacks. Source: Mak Abellon.

Photo 4. Slum tenements. Notice a small variety store operating out of one of the homes on the ground floor, providing many ultra-processed foods from instant noodles to junk snacks. Source: Mak Abellon.

Photo 5. Beverages made from packets of fruit-flavoured and high-sugar powders. Source: Mak Abellon.

A special but fairly low-cost street food is called *pagpag* (see Photo 6) which is made from what food restaurants (mostly fast-food places) throw out at the end of the day. It is scavenged and recooked, usually by frying. *Pagpag* originally meant shaking clothes or linen to remove dust. Another term for this treat is *tirtir* from *tira-tira*, which means leftover food (Chua et al. 2018; Martinez 2021).

Photo 6. *Pagpag* or scavenged foods that are recooked. We cropped the photo to focus on the *pagpag* chicken meal. Source: Mak Abellon.

The poor, especially those who migrated from rural areas, will look for fresh vegetables but complain that they are expensive. If they have some empty space around their homes, they will plant vegetables like *kangkong* (water spinach), *kamote* (sweet potato), or *kamoteng kahoy* (cassava) (see Photo 7).

Photo 7. Gathering cassava planted in the backyard. Source: Mak Abellon.

Overall, the food situation among the poor is one of precarity and day-to-day uncertainty because nearly all food and beverages, including water must be bought. Just as jobs have to be sought (*hanap-buhay*), a meal must be scrounged together with whatever the day's budget is. With jobs so scarce, the poor assure themselves and their loved ones, *hahanapan ng paraan* (we will look for ways to survive).

Likewise little known in the plight of poor Filipinos and their meals are the many decisions that have to be made about who gets to eat what. Photo 8 shows an elderly man with a cigarette and coffee, that unhealthy combination a typical meal across all age groups, but more so with the elderly, who, believing they need less to get by, give way to younger household members. The coffee is usually prepared from 3-in-1 packets of coffee, dairy substitute powder, and sugar, lots of sugar.

Decisions regarding food will even involve lifeboat ethics, as we find in narratives by Taqueban (2010): who has the chance to eat more and who eats less, if at all. In one particularly heart-breaking account, a mother tells Mai how she had to move away from a meal so her

Photo 8. Elderly man taking 'breakfast': a cigarette and instant coffee. Source: Mak Abellon.

two children could be the ones to take the little rice they had left. Her husband joined them and she fell silent as she watched him and the children picking at tiny pieces of chicken.

She cries as she recalls that meal, which she recounted as context for her dilemma in having to make a bigger decision, whether or not to terminate a pregnancy during an economic crisis, when she can barely feed the children she already has.

3
Attributing therapeutic efficacies to plant materials

In Chapter 1, we described in historical perspective how Spanish and American colonizers' dismissal of traditional uses of plants for therapeutic purposes as 'quack medicine' disrupted plant sovereignty in the Philippines. Michael's first job after graduation, in 1977, was to document the most commonly used Filipino plants and produce a manual about them (Tan 1977). This was for a network of non-governmental community-based health programmes (CBHPs) that sought to re-establish plant sovereignty. The CBHPs advocated self-reliance in healthcare and therapeutic needs. Inspired by the 'barefoot doctors' (peasants who became health workers) model that evolved in China, they promoted the cultivation and use of plant medicines for the treatment of common disorders, as alternatives to pharmaceuticals produced by multinational, usually American, pharmaceutical companies.

To reconnect Filipinos with the therapeutic potential of plants, CBHP staff needed to re-articulate the benefits of plants, which they did by conducting ethnographic and botanical research on how people use them. In this chapter, we show how, building on the work of CBHP ethnographers, government-sponsored research and development projects expanded the search for effective plant medicines and their therapeutic potential, with the aim of mass-producing plant medicines. In the process, plant sovereignty was lost, as people no longer cultivated plants for therapeutic purposes.

The commercial production of medicines exploited plant-derived chemicals but, in the post-World War II period, increasingly adopted synthetics. Starting in the 1990s, there was revived interest in plants as sources of medicines, especially with the rise of 'back-to-nature' movements with large Western companies dominating production. In the twenty-first century, Philippine government-sponsored projects revived research on the medicinal use of plants, while private companies, both Western and local, began to cash in on producing food supplements, with claims they were derived from plants and therefore 'natural'. This further disrupted plant sovereignty. The current situation in the Philippines is that state health programmes and private companies encourage people to use packaged medicines for therapeutic purposes and to supplement their deficient diets.

The CBHPs promote plant sovereignty

Inspired by liberation theology developed in Latin America that drew on official Roman Catholic documents on social justice and called for a preferential option for the 'poor, deprived and oppressed' (Freire 1970; World Synod of Catholic Bishops 1971), the CBHPs emerged in the 1970s under the Marcos dictatorship. Their aim was to provide community-based healthcare for most of the population, which did not benefit from the country's economic development and were not adequately served by its health system. The CBHPs' efforts slowly gained support among the Philippines' Catholic Church hierarchy and its social action agencies, and reoriented health and other social services away from hand-outs that kept people dependent on a system of noblesse oblige.

Despite (or, perhaps, because of) the oppression of progressive movements under the Marcos regime's martial law, the CBHPs flourished: in the 1970s and 1980s, hundreds of community health workers (CHWs) were trained in primary healthcare, becoming adept at health education, preventive measures and even minor surgery. Brazilian educator Paolo Freire's (1970) 'conscientization', which emphasizes communities 'decoding' problems and generating solutions, provided the model for the CBHPs' teaching methods. The CBHPs produced handbooks and manuals influenced by David Werner's (1970) *Donde No Hay Doctor* (Where there is no doctor), based on Proyeto Piaxtla's experiences in Mexico's Sierra Madre. Werner's book was reprinted in English in 1977 and translated into Tagalog in the Philippines in 1982. The CBHPs created other manuals in various Filipino languages, with content based on local needs.

When Michael started studying the use of medicinal plants in his work with the CBHPs, many Filipino health professionals still dismissed plant medicines as 'quack medicine'. Working in rural communities, he noticed that villagers would sometimes deny using medicinal plants for fear of being perceived as ignorant. Decades of Spanish colonization and US 'modernization' had led to the use of medicinal plants becoming a marker of 'backwardness' (Tan 1986).

In 1977, Michael published *Philippine Medicinal Plants in Common Use: Their phytochemistry and pharmacology*. In it, he asserted that 'the starting point and continuing guide for research must be the communities themselves. We have to work on existing local uses because these are reflective of local needs and because of the strong empirical (experiential) basis of these practices' (Tan 1977, ii). Following this manual of commonly used Filipino plants, Leonard Co (1977; 1989), a botanist affiliated with the CBHPs, published even more extensive studies. The military killed Co in 2010, while he was conducting fieldwork, allegedly mistaking him for an insurgent from the New People's Army.[1]

Most of the knowledge Michael had acquired about local plants came from travelling the country interviewing *albularyo* (herbalists), mothers and grandmothers (and the occasional father or grandfather). He listened intently, learning the local names for plants and their various applications. Viewed with mistrust by the Spanish and American colonizers, and hounded in the 1950s by the Philippine government and the Philippine Medical Association (Stauffer 1966), traditional medical practitioners working with the CBHPs were reassured that their knowledge was respected and they were considered partners in healthcare. Within a few weeks of beginning his interviews, Michael noted emerging patterns in the plants the healers enumerated: names for plants might differ, but their uses were fairly consistent in various regions of the country. He learned, too, that the plants were easy to obtain, were often cultivated in backyards and served multiple purposes, as medicines, food and spices – a practice we noted in our introduction (Etkin 2006; Tsing 2004). There was little of the esoterica the colonizers had so feared, except for occasional prayers and incantations that herbalists invoked, which Michael came to accept as part of their therapeutic touch.

It helped his research that Michael was in many ways a 'naïve' ethnographer who, born and raised in Manila, and exposed to Chinese traditional medicine at home, knew almost nothing about Filipino traditional medicine and medicinal plants. After graduating from veterinary school, he took a non-degree university course in economic botany. He discovered that while there were many 'preliminary' studies of medicinal plants, each presenting similar findings, there was no research that built on these. He benefited from the generous expertise of pharmacists like Beatrice Guevarra at University of Santo Tomas and the Centro Escolar University, which had programmes for training and research in pharmacognosy (the study of the properties of drugs derived from natural sources).

Michael noticed that women were usually the gatekeepers and culture-bearers, passing on knowledge about plants and their preparations, usually decoctions, infusions and oils, to their children and neighbours. Many applications, he discovered, were specific to particular stages of life: the colicky infant, the child's cuts and bruises, the adolescent's puberty, the new mother's recovery from birth and the middle-aged person's body aches. He learned of other forms of traditional healing, mainly massage, and magical utterances to ward off evil, sorcery and surrounding spirits.

He also learned, early on, to be realistic in his expectations of plants as medicines. The most frequently used herbal remedies employed essential oils and astringents. Many plants acted as diuretics (increasing urination) which did not necessarily cure disease but provided relief while the body healed itself. He was aware of the many laboratory studies working on the isolation of active ingredients, some of which were already in use in China. He could only hope that research on local Filipino plants would produce medicines, as had occurred in China, to treat serious ailments, including asthma and infectious diseases such as malaria and tuberculosis, both prevalent causes of death at the time.

In 1981, Michael was pursuing a graduate degree in the United States when the US development organization World Neighbors invited him to produce educational materials on medicinal plants. While organization staff recognized that the featured plants would necessarily be ones available in the Philippines, they requested that Michael use a generic approach so the materials could be efficacious in other countries. He took this as an excellent opportunity to promote plant sovereignty, and to discuss why plant remedies worked in terms of general categories of phytochemicals with pharmacological effects.

On returning to the Philippines, Michael received a more down-to-earth request from the CBHPs: to produce an illustrated guide, entitled *Lampuyan* (a local name for one type of ginger), for preparing medicinal plants in the emerging CBHPs. A Brazilian non-governmental organization (NGO) later translated *Lampuyan* into Portuguese, an indication of the ecumenical approach to plant medicines in community-based programmes. More than recipes, Michael argued that communities should receive support preparing the medicines themselves, from growing the plants to 'cooking' and packaging them. Subsequently, throughout the 1980s, the CBHPs developed several preparations based on the therapeutic potentials of medicinal plants. *Lagundi*, a plant documented by Spanish botanists, was developed into a syrup for *hika, ubo*, and *trangkaso* (asthma, coughs and influenza). A tannin-rich preparation for diarrhoea earned the name ABC, for avocados, *bayabas* (guava), and *caimito* (star apples). Again using the initials of the ingredients as a name, SLK cough syrup combined essential oils from *sampalok* (tamarind), *luya* (ginger) and *kalamansi* (a Filipino lime variety). For the many body pains that result from heavy physical labour and age, there was BLS oil, made from *bawang* (garlic), *luya* (ginger) and *sili* (red pepper), a preparation that, we joked, would also serve well as a dip for various foods.

Galvez Tan (no relation to Michael) was a student leader in the years preceding the declaration of martial law in 1972. After finishing his medical studies, he decided to work in a remote rural area, where he learnt a lot about the traditional use of herbal medicines. He subsequently worked with the CBHPs. After reading Anita's 1987 article on Filipino villagers' practices of self-medication with modern pharmaceuticals, Galvez Tan invited her to conduct a study for the CBHPs. He proposed she come to the Philippines to work with CBHP staff to help them understand why poor people kept on buying pharmaceuticals when the CBHPs were presenting them with cheap herbal alternatives they could grow in community gardens.

Challenges restoring plant sovereignty to urban poor communities

Anita was affiliated with Health Action Information Network (HAIN), an NGO established to meet the research and information needs of CBHPs, and which at that time was headed by Michael. In 1985–8 she conducted fieldwork in Marikina, on the outskirts of Metropolitan Manila – dense urban communities, very different from the rural communities where Michael had worked on herbal medicines. Her aim was to compare self-care practices in two communities: one engaged in a CBHP run by the Maryknoll Sisters, and the other covered by ordinary urban health services. She noticed that mothers of preschool children in both communities relied on self-medication to treat common health issues in their families. They tended to use a limited range of around 10 relatively affordable modern pharmaceuticals, all of which were available in community sari-sari stores. The women running the stores sold the drugs as single tablets (on a *tingi* basis) after purchasing larger quantities from pharmacies downtown. These medications were complemented by herbal home remedies (such as ginger for sore throats and guava for diarrhoea), knowledge of which mothers had acquired in the rural communities where they had grown up before migrating to the city.

At that time, modern pharmaceuticals for common health problems were heavily advertised on popular radio stations, encouraging people to take medicines at the first sign of a cough, cold, fever or diarrhoea, to prevent it from becoming worse. Anita argued that radio advertising contributed to the growing commodification of health (Hardon 1987), given that young mothers listened to the radio constantly at home while minding their children, doing household chores or doing low-paid piece work for Marikina-based shoe manufacturers.

The Marikina CBHP promoted SLK syrup (made from locally sourced *sampaloc* leaves) for treating coughs and colds, *lagundi* leaves (grown in the local medicinal garden) for fever, asthma, cough and flu, and *bayabas* (guava) for diarrhoea. Some of the herbal remedies resonated with the traditional knowledge of Anita's interlocutors, who had come to Manila from all over the Philippines. In promoting these herbal medicines, community health workers asserted that they had been in use for a long time and were proven safe and effective. While some mothers took and administered the herbal concoctions the community health workers promoted, many complained it was time-consuming to prepare them and that finding some of the herbs could be difficult. They were also worried about pollution of the soil and water in their poor urban community. The stream running through the neighbourhood regularly turned red and yellow due to runoff from an upstream paint factory.

To further examine the advantages and disadvantages of medicinal plants, Anita organized two theatrical debates between the community health workers (CHWs) and mothers, concerning the pros and cons of modern pharmaceuticals versus plant medicines for treating common disorders. Elementary school children would act out common health problems – in one case a preschool child with a cough and slight fever; in another, a baby with diarrhoea – and ask the audience for advice. She assigned a group of mothers the role of promoting use of *gamot botika* (pharmaceuticals) and the CHWs the role of advocating for herbal medicines. A jury, including a CBHP doctor, deliberated on the quality of the arguments and decided in favour of the mothers in each case. A seemingly convincing argument against using plant medicines that mothers had frequently expressed was that they might be 'dirty'; as one woman said:

> Herbal medicines are dirty, they make you extra sick; [pharmaceuticals] have been made in laboratories. They are clean ... The medicinal plants come from the roadside; sometimes you don't even know where they come from. So our advice is you use the better drugs, the one from the *botika* (pharmacy). (Hardon 1991, 121)

So it seemed that, in this urban community, concerns about plants as medicines did not focus on their backwardness, but rather on the environment in which they grew – by the roadside in a densely populated, heavily polluted city.

The contrast was therefore not between plant-based and synthetic drugs, but between unprocessed plants from polluted environments and medicines from clean laboratories and shops. Moreover, preparing SLK syrup for alleviating coughs meant spending money to buy tamarind, ginger and lime at the market and using fuel and sugar to boil the syrup. *Lagundi* could be sourced at the medicinal garden of the Maryknoll Sisters, a few kilometres away, but supplies were limited. For mothers, giving their children cough tablets, which they purchased *tingi* from a sari-sari was both more convenient and affordable.

Anita's observations in Marikina point to the pragmatic challenges to promoting self-reliance via use of herbal medicines in poor urban areas. These include the pervasive influence of consumer advertising of pharmaceuticals, the convenience of commodified health products and the popularity of *gamot botika* ('medicines from the pharmacy'). In an effort to mediate this popularity, CBHPs packaged plants to make them appeal more to the people they served.

Figure 3.1 shows packaged *lagundi*, which the Marikina CBHP sourced from a sister programme in nearby rural Munoz. Note how the bottle's label mimics those of commercial syrups, including details on potency (250 mg/5 ml) and indications for use: *hika, ubo, trangkaso* (asthma, cough and influenza). Not visible in the picture, the label also includes information on dosages: Adults: 2 teaspoons three times a day; 7–12 years of age: 1 teaspoon three times a day; 2–6 years of age: ½ teaspoon three times a day. The information is provided in Tagalog, rather than English as is usually the case for *gamot botika*. Over time, Anita observed, mothers in Marikina began to integrate *lagundi* and SLK syrup into their treatment of common childhood illnesses but did not use them to replace *gamot botika*. Instead, they were pragmatic and used both.

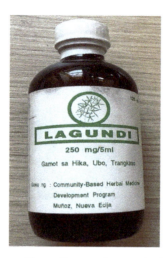

Figure 3.1 Locally sourced lagundi syrup. Source: Author (Hardon), 2017.

Scaling up R&D on plant medicines

While the CBHPs promoted community-sourced and locally produced herbal medicines, the Philippines Department of Science and Technology (DOST) embarked on an ambitious programme to scale research and development (R&D) of medicinal plants. In 1974, the DOST sponsored the creation of the National Integrated Research Program on Medicinal Plants (NIRPROMP) formed jointly by University of the Philippines Manila and several other universities and government research agencies. In so doing, they followed an Asia-wide trend, according to which governments began to generously fund research programmes to screen plants for valuable phytochemicals, conduct clinical research to test them for specific health outcomes and market them to meet the needs of contemporary consumers (Hardon et al. 2008; Ma et al. 2020) – processes that Pordié and Gaudillière (2014) refer to as 'reformulation regimes'.[2]

The CBHPs encouraged people to use plant medicines that had been tried and tested over generations of community and home use. NIRPROMP set out to validate the safety and efficacy of those commonly used medicinal plants through clinical trials. Dr Conrado Dayrit, one of the programme's directors, emphasized that NIRPROMP should focus on medicinal plants that were well known and trusted among the population. While Michael and Leonard Co had studied indigenous applications of plants through participant observation,

Dayrit organized a quantitative survey of 1,000 traditional healers from across the Philippines (Dayrit et al. 2018). As a result, the research team identified 1,500 different plants and discovered that one-third possessed beneficial medicinal properties. To select plants for in-depth testing, the researchers assessed their safety and efficacy and likewise considered availability to ensure the sustainability of supplies. This resulted in prioritizing 10 plants for development as herbal medicines.

Lagundi, which the CBHPs had adopted for the treatment of asthma, coughs and influenza, was among the plants selected. Seventy per cent of the herbalists surveyed had mentioned the plant's efficacy in treating coughs. Moreover, the lack of any reports of adverse side effects and the plant's abundance throughout the Philippines made it an ideal candidate. Note how the researchers built on indigenous notions of efficacy in selecting plants for inclusion in the trials and used the survey results to define outcome measures for their clinical experiments.

The researchers dried *lagundi* leaves and ground them into a fine powder. In the first trial, 119 patients who suffered from mild to moderate coughs received either the *lagundi* medicine or a placebo (both were given in tablet form to facilitate 'blind administration'). Those who received the *lagundi* exhibited substantial positive medical responses without any adverse reactions or side effects. Pharmacological research identified four active ingredients in *lagundi* and suggested that the phytochemicals together acted to (1) relax air passages in the lungs, (2) counter histamine, (3) reduce inflammation and (4) lessen asthmatic responses. The researchers observed that each of the active ingredients worked weakly when administered on its own but produced a powerful cough-suppression effect when combined, again without any adverse side effects (Payumo et al. 2012). Here again, the researchers drew upon indigenous practices, in which the whole plant is administered as medicine.

Eventually, in 1995, the NIRPROMP registered *lagundi* with the Food and Drug Administration of the Philippines as a clinically proven medicine for treating coughs and asthma. NIRPROMP signed an agreement stipulating that all royalties would be used to fund further investments in research and development at DOST and the University of the Philippines (Payumo et al. 2012). The first licensee to receive the *lagundi* tablet technology was Herbafarm, a Philippine pharmaceutical company. Others soon followed, including one to Pascual Laboratories, a large Philippine pharmaceutical company that would become *lagundi*

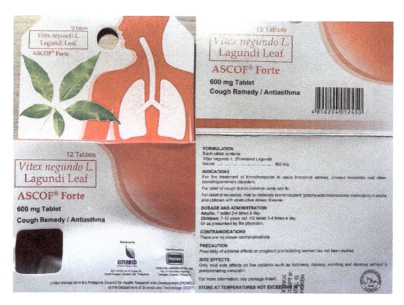

Figure 3.2 Lagundi Leaf, ASCOF Forte package (front and back).
Source: Author (Hardon), 2020.

technology's most successful licensee (see Figure 3.2 for Pascual's popular Lagundi Leaf brand).

On the label, the text '*Vitex negundo L.*/Lagundi Leaf' is printed in larger font than the brand name, ASCOF. This adheres to the Philippines' law regarding generic medicines, which requires brand name medicines to display the drug's generic name on the package in large letters. The package insert attests to the hybrid (modern and traditional) nature of the drug and provides the plant's name in several major Filipino languages: *kemala* (Tagalog), *kalipapa-madam* (Maguindanao), *tugas* (Cebu, Samar), *dangla lini-lino* and *lingo-lingo* (Ilocos), *molave-aso* and *magupay* (Sulu), and as 'five-leafed chaste tree' (English). The insert also provides a botanical description:

> … an erect, branched shrub that grows up to five meters high and is found in all regions of the Philippines. Its leaves are green and composed of five leaflets which are pointed at both ends. The middle leaflets are larger than the others. It has small violet flowers (6mm) and bears tiny, black, succulent fruits.

There is in addition a statement regarding the preparation's scientific validation:

The National Integrated Research Program on Medicinal Plants (NIRPROMP) has scientifically validated the ancient popular knowledge and practices of our traditional healers. They have established in both animal and human studies, the wide margin of safety and efficacy of *lagundi* as Cough Remedy and Antiasthma medicine. Phase III double blind placebo-controlled trial has shown bronchodilator effect and antitussive effect.

The ASCOF-branded *lagundi* product that Pascual manufactured became a bestseller in the Philippines, available in pharmacies throughout the country. By 2019, ASCOF was identified as one of the most trusted brands in Asia, based on a survey of ordinary consumers that Catalyst Research had conducted. Pascual's product received a gold rank, just below US-based USANA, which distributes food supplements in the country through multilevel marketing (Euromonitor International 2019). The manufacturers seemed to have earned this trust by referring both to the traditional use of *lagundi* and to the modern clinical trials proving it works.

Mainstreaming applications of medicinal plants

The 1990s were a period in which the Philippines government embraced the medical properties of plants. The Department of Education (DOE) set up a programme to integrate information about medicinal plants into health education, while the Department of Health (DOH) set up medicinal plant processing factories (Tan 1999). In 1992, under the leadership of Juan Flavier (a physician and politician who was a driving force behind the government nutrition policies described in Chapter 2), a traditional medicine unit was created and the Botika sa Paso (Drugstores in Flowerpots) programme established to encourage Filipinos to grow medicinal plants in their own backyards. With the intention of professionalizing the practice of plant-based medicine, the DOH set up the Philippine Institute of Traditional and Alternative Health Care (PITAHC) in 1997. The institute had the mandate to encourage scientific research on and development of traditional and alternative healthcare systems with direct impact on public healthcare and to promote traditional, alternative, preventive and curative healthcare modalities established as safe, effective, cost effective and consistent with government standards for medical practice. It endorsed the 10 plants mentioned above, which the NIRPROMP had vetted, for their safe medicinal properties: *lagundi, akapulko, ampalaya, bawang, bayabas, niyog-niyogan, pansit-pansitan, sambong, tsaang-guba,* and *yerba buena* (Department of Health 1995).

As secretary of health under President Fidel Ramos, Juan Flavier also consulted with CBHPs while drafting the Traditional and Alternative Medicines Act (TAMA). A coalition of multinational pharmaceutical companies and the Philippines Medical Association opposed the act, on the grounds that the plants' safety and efficacy remained unverified. The Philippine Federation of Natural Health and Environment Associations maintained that the pharmaceutical companies' and physicians' real concern was that, if medicinal plants were allowed to compete with Big Pharma drugs, it would diminish their profits and earning capacity (Lee Mendoza 2009). However, the TAMA became law in 1997, thanks to grassroots support from the CBHPs and endorsements from the World Health Organization and the United Nations Development Programme.

Once the TAMA passed, controversy arose over the medicinal properties of one of the plants the DOH was testing, *ampalaya* or bitter melon (*Momordica charantia linn*), which was considered an affordable alternative to diabetes drugs. Several *ampalaya*-based food supplements had entered the market, touted for their beneficial effects on glyco-metabolism (Mercado 2003).

Inventing First Vita Plus

Dr Galvez Tan came up with the formula for First Vita Plus. His 'five power herbs' formula, which became First Vita Plus, also involved 'mixing' medicinal plants, but the fundamental principle behind doing so differed from that of the CBHPs. While the CBHPs aimed to help communities learn to prepare plant medicines themselves for distribution at low cost for self-care, and used local terms to describe their health properties, First Vita Plus was mass-produced for wide distribution and sales.

In a 2017 interview with Anita, Galvez Tan stated that he invented the formula while temporarily serving as secretary of health in the national government and acting as vice chancellor for research at the University of the Philippines. Representatives of a Philippine company approached him, seeking to develop a food supplement based on Filipino plants, given the positive regulatory environment for such products. He had previously declined requests from several multinational corporations to exploit the medicinal plant heritage of the Philippines, hoping instead to collaborate with Filipino firms. But large Filipino pharmaceutical companies like United Laboratories worked closely with the Marcos regime and were not interested in his work. Consequently, when representatives from another Philippine company contacted him, he responded positively.

Two company representatives set out to design the product with him, and he recalled that:

> ... they wanted a truly Philippine product. They were looking for a product that could easily be carried to a picnic or used after sports ... I was initially thinking it should be a tablet. Over some time, we came up with the idea of a drink – not a juice, but a powder. (Interview with Hardon, 2017)

He told his co-designers that he wanted to develop a 'true wellness product, a symbol of wellness for the Philippines'. This was how they developed the brand name, he explained: 'Vita Plus – so it's "life" plus "plus", and it means vitality, it means life, it means wellness, really.'

Galvez Tan selected five common plants (from the genera *Ipomoea*, *Amaranthus*, *Corchorus*, *Capsicum*, and *Moringa*) that research programmes at the University of the Philippines had found to be high in antioxidants, vitamin A, iron, calcium and a host of other nutrients. During our interview, Galvez Tan asserted that these were things 'our normal body needs, plus they also had phytochemicals that were ... going to help prevent hypertension and diabetes, anaemia and other inflammations of the body.' He said his exposure to medicinal plant practices among the indigenous communities of Kalinga (the abundant foodscapes of which we discussed in Chapter 1) inspired the formulation of First Vita Plus. He recalled:

> I really chose this product [based on what] I learned from the Kalinga. When I went there as a young doctor ... I discovered that they ate a lot of natural leaves around that environment. They are one of the strongest and mightiest and tallest Filipinos. I said, 'This must be a true wellness product. The symbol of wellness for the Philippines'. (Interview with Hardon, 2017)

He told his co-designers they should select a good natural flavour; they chose a Philippine citrus fruit, the *dalandan*. Galvez Tan also proposed

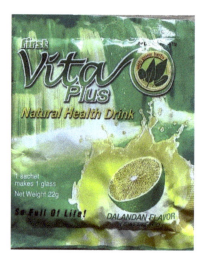

Figure 3.3 A First Vita Plus sachet, designed to meet consumer preference for small packages of specialty goods. Source: Author (Hardon), 2020.

the company use raw cane sugar to sweeten the product, in line with Filipinos' preference for sweet drinks, but admitted that, in retrospect, he should have instead suggested coconut sugar, dehydrated honey or stevia as a natural sweetener.

The contents of the sachet pictured in Figure 3.3 taste similar to the fruit juice powder Tang, although *dalandan* replaces the Western 'orange' flavour. The sachet fits well into the larger landscape of consumption, in which poor Philippine households economize by buying small quantities of desirable consumer goods, as a way to enjoy small pleasures in daily life (Sy-Changco et al. 2011).

After Galvez Tan had helped to design First Vita Plus, the company asked him to market it. He featured in a promotional video (see Figure 3.4) asking 'How are your children? Are they healthy and happy? Do you want to be happy, healthy, and wealthy?'

The first part of the promotional video features Galvez Tan seated, in a dark business suit and speaking in English. He then repeats the same message in Tagalog, this time standing and wearing a white laboratory coat. In both segments, he describes the health potentials of First Vital Plus with reference to the benefits of the five 'power herbs' in his recipe:

> Five unique Philippine herbs, truly Philippine. It is the first time that we are going to have five herbs in one Vita Plus drink. Ipomoea is a diuretic, maintains normal blood pressure. Moringa is

Figure 3.4 Screenshots from promotional video 'First Vita Plus – Dr Jaime Galvez Tan' posted by a First Vita Plus distributor, 2010. Source: https://www.youtube.com/watch?v=XwZayb8pBkI (Accessed 6 June 2024).

anti-anaemia, it enhances red-blood cells, as well as the production of breast milk. Capsicum is good for muscle and joint health. It protects you from rheumatism as well as arthritis and also good for digestion. Corchorus regulates bowel movement aside from [having] a large reserve of calcium and phosphorus. Amaranthus contains vitamin A that protects your eyes and skin.

He then repeats the message with slightly different wording:

First Vita Plus is unique, as well as its five characteristics. First, it is the first product that contains five power herbs. Secondly, it is the first time in the Philippines that this product has been introduced. Thirdly, it contains the complete line of vitamins, minerals, micro-nutrients, fibre, anti-oxidants, and phytochemicals. Fourthly, it is definitely uniquely Philippine from beginning to end, maybe because it is planted by Filipino farmers, processed by Filipino farmers and processing machines. It is manufactured by a Philippine company and also sold by a Philippine company. And lastly it has a Philippine flavour, *dalandan*.

Next, he specifies the health benefits:

First Vita Plus has all of the five useful benefits to the body. It maintains and enhances your health, wellness, and wellbeing. It enhances immunity against diseases and protects us from many illnesses. It preserves youth, beauty, and vitality by repairing the tissues and cells in the body ... it provides the energy boost and the needed stamina to fight daily stress. And lastly, it regulates, normalizes, and balances all the different systems in the body, from digestive, nervous, to reproductive health.

At the end of the video, he says: 'Drink First Vita Plus every day for your total health, wellbeing, and wellness. For your holistic health, body, mind, and spirit. First Vita Plus, so full of life.'[3]

In promoting First Vita Plus sachets for holistic health, Galvez Tan appears to have drifted away from the emancipatory aims of the CBHPs. The CBHPs sought complete restructuring of the health system alongside socioeconomic transformation. When collaborating with them in the 1970s and 1980s, Galvez Tan advocated for self-reliance by using plants from forests, backyards and community gardens (Galvez Tan 1987). A website promoting his life's achievements (http://docjimmygalveztan.com/) explains at length how the experience of serving poor communities in Samar and Leyte (islands in the Philippines' Visayas Region) as a young doctor led to his interest in herbal medicines.

In the 1990s, building on decades of experience in the CBHPs, 'Dok Jimmy' as Galvez Tan is sometimes known, became an international consultant on primary healthcare. He joined UNICEF's Manila office, which at the time was promoting targeted community health interventions, such as pre-packaged oral rehydration solution for the treatment of diarrhoea and vitamin A to prevent blindness. This approach, referred to as 'selective' primary healthcare (SPHC), was an attempt to speed up efforts to meet the health needs of the poor (Newell 1988), often through social marketing programmes set up to distribute commodities through private sector channels. Galvez Tan's promotion of a sachet with five power herbs was in line with UNICEF's pragmatic approach.

Scaling up research on medicinal plants

When plant materials enter the market as capsules, tablets, syrups and powders, the Philippines Food and Drug Administration demands that the companies manufacturing them make a choice. They may register the products as medicine (but only if the manufacturers provide clinical proof of therapeutic potency, as for *lagundi*), or as food supplements. When registering a product as a food supplement, manufacturers must include a disclaimer on the packaging regarding any therapeutic claims and note its nutritional value in a declaration of content.

A key historical moment in the growth of the worldwide food supplements industry, with which the DOST seeks to align, was the US

Dietary Supplement and Health Education Act, sponsored in 1994 by US Senator Orrin Hatch, which eased regulation of supplements in the United States. Under the act, food supplements are assumed to be safe, and require no laboratory testing, unless evidence of harm is documented in users, a regulatory stance that the Philippines also adopted (Cohen 2016; Lipton 2011; MacKendrick 2018; Mayer, Scammon and Hatch 1994). Moreover, manufacturers of supplements do not need to submit any clinical evidence of their products' effects. All they need to do is declare their contents.

Since 1994, a wide range of supplements touting a range of nutritional and health claims, interacting with distinct medical systems and cultures, and marketed through different types of direct-selling schemes and multilevel marketing, have appeared across the world. In the United States, lax regulation led to a 20-fold increase in the number of supplements on the market, from 4,000 in 1994 to 55,000 in 2012 to 75,000 in 2018 (Gurley, Yates and Markowitz 2018). The supplements industry's boom has occurred against a backdrop of stringent regulations for promoting pharmaceuticals which, when sold to consumers in US pharmacies and supermarkets, must list all possible side effects.

The global supplements industry uses evidence generated from the subdiscipline of nutritional science in research trials that examine the health benefits of 'functional' foods (Eussen et al. 2011). While there is no requirement for randomized controlled trials (RCTs) to prove efficacy for food supplements to enter the market, their marketing draws on scientific terms and principles. Adopting language from the newly defined sub-discipline of functional food studies (clinical studies of foods that provide benefits additional to nutritional value), manufacturers bolster advertising campaigns; especially those promoting botanicals (plant-derived products with health benefits).

In the field of pharmaceuticals, regulators scrutinize claims of health benefits for potential conflicts of interest, but this is not common in the field of nutrition science. In consequence, marketing campaigns of plant-based food supplements emphasize their beneficial effects without drawing attention to possible risks caused by interactions with other foods or medication consumers may take or the presence of heavy metals or pesticide pollutants in the supplement preparations (Government Accounting Office 2010).

As a result, we can now purchase packaged Lagerstroemia leaves (known in the Philippines as *banaba* – a common roadside tree) as a supplement to treat diabetes and dried and ground Garcinia (*mangosteen*, a popular fruit from the southern Philippines) to lose weight, without companies being required to provide clinical evidence for any of these claims to the US Food and Drug Administration or to list any possible side effects. Scrinis (2013, 8) raises concerns about the dynamics surrounding this trend: 'Food corporations have colonized the nutriscape, flooding the food supply with nutritionally engineered products and marketing claims and accentuating the nutritional anxieties and nutritional needs of consumers.'

Examining a product sold by the Filipino multilevel marketing company AIM Global illustrates the use of functional food research to exaggerate health claims. Marketed as a preventive supplement to keep your heart in 'tip-top shape', Vida! is a 'cardio-ceutical' drink containing resVida (Figure 3.5).

The chemical name of resVida is resveratrol, which is found in grapes. The Dutch multinational DSM acquired the patent to manufacture this phytochemical, which it advertises as being free of impurities, including herbicides and pesticides. DSM claims that customers can 'uncork' the health benefits of red wine with resVida (see Figure 3.6). Online product information about the supplement emphasizes its preventive properties by referring to results of clinical studies demonstrating that 75 mg of resVida consumed twice a day normalizes blood pressure, blood sugar and insulin levels. Referring to clinical studies gives the supplement an aura of authenticity and modernity (DSM 2014).

Intrigued by the presence of this Dutch phytochemical in a supplement popular in Puerto Princesa (see also Chapter 5), we conducted some research into DSM's efficacy claims regarding resVida. DSM's website declares resVida is 99 per cent pure, states that comprehensive data prove it safe, and that the compound emerges from 10 years of development and testing. DSM also states that resVida 'has obtained self-affirmed Generally Recognized as Safe (GRAS) status', referring to a United States and European regulation, whereby corporations can market food supplements using this statement to refer to research the manufacturers have performed themselves. DSM's product leaflet, which can be downloaded from the company's website, lists the functional studies that have been conducted on resVida (DSM 2014); see Figure 3.7.

These graphs represent placebo-controlled clinical trials that demonstrate improved 'vascular reactivity in humans', decreased insulin sensitivity and reduced blood pressure. Such graphs suggest to consumers and health professionals, should they take the time to read the product information DSM provides online, that scientific studies prove resVida works, positioning the preparation as a useful tool in the pursuit of protective shields against future metabolic health problems.

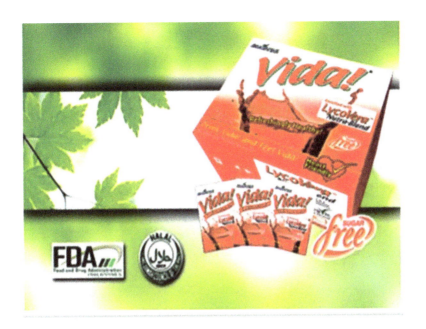

Vida! Enriched with LycoVera Nutra-Blend

Vida! is a refreshing instant cardio-ceutical drink that combines the power of resVida® and quality carotenoid lycopene to keep your heart in tip-top shape. Vida! has the highest resVida® content in instant powdered functional beverage and thus the most potent drink to give you the maximum health benefits your body needs.

Figure 3.5 An information leaflet for Vida! supplement. Source: Author (Hardon), 2016.

But how were these placebo-controlled studies carried out and do they really prove that resVida is efficacious? To answer these questions, we need to take a closer look at the studies DSM cites as the sources for the graphs.

We reviewed the full publication of the clinical study Wong et al. (2011) conducted, cited by DSM to support claims about resVida's benefits (see Figure 3.7, upper graph). The sample for the study comprised

Figure 3.6 Image heading the DSM leaflet for resVida. Screenshot by Anita Hardon, 15 June 2024 from resVida Health Benefit Solutions pamphlet. Source: https://www.dsm.com/content/dam/dsm/human-nutrition/pdfs/resVida_A4_2pp_leaflet_08_09_2014_Final.pdf (Accessed 6 June 2024).

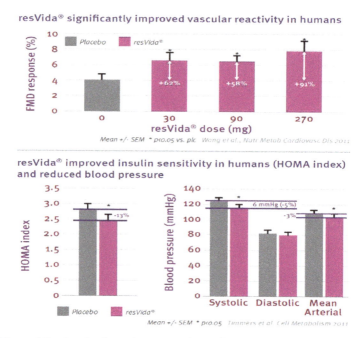

Figure 3.7 Graphs shown in DSM product information for resVida. Source: https://www.dsm.com/content/dam/dsm/human-nutrition/pdfs/resVida_A4_2pp_leaflet_08_09_2014_Final.pdf (Accessed 6 June 2024).

19 obese adults in their fifties (14 men and 5 women), all with borderline hypertension (high blood pressure). Participants fasted for four hours before receiving one of four capsules (0 mg, 30 mg, 90 mg and 270 mg dosages of resveratrol). The capsules' effects were measured with an

ultrasound assessment of flow-mediated vasodilation, 45 minutes after dose administration.[4] The results of the study are not concerned with the effects of resVida when consumed along with food in everyday life, or by people who are not obese and in their fifties. Nor do we know how long the vasodilatory effects last; they could wane after two hours. Moreover, the sample size is too small for the results to be considered as clinical evidence, if an application were to be made to register the product as a medicine with the Food and Drug Administration of the Philippines.

The other clinical study represented on the bottom chart, conducted by Timmers et al. (2011), was run with an even smaller sample: 11 obese but otherwise healthy men without a family history of diabetes. The men received either a placebo or a 150 g dose of resveratrol over the course of 30 days. The study found 'modest' effects on glucose homeostasis – measured using the Homeostasis Model Assessment (HOMA) index – and a slight decrease in blood pressure, measured on day 1 and day 30 after an overnight fast, in the subjects who received the active ingredient. Again, the study does not provide information on the product's efficacy as a preventive medication in non-obese people; nor does it provide evidence of the effects the product has on women. These two studies do not support the claims the advertising in the Philippines makes for Vida! Moreover, examination of the study's authorship and acknowledgments reveals that DSM employees co-wrote the article, while DSM funded the study by Wong et al. (2011), implying a clear conflict of interest.

The resVida studies we examined reflect a growing body of globally circulating functional nutrition studies organized to provide companies that sell food supplements with evidence for the health claims those companies make. While materials advertising the products present such findings as evidence of efficacy, DSM's claims – along with those of other food supplement manufacturers – have not been reviewed by independent bodies. Moreover, such studies play no role in obtaining the products' registration as food supplements. They are simply marketing tools created to generate demand.

In the early years of medicinal plant research in the Philippines, researchers demonstrated interest in the ways locals used plants to treat common health problems. Now, we observe the emergence of a globally connected field of studies, guided not by healthcare needs, but by the potential for marketing plants to treat a wide range of health concerns and thus expand sales and increase profits. The process disrupts plant sovereignty in multiple ways. People lose knowledge of how to use the plants that grow around them. Impressed by the marketing claims made regarding the five power herbs contained in First Vita

Plus sachets, they do not realize that most of those herbs can or do grow in their own backyards. Enthralled by the graphs embedded in Vida! promotional materials, they are unaware the supplement's main ingredient is grapeseed. They lose the pleasure of putting mangosteens in their mouths and tasting them, instead consuming them as capsules. Most significantly, they forgo the social connections of caring for each other that emerge from preparing the wide range of fruits and vegetables traditionally eaten as ordinary Filipino meals and cherishing the culinary value of doing so.

In recent years, Philippine research into exploiting natural products for medicines has turned to the marine environment. In 2017, the Philippines Department of Science and Technology substantially scaled up its R&D efforts related to the health properties of plants, by starting to include medicinal resources found in the sea as part of its new *Tuklas Lunas* (discover remedies) programme. The programme's agenda states that 'being one of the megadiverse countries in the world in terms of species thriving makes it favorable for the discovery of novel compounds from indigenous/endemic terrestrial and marine species' (Tuklas Lunas 2017, 2). With *Tuklas Lunas*, the DOST sought to reduce the country's dependence on imported pharmaceuticals and to exploit its abundant natural resources.

The *Tuklas Lunas* programme has three discrete outputs: synthetic drugs, designed to mimic bio-active compounds, standardized herbal drugs, and standardized 'herbal' supplements (see Figure 3.8). The latter (see the figure's upper right corner) is a new category for the DOST, which initially focused solely on developing herbal therapeutics. It is possible to develop such supplements into economically viable health products without doing clinical studies. Instead, manufacturers can create them through a straightforward process of sample collection, extraction, and standardization.

The seas are seen as a new resource for planetary health, given the declining availability of terrestrial resources, due to the loss of forests and excessive use of pesticides and herbicides in agriculture. In the relatively short period since research began in 2008, a project called Pharmaseas at the University of the Philippines has yielded several potential drugs with powerful effects: anti-infectives, analgesics, and other neuroactive compounds, as well as anticancer agents (PhilStar Global 2008). The Pharmaseas project is logical, given that the Philippines has a land area of 300,000 square kilometres but, as an archipelago, oceanic waters with a total area of 1.9 million square kilometres (Ministry of the Environment 2003). The supplement industry has cashed in on seaweed, particularly

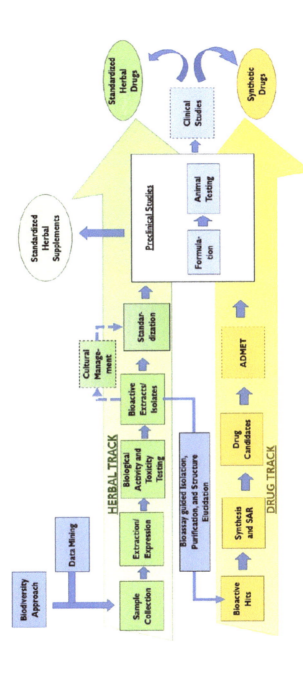

Figure 3.8 The *Tuklas Lunas* program framework, 2017–22. Source: screenshot by Anita Hardon.

kelp. Chlorella growth factor, an ingredient of Cherifer, the multivitamin that claims to stimulate growth, derives from algae, albeit from freshwater sources.

In the next chapter, we take a closer look at the marketing of packaged plants, showing how it attributes efficacies to plant-based supplements that speak to Filipinos' contemporary health concerns.

Notes

1 https://www.rappler.com/nation/four-year-death-anniversary-leonard-co-botanist (Accessed 25 January 2020).
2 Pordié (2015) describes an interesting example of reformulation in India, in which the Himalaya Drug Company reconstituted its blockbuster ayurvedic medicine LIV.52 as Partysmart. In so doing, the company created a new niche market of young professionals who want to enjoy evenings out with friends, while remaining able to perform their demanding daytime jobs. The reformulated plant medicine was promoted on a dedicated website, as well as in trendy bars and clubs that were popular among middle-class youth. Aiming for a medical aura, the company provides directions regarding how to take the drug, instructing users to take a dose an hour before their first glass of alcohol. But because its effects have never been proven in randomized controlled trials (RCTs), the substance could not be registered as medicine; instead, the company registered it as Ayurvedic medicine, which, in India, is possible for packaged plants that use ancient Ayurvedic recipes. The company wanted to expand the market for Partysmart globally, but there is no recognized regulatory category for Ayurvedic products abroad (Dwyer, Coates and Smith 2018). See also Pordié and Hardon (2015) for examples of similar processes elsewhere in Asia.
3 Transcribed from 'First Vita Plus – Dr Jaime Galvez Tan', https://www.youtube.com/watch?v=XwZayb8pBkI (Accessed 6 June 2024). In the Tagalog segment, he repeats this message, but also adds that First Vita Plus is good for sex and can help protect against avian flu.
4 Flow-mediated dilation (FMD) refers to a vascular function test that measures the change in artery diameter.

4
Reading the scripts

In this chapter, we examine the burgeoning popularity of food supplements in the Philippines, where they are ubiquitous. Supplements may be bought in drugstores, market stalls, and are increasingly sold directly to consumers through multilevel marketing. Malls typically house retailers who rent small spaces to sell supplements imported from all over the world, mostly without Philippine Food and Drug Administration (FDA) registration. They can do this because the borders of the Philippines archipelago are porous.[1]

In practice, despite the obligatory disclaimer disavowing any therapeutic claims, supplement manufacturers promise a wide range of health benefits in the package inserts and the marketing collateral that accompany their products. They have found ways to use the language of pharmaceuticals to promote totally untested supplements. In this way, they cash in on both the national increase in metabolic disorders and desires for natural products, and on national economic ambitions. They exploit neoliberal trade policies that globalize markets and deregulate trade in supplements. Leveraging Filipinos' worries about metabolic disorders to make health assertions with impunity, manufacturers package local and foreign plant materials in ways that mimic pharmaceuticals' packaging, including dosage information stating that supplements should be taken at regular intervals throughout the day. The 'scripts' printed on the packages emphasize the naturalness of their contents and reassure consumers that the products are safe (Idrus and Hardon 2015); some add allure to products by using scientific terms like 'phytochemicals' (which, as noted in Chapter 3, simply means 'chemicals found in plants').

We conducted an ethnography of labels that involved visiting market stalls, sari-sari stores, malls and pharmacies to observe the kinds of food supplements on sale. We were most interested in supplements close to the sales counters, which sold at higher rates than other supplements, and those advertised through billboards and posters. We asked the clerks behind the counters which food supplements were popular and why. In addition to interviewing salesclerks and customers, we sampled popular products from drugstores, malls and markets during periods of intermittent fieldwork in the Philippines, from 2014 to 2021, to conduct detailed analyses of their efficacy claims. We examined the packages, front and back, along with any package inserts. We considered the material content of the supplements – powders, leaves, syrups or capsules – and scrutinized any information provided on blister packages. What can an ethnography of the labels of Filipino food supplements teach us about how people experience the rapidly changing socio-metabolic conditions we described in Chapters 1 and 2? Our three main research questions were: Why are the products appealing to customers? What kinds of effects are promised and what kinds of metabolic, dietary, and societal concerns do efficacy claims reflect? How do supplements create new needs and new ways to 'treat' the experience of contemporary life?

Surveys confirm the popularity of food supplements in the Philippines. The Philippines National Nutrition Survey, reporting on a study conducted in Metro Manila among 502 respondents, demonstrates a rapid increase in awareness of and the perceived need for food supplements (Cruz et al. 2011). In 1998, only 37.5 per cent of respondents were aware of supplements. By 2008, that figure had grown by nearly 50 points to 85.6 per cent. There was also a reported increase in the number of respondents who stated that the nutrients food provides require supplementation. In 1998, 41.9 per cent of respondents said that ordinary meals needed supplementation. By 2008, 69.4 per cent of respondents responded that this was the case.

A recent research report on ageing in the Philippines notes that supplement sellers have become mobile, going on weekends to visit communities where they target the elderly. One senior citizen interviewed as part of the research described various supplements, including *panyawan*, a packaged plant which she said had become very popular in her community. A website which celebrates the plant listed its many beneficial effects, including pain relief, improved digestion, stress reduction and the boosting of immunity.[2] When asked why she did not prepare the herbal concoctions herself, she responded that the herbs were not readily available (Ladia 2024).

Sales figures support these findings regarding the increased popularity of food supplements. In 2016, sales of supplements increased

10 per cent over the previous year (Euromonitor International 2016). Market researchers attribute the surge in use to the expanding range of wellness claims companies make, including those related to beauty, weight management, memory, energy, eye health, heart health, muscle density, immune strengthening, mood improvement, relaxation, virility and liver health (Euromonitor International 2016).

The Asian Pacific region accounts for 57 per cent of global supplements sales, exceeding sales both in Europe and the United States (Euromonitor International 2019). The Euromonitor (2019) survey attributes the popularity of supplements in Asia to three factors: the long history of traditional medicine use in the region, prevailing concerns that modern pharmaceuticals have too many side effects and increased health consciousness among a growing middle-class population.

Drugstores play a pivotal role in promoting supplements, as well as snack foods and cosmetics. They also allow sales agents for supplements and 'nutritional formulas' (for children and the elderly) to approach drugstore customers directly with free samples and offers for 'discounted' packages of their products. The agents can be very aggressive in pushing their products, declaring that they prevent and treat a multitude of illnesses.

Pharmaceutical companies likewise deploy sales agents inside drugstores to pressure customers to purchase their products. One time, an agent approached Michael offering to test his hand grip. After doing so, she declared that his grip was too weak and that her company's product could remedy the problem with three months of consumption. When Michael asked if her assertions were guaranteed, with money back if the product did not work, the agent just laughed and said the company could not do that. Michael asked why most of the sales agents were approaching elderly customers. 'Was it', he joked, 'because the elderly can't run away from them?'

The supplement packages and promotional materials intentionally promote a return to nature (in contrast to what synthetic drugs offer), touting the herbal remedies in their products, often in combination with vitamins and minerals. They implicitly suggest that the supplements combine the best of two worlds: the bounties of 'natural' plant-based medicines and the 'miracles' of modern vitamins, packaged into pills and powders – issues to which we will return, reflecting on redefinitions of 'health' fuelled by the vibrant sales of supplements and also by government-sponsored development of food supplements.

Below, we present findings with regard to three aspects of food supplement efficacy that manufacturers consistently allege: (1) boosting sexual stamina and energy; (2) improving diets with minerals and vitamins; and (3) optimizing metabolic health, including controlling blood sugar levels, to improve health. (Supplements for fitness and losing weight are likewise marketed in the Philippines but are not included here because the focus of our book is on the effects of metabolic shifts on dietary deficiencies and metabolic health.)

We demonstrate how manufacturers carefully tailor the efficacy claims for their products to meet prevailing dietary and health concerns. In so doing, we are inspired by Lyon's studies of *jamu* – a generic term used to refer to Indonesian herbs (roots, bark, flowers, seeds, and leaves mixed with honey or palm sugar and eggs), which have long been part of popular Javanese culture and which nowadays are mass-produced and exported throughout Asia, including to the Philippines (Afdhal and Welsch 1988). In Indonesia, *jamu* used to be sold mainly by ambulant vendors, usually women, to boost beauty, virility and sexuality, as well as to manage hot–cold balances and treat a local condition called *masuk angin* (wind entering the body). Lyon (2005) notes that *jamu* has something important to teach us about how people manage rapidly changing social and economic conditions, which generate new needs and new ways to 'treat' the experience of contemporary life. More specifically, Lyon points to the economic insecurities following Indonesia's economic collapse in the late 1990s. There, worsening economic conditions engendered 'a sense of fruitless struggle and the sapping of one's energy', which found a voice in advertising campaigns and product packaging that promised 'the renewal of the body in the face of depletion caused by work and strain' (Lyon 2005, 14). Figure 4.1 features an example of an Indonesian energy drink popular in the Philippines that is sold using images of male power.

Boosting energy and sexual stamina

Similar to what Lyon observes in Indonesia, consumers in the Philippines seek to boost their sexual energy and stamina. While Extra Joss, a popular Asian tonic drink, is sold on market stalls in the Philippines, the Filipino brand Cobra is the market leader among Filipino energy drinks, accounting for 74 per cent of all sales (Euromonitor International 2020). Similar to Extra Joss, Cobra contains caffeine, along with B vitamins, ginseng and sugar. Sari-sari stores sell the brand, and it is heavily advertised on TV and through X (previously Twitter), Facebook and YouTube. Everyone in the Philippines knows Cobra's advertising

Figure 4.1a & b Front (top) and Back (bottom) of Extra Joss Suplemen Makanan (food supplement) sachet, sold in Indonesia, Malaysia and the Philippines. The product contains Korean Ginseng, Royal Jelly, high levels of Taurine (1000 mg) and several B vitamins. Note how the sachets mimic modern medicine by suggesting the dosage of 3× sehari (to be taken three times a day). Source: Author (Hardon), 2021.

slogans: *May Laban Ka* (You're up against it) and *Tunay na Lakas* (Full of strength). Its popularity is aided by the use of award-winning Filipino actor Coco Martin (who is attractive and muscular in appearance) to promote it (see Figure 4.2).

The supplement Robust is very popular for promoting sexual stamina. It contains several packaged plants: *Cnidium monnieri*, tea, ginseng, *Ginkgo biloba* and the roots of Dahurian angelica and danshen (see Figures 4.3–4.4).

Figure 4.2 Cobra advertisement. Source: https://www.youtube.com/watch?app=desktop&v=D-5TREqwyPo (Accessed 14 December 2020).

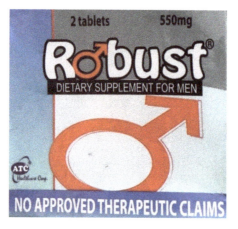

Figure 4.3 Robust, a supplement for sexual stamina (product sample, front). Source: Author (Hardon), 2021.

Available for purchase in pharmacies across the country, Robust is usually placed near cash registers, so that people notice it while waiting to pay. It is distributed by ATC Healthcare Corporation, which states as its mission: '… one goal for every Filipino and that is spreading the idea that "we are the boss of our health"'.[3] The package insert includes an alluring image of an attractive, well-endowed woman in provocative lace underwear, to get users in the mood to boost their virility.

Figure 4.4 Package insert for Robust, a supplement for sexual stamina.
Source: Author (Hardon), 2021.

Augmenting diets

Supplements that are supposed to increase stamina and vitality are common. In the Philippines, we found that supplements purported to bolster diets deficient in nutrients are equally present. Among the huge number of supplements on the market making such claims, we decided to focus on a selection that contain *malunggay* (Moringa oleifera). *Malunggay* is a common plant, the leaves of which are widely eaten as a vegetable and are likewise common in Filipino soups, such as *sinigang*. *Malunggay* trees grow even in the most densely populated urban environments. In recent years, after government nutritionists decided *malunggay* should be promoted for its relatively high protein content, the plant has transformed into a supplement about which there are all kinds of therapeutic claims.[4] It is one of the five 'power herbs' in First Vita Plus (previously discussed).

In Chapter 1, we discussed how generations of nutritionists and policymakers promoted the use of *malunggay* by distributing seedlings, promoting the plant's inclusion in home-cooked meals, and adding its dried leaves to dietary supplements. The tree's transformation into a food supplement was easy enough: it simply required packaging it in capsules, or in powder form and the obligatory message: 'NO APPROVED THERAPEUTIC CLAIMS'.

In Chapter 3, we saw Jaime Galvez Tan featured in a video where he outlines in detail the nutritional value and health benefits of each of the five plants comprising First Vita Plus, including *malunggay*. An examination of the packaging reveals assertions that the product is a 'natural health drink', 'So Full of Life' (see Figures 4.5a & b). In addition to *malunggay* (Moringa), the drink's wrapper lists four other plants, using their Latin names: Capsicum (red peppers), Amaranthus (locally called *kulitis*, a leafy green vegetable), Ipomoea (sweet potato or *kamote*) and Corchorus (jute or *sayote*). The sachet indexes quality and value by stating that it contains 'selected premium leaves' that are 'packed to meet your daily requirements of vitamins, minerals, micronutrients, anti-oxidants and immunity enhancing phytochemicals'. Likewise listed as 'ingredients' are cane sugar, instant spray-dried *dalandan*, 'nature-identical flavors', FD & C yellow and 'power herbs'.

The sachet also provides information on how to prepare this 'natural health drink': 'empty contents into 8 oz glass of water. Stir until contents are completely dissolved. Relax and enjoy the healthy taste of First Vita Plus!'

Closer examination of the sachet's labelling reveals contradictions between the nutritional benefit it allegedly provides to consumers and the nutritional content declared in the white nutrition information box on the back of the packet. How can there be claims on the front of the sachet that the drink is 'so full of life' when there is very low content of vitamins A and C: respectively just 2 and 3 per cent of the recommended daily allowance for every 100 g of powder. Since one sachet is only 22 g, you have to divide that percentage by five. The quantities of vitamins and minerals are minuscule. Moreover, given that the sugar content is very high (94 out of 100 g) and there is no fibre in the drink, we can surmise that the main plant-based substance in this product is cane sugar.

In contrast, let us look at a different *malunggay* project, developed by Galvez Tan more recently. After he became disappointed by how First Vita Plus had been 'reformulated' he created moringa-only capsules, which he sells to clients in his acupuncture clinic in downtown Manila.

Figure 4.6 shows a simple plastic zip bag containing capsules of 'air-dried' *malunggay* leaves (also referred to by their Latin name,

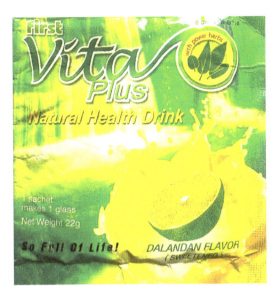

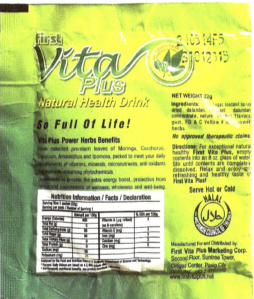

Figure 4.5a & b Front (top) and back (bottom) of a First Vita Plus sachet, in dalandan flavour. Source: Author (Hardon), 2019.

Moringa oleifera). The label states that the leaves are 'organic' (as expected when harvested directly from a tree) and that they have 'balanced combinations of just right amount of real natural vitamins and minerals', which, the label suggests, 'may possibly explain the

Figure 4.6 Malunggay capsules. Source: Author (Hardon), 2017.

many health benefits that *malunggay* gives as confirmed for generations by our ancestors'. Consumers are advised to 'take it liberally'. The capsules are made in the clinic with locally sourced leaves (the green leafy content is visible in the capsules), making them low cost to consumers.

Watsons – a pharmacy chain – sells a product that is labelled *Mangosteen + Malunggay*. (Mangosteen is a Filipino fruit said to have many health benefits, see Figure 4.7). The capsules sold by Watsons contain a specified amount of mangosteen fruit pulp powder (450 mg) and *malunggay* leaf powder (50 mg). Recommended use is one capsule a day 'or as recommended by your healthcare professional'. The packaging also lists 'benefits', including that the product 'promotes a healthy body by providing some nutrients needed'. Note the use of 'some' in this health claim, which suggests that the company does not want to overstate the nutritional value of this reconstituted plant.

In 2015, a new food supplement for children, Manna Plus, entered the Philippines' market. It contains, in addition to multiple vitamins and minerals, a chlorella extract for growth, as well as *malunggay* (see Figure 4.8).

The existence of this product reflects attention among food supplement marketers to the latest nutrition policy in the Philippines, which recommends the use of locally sourced ingredients and recognition of the importance of micronutrients to children's health and cognitive

Figure 4.7 Watsons Mangosteen + Malunggay capsules, with the image of a mangosteen fruit. Source: https://www.watsons.com.ph/mangosteen-malunggay-50mg-1-capsule/p/BP_10096074 (Accessed 14 October 2020).

Figure 4.8 Manna Plus with moringa, online advertisement. Source: http://www.mannaplus.ph/ (Accessed 14 October 2020).

abilities (Department of Health 2017). The online advertisement for Manna Plus stresses that children need nutrients to:

> … aid in their muscle and bone growth, brain development, mental clarity, healthy skin, hair, and nails, and to strengthen their immune system. Children deprived of nourishment during these intensive growth cycles may show lower IQ levels, speech and language difficulties, and slower motor skills. With Moringa, you can give your child a head start to a healthy life.

The advertisement also contains amazing nutritional claims for Manna Plus: the calcium four times higher than found in milk, iron levels three times higher than that in spinach, three times more potassium than bananas, two times more protein than eggs, and seven times more vitamin C than oranges. It is noteworthy that the manufacturer of Manna Plus, the MLA Corporation, presents itself online emphatically as '100% Filipino-made very much affordable yet beneficial for the growth and development of Filipino children' (MacKay Foundation 2018). Support for local farmers is also a prominent feature of their marketing (see Figure 4.9).

Scheele Laboratories, a local company, launched this brand seeking to acquire a share of the Philippines' 'child growth' market from the dominant Cherifer, a product manufactured by another Filipino company. As a supplement, Cherifer enjoys great popularity among parents who believe that 'height is might' (see Figure 2.6), with a reason: many jobs in the Philippines have height requirements (Lasco 2017).

Figure 4.9 Manna Plus supports farmers and plants malunggay trees.
Source: http://www.mannaplus.ph/our_advocacy.html (Accessed 14 October 2020).

Improving metabolic health

Examining the packaging materials and promotional assertions attached to food supplements uncovered a third category of efficacy claims, which we loosely refer to as those alleging to improve metabolic health. We wondered, do these claims reflect recent understanding of how metabolisms function, emerging from biochemistry and the nascent field of functional nutrition?

In the nineteenth century, when Marx analysed metabolisms, bodies were conceptualized as factories that harboured machines that required fuel in the form of calories (Foster 2000; Moore 2015). Nutritionism, one of the metabolic shifts discussed in Chapter 1, became a driving force in the food industry and in nutrition policies in the post-World War II period, which led to a focus on the body's needs for individual vitamins and minerals, reflected in the efficacy claims for the *malunggay* supplements presented above. In the late twentieth century, due to advances in biochemistry, the concept of metabolism was redefined as interconnected biochemical pathways in cells and organs, linked through flows of blood and other fluids. More recently, in the early twenty-first century, metabolism has been reconceptualized again, as an unstable information-driven regulatory system that reacts to environmental signals (Landecker 2013; Saldaña-Tejeda and Wade 2019). We see efficacy claims related to metabolism in an increasing number of supplements, the sellers tending to back up their assertions with references to clinical research (which may not be necessarily understood by their customers). One example is C24/7, a supplement imported from the United States that supposedly helps people take charge of their bodies by improving *cellular health* (see Figure 4.10). AIM Global

Figure 4.10 Promotional leaflet for C24/7 including information on its metabolic action, contents and benefits. Source: Author (Hardon), 2019.

sells the supplement in the Philippines using multilevel marketing. Its marketing collateral purports that C24/7 contains over 100 ingredients, including 14 'superfoods' in a spirulina blend, a 12 whole fruit juice blend, a 12 whole vegetable juice blend and 12 kinds of mushrooms. The number of ingredients is mind-boggling.

The marketing materials for C24/7 emphatically state that the preparation bestows a multitude of metabolic effects on consumers, including cellular protection, immunity, energy and longevity, which results in a whole range of health benefits, including controlling blood sugar, regenerating liver cells, detoxifying the body, reducing fatigue and enhancing sexual vitality. In claiming to possess this range of metabolic health benefits, the product appears to outdo all the other supplements on the market. Its 'scientific' references to cellular metabolic pathways lend credibility, while its statements on nutritional content feed into people's concerns about deficient diets. What else could a consumer desire, especially in the light of current concerns about the low nutritional value of fast food and increasing rates of chronic metabolic diseases? Examining the capsules, we see green fibres, as is the case with the *malunggay*-filled capsules prepared by Dr Galvez Tan's clinic. But one wonders, how much vegetable, fruit and mushroom content can one small capsule contain? Surely, if the package inserts are accurate, only traces of each.

Glomar Herbal Philippines Corporation, which manufactures products for local entrepreneurs seeking to develop their own brand, makes GDetoxPlus.[5] We purchased a package of GDetoxPlus from a pharmacy in Cagayan de Oro, a town on the Philippines' southern island of Mindanao.

Note that this supplement contains fennel, ginger, garlic and mustard seeds. The leaflet we received with our purchase reads: 'Toxins are everywhere in our environment. They are in the air we breathe, the water we drink, and the foods we eat – polluted air, contaminated water, preservatives, pesticides, fertilizers, drugs, alcohol, cigarettes, cosmetics, household cleaning products and other chemicals' (see Figure 4.11.) The information on the right-hand panel declares that the GDetoxPlus Herbal Capsule 'has been proven effective, through clinical studies', for relieving multiple disorders, including digestive problem, dysmenorrhea and liver diseases. Detailed dosages are provided, for use as a remedy (1–2 capsules, three times a day) and for maintenance treatments (1 capsule per day). Here, again, a manufacturer references scientific studies to bestow credibility on a product. In the Philippines, more than 90 per cent of schoolchildren

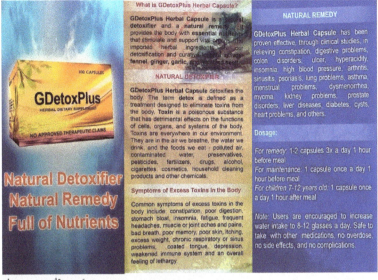

Figure 4.11 GDetoxPlus product information. Source: Author (Hardon), 2020 and http://gdetoxplus.com/ingredients.php (Accessed 15 May 2024).

attend secondary school (Education Policy and Data Center 2018), where they learn biology and the importance of scientific evidence. This makes such claims a powerful sales technique. Because there is no regulatory mechanism to scrutinize the evidence manufacturers mobilize to promote the sales of their products, they can make claims with impunity.

Supplements during the COVID-19 pandemic

The COVID-19 pandemic presented supplement manufacturers with an opportunity to tailor their supplements to a new set of consumer concerns. During the pandemic, Michael led a research project entitled, 'Navigating environments of COVID-19 risk', which included asking if people were taking any products to prevent COVID-19. The responses included the usual 'multivitamins' and specific ones like vitamin C and vitamin D, and the mineral zinc. But respondents also mentioned two plant-based supplements that tend to be specific to certain Filipino ethnic communities. These were Lianhua Qingwen capsules among ethnic Chinese and 'black seed' among Muslims.

Lianhua Qingwen first came into the public eye in newspaper articles about government raids on illegal clinics and pharmacies that had opened during the COVID-19 lockdown. These establishments were catering to the 'new Chinese': business people and office workers from mainland China who had started entering the country in large numbers from around 2010, mainly for short-term business engagements. The raids yielded stocks of Lianhua Qingwen, capsules containing extracts from 13 plants. The Chinese government had approved the product for mild cases of COVID-19, using traditional Chinese medicinal principles indicated, in Chinese, on the packaging: 'clearing scourge, removing toxins, diffusing the lungs and discharging heat'.

When word of Lianhua Qingwen spread among the local ethnic Chinese population who were not 'new Chinese', the product began appearing in some Chinese drugstores and even at grocery stores. In May 2020, the Philippines' Dangerous Drugs Board (DDB) issued a memo noting that the Chinese government had donated 700,000 Lianhua Qingwen capsules to the Philippines, which had been asked to render an opinion on the preparation. The DDB was caught in a dilemma, given that the product contained ephedra, a stimulant banned in the Philippines because of its potential for abuse.[6] Despite noting that each dose contained as much as 85 mg of ephedra, the DDB nonetheless decided to endorse use of the medicine.

The Philippine Food and Drug Administration (FDA) seemed unaware of the DDB's decision. In July 2020, the FDA issued a warning that the drug was not approved in the Philippines. A month later, the Chinese Embassy in Manila issued a statement welcoming the Philippine FDA's approval of Lianhua Qingwen as 'important progress in the entry of TCM (traditional Chinese medicine) into the Philippines'. The embassy also stated that the drug was approved in China for mild and moderate COVID-19.[7] The Philippine FDA quickly issued a statement clarifying that the drug was indeed approved, but only as a 'traditionally used herbal product [that] helps remove heat-toxin invasion of the lungs, including symptoms such as fever, aversion to cold, muscle soreness, stuffy and runny nose', and not as a treatment for COVID-19.[8] The drug is now sold in various outlets, (traditional Chinese) pharmacies and groceries, without warning labels about its high ephedra content. Indeed, the Lianhua Qingwen sold in traditional establishments comes directly from China, and its packaging has no English labels or package inserts.

The other product that became popular in response to COVID-19 was 'black seed', brought to our attention by a member of Michael's research team in Zamboanga City in the southern Philippines. The research assistant saw that people in his fieldsite considered this 'black seed' a powerful drug, citing a hadith (sayings attributed to the Prophet Mohammed) that it cures all illnesses except death. The research assistant's source of black seeds was a Filipino who had worked in Saudi Arabia. Michael was able to establish that the 'black seed' was Nigella sativa, also known as 'black caraway' and 'black cumin' and was sold raw or as oil in capsules.

A Muslim faculty member at the University of the Philippines provided an elaborate account of the uses of these packaged seeds, confirming their popularity among local Muslims, and increasingly so when the pandemic began in 2020. She also said that many of her friends and relatives believed the medicine could prevent and cure COVID-19, but also warned Michael to be careful when purchasing black seeds because there were many fake preparations. Concerned he would unknowingly purchase one of these, she sent him a package of black seeds capsules (with the brand name Habbasy ibnuafif) which, it turned out, came from Indonesia. The package's insert called the seed 'prophetic medicine' (see Figure 4.12).

Note that the branded capsules are referred to as *jamu* (top left-hand corner) and that the oil (*minyak*) contained in the capsules is said to be cold pressed, perhaps referring to the beneficial health properties of cold-pressed olive oil.

Michael also performed his own observations in local malls and pharmacies. During a visit to a local mall before the pandemic, Michael received a free sample of a product called Lola Remedios – see Figure 4.13 – which means Grandmother Remedios. Remedios is an (originally Spanish) woman's name that also means 'remedy'. He set the sample aside without reading the package and forgot about it.

Figure 4.12 Black seed capsules and seeds used to prevent COVID-19. Source: Author (Tan), 2020.

Figure 4.13 Lola Remedios. Source: Author (Tan), 2021.

When his housekeeper found it and asked him if he had tried it (he had not), she said she had been using a similar product called Tolak Angin, a *jamu* imported from Indonesia, to rebalance problems of cold entering her body. The product's name caught Michael's attention since he recognized its meaning – 'to push wind' in Indonesian. That was when he examined the Lola Remedios and realized it was actually imported *jamu*. Later, during the lockdown in 2020, Michael went to a Mercury Drugstore to purchase both Tolak Angin and Lola Remedios, and asked the cashier how sales had been for the two products since the onset of the COVID-19 pandemic. She replied 'mabenta', meaning they sell well, and speculated that maybe this was because the products contain *luya* or ginger. Ginger is used in popular medicines as treatment for coughs and colds, and many Filipinos touted ginger drinks during the lockdown as a means to prevent COVID. A November 2020 report from the Euromonitor marketing firm, 'Herbal/traditional products in Indonesia', observed that Tolak Angin and another product, Antangin, were expected to surpass traditional products in value terms, since they are 'leaders in the same category, herbal/traditional cough, cold and allergy (hay fever) remedies, as consumers look to herbal formulae to effectively alleviate colds, coughs, fevers, nausea, and fatigue'.

A box of Tolak Angin, which bears the required 'No Approved Therapeutic Claims', contains 12 sachets of a liquid that its packaging describes as a 'secret recipe of natural herbs'. The ingredients are listed as Asian rice, fennel, Indian screw tree, clove, mint, ginger, cardamom, nutmeg, Indonesian cinnamon, gotu kola, tree bean, usnea and some food additives (see Figure 4.14).

One side panel of the Tolak Angin box shows a pot, above which is written the word 'honey', surrounded by pictures of plants labelled ginger, fennel, mint and clove. The other side panel gives a brief history of this *jamu*, referring to its 'secret recipe' of natural herbs trusted in Indonesia for many generations, stating that it was 'first produced as liquid and packaged in a practical sachet in 1992'. The dose recommendation is one sachet three times a day.

Returning to look closely at his box of Lola Remedios, Michael noticed a Filipino text: *Hagod-Ginhawa, pag napasukan ng lamig* (Bringing relief when wind enters [the body]). Opening the box top, he found another text: *Mabigat na pakiramdam ngunit wala namang sakit?*

Figure 4.14 Tolak Angin, repackaged for the Philippines, including a front image of the package, and one side panel. Source: Author (Tan), 2021.

Figure 4.15 Text provided inside the packaging of Lola Remedios. Source: Author (Tan), 2021.

Baka LAMIG 'yan! (Do you have heavy symptoms but no illness? Maybe that's the COLD – see Figure 4.15).

Lola Remedios' marketing pitch is clever. It highlights *lamig* (cold) rather than *hangin* (wind), recognizing that the latter's Indonesian cognate *angin* (as in the product Tolak Angin), which is blamed for a wide range of ailments from body aches to rheumatism, arthritis, coughs and runny noses, isn't quite as virulent in the Philippines. Instead, Filipinos tend to blame *lamig*, and so this is used in Lola Remedios. The marketing of Tolak Angin has likewise been tailored to the Philippines, reflecting a trend of expanding products to a large regional market – a process that Pordié and Gaudillière (2014) refer to as a 'reformulation regime'.

Health claims and regulatory actions

Many of the plant ingredients we reviewed above are easily grown and harvested – even in urban communities – with minimal space and effort. Nutrients abound in the natural plant, but not in these little sachets. Less obvious than the promises of vitality, health and longevity made on the wrappers of these packaged plants is another, more troublesome assertion: you can keep living however you want, if you just drink your sachet. The illusion of easy cures displaces important aspects of maintaining health, particularly the prevention of disease through exercise and proper diet. Moreover, advances in nutritional science and ethnopharmacology that highlight synergies among constituents, rather than isolating individual nutrients and phytochemicals, call into question the fragmented approach to health and nutrition reflected in the nutritionist promotion of supplements (Etkin 2006; Jacobs et al. 2009). A renewed interest in the value of fresh vegetables and fruits in maintaining a healthy diversity of micro-organisms in our guts likewise renders questionable the value of supplementing (Thursby and Juge 2017).

The Philippine Department of Health and the Food and Drug Administration (FDA) share our concerns about the plethora of health claims manufacturers make when promoting plant-based supplements. Former FDA director Dr Kenneth Go told Anita that he is concerned that consumers taking supplements such as C24/7 that purportedly stabilize blood sugar will postpone preventative doctor visits. Go's peers who work as medical specialists in hospitals across the Philippines inform him that patients trust the efficacy claims regarding plant-based supplements, to such a great extent that they often stop taking the prescribed medications that manage their conditions. The problem, Go disclosed to Anita, is that supplements are sold as wondrous cure-alls that can prevent cancer, diabetes, improve memory and increase height, but medically these presumptions are all nonsense. He says: 'These misleading claims ... can be dangerous especially for patients who really need healthcare but then choose not to because they believe what is being offered to them as an alternative approach to healthcare' (interview with Hardon). He notes that plant-based supplement merchants often assert that they are safe because they are natural. But, he says, perhaps they are safe because they have no effects at all. 'How would you have side effects if you don't even have any real beneficial effects to begin with? If the product doesn't work, there's no safety issue. But then you delay diagnosis, you delay interventions. And then complications set in. Then you end up spending more, and you destroy your quality of life' (interview with Hardon).

The main concern at the FDA appears to be that manufacturers do not register food supplements with the authorities. In a series of posts on its website and a dedicated Facebook page, the FDA warns against plant-based supplements that are unregistered, the safety of which it can therefore not guarantee. See Figure 4.16 and the FDA following statement:

> In light of the foregoing, the public is advised not to purchase the aforementioned violative products. Moreover, the public is advised to always check if a food product/food supplement is registered with the FDA. The FDA website (www.fda.gov.ph) has a Search feature which may be used by typing in the name of the product before purchasing.
>
> All concerned establishments are warned not to distribute violative food supplements until they have been issued the appropriate

authorization, a License to Operate (LTO) for the establishment, and a CPR for the food product.

All FDA Regional Field Offices and Regulatory Enforcement Units, in coordination with law enforcement agencies and Local Government Units, are requested to ensure that violative products are not sold or made available in the market or areas of jurisdiction.

To report any sale or distribution of unregistered food products/ food supplements, kindly email us through ereport@fda.gov.ph.

Dissemination of this advisory to all concerned is hereby requested. (Department of Health. Food and Drug Administration 2020)

Figure 4.16 FDA warning about unregistered food supplements (Department of Health 2020). Source: Republic of the Philippines Department of Health. Food and Drug Administration. FDA Advisory. https://www.fda.gov.ph/wp-content/uploads/2020/07/FDA-Advisory-No.2020-1335.pdf (Accessed 15 May 2024).

We return to the problem of packaged plants becoming globalized and evading regulatory controls. Dr Go says that the Philippine FDA does not test the products because it lacks the laboratory capacity and funds to do so. In the rare cases when the FDA can research a supplement's contents, it regularly finds that plant-based food supplements are adulterated with synthetic pharmaceutical ingredients, such as steroids and ephedrine, to enhance efficacy. A study from the Pharmacy Department of the University of Porto in Portugal confirmed the synthetic adulteration of plant-based food supplements, which many consumers believe are safe because they are 'natural' products, especially in supplements marketed for weight loss (amphetamines and ephedrine are added), muscle-building (anabolic steroids added) and sexual performance (sildenafil, the active ingredient of Viagra, and its analogues are added). The study's researchers relate this adulteration to a lack of the requirement for pre-approval for plant-based supplements prior to marketing in both Europe and the United States (and indeed also in the Philippines), stating that 'this allows for unscrupulous manufacturers and distributors to deliberatively adulterate supplements through the addition of pharmaceutical drugs or analogue substances (designer drugs, often not characterized for their safety and toxicity) in order to increase product effectiveness' (Rocha et al. 2016, 58). Rocha et al. (2016) argue that the growing consumption of these products, coupled with global distribution, creates an urgent need for better control than currently exists.

The US Government Accounting Office (2010) makes similar recommendations. It tested 40 herbal dietary supplements and found 37 of them to be contaminated with potentially hazardous heavy metals: 32 contained mercury, 28 cadmium, 21 arsenic, and 18 possessed residues from at least one pesticide. While the agency reports that the levels of heavy metals do not exceed the standards outlined in US FDA or Environmental Protection Agency regulations governing dietary supplements, we imagine that supplement consumers would want to know that the 'natural' products they take may have traces of synthetic, and sometimes dangerous, chemicals.

Questionable panacea

Plant-based supplements are attractive health commodities with the appearance of natural, scientifically proven potencies in modern packaging. They promise to bestow stamina and vitality, to augment diets composed of overly processed foods that are deficient in key nutrients and to enhance metabolic health through their physiological and cellular effects. They pledge to protect users against pollution, diabetes and cardiovascular disease.

Reflecting on the historical exchanges of plants across vast territories, we observed a vibrant transnational trade in packaged plants. Our close reading of the supplements on the Filipino market indicates both intense intra-Asian reformulations of these packaged plants and global flows. Plant materials like Nigella sativa seeds (packaged as black seeds) make 'stopovers', transiting through Indonesia from the Middle East or Eastern Europe, before arriving in the Philippines. We learned about a grey market of products not officially registered or approved by Philippine regulatory authorities, and about consumers, some in their own ethnic communities, with their own standards and senses of caution regarding 'fakes'.

Manufacturers skilfully fuel demand by associating their packaged plants with prevailing concerns about pollution, diets, metabolic health and COVID-19. Our observations echo those of Pordié (2015), who presents an insightful analysis of the ways in which an Indian Ayurvedic medicine manufacturer reformulates its drugs to match changing health concerns. He describes how the Himalaya Drug Company first reconstituted its blockbuster ayurvedic medicine LIV.52 as a hangover drug called Partysmart. The company tailored its product to meet the concerns of a new niche market of young professionals who want to enjoy evenings out with friends and still be able to perform their demanding daytime jobs. Himalaya Drug Company promoted the reconstituted plant medicine on a dedicated website, as well as in trendy bars and clubs, popular among middle-class youth. Aiming for a medical aura, the company's marketing materials provided advice on how to take the drug, instructing users to take a dose an hour before their first glass of alcohol.

The company next wanted to expand the market for Partysmart in Asia, but to do so it would have needed to meet regulatory categories abroad (Dwyer et al. 2018). Plant-based supplements go by different names, for example, as herbal dietary supplements (the United States), natural health products (Canada) and food supplements (the Philippines, Indonesia, Malaysia and Mongolia). The Himalaya Drug Company's international regulatory department decided to export Partysmart to Mongolia as its first area of expansion, given the high alcohol consumption in that country among the general adult population. To meet Mongolia's regulatory requirements, Partysmart was reformulated to include just six herbs, which made it possible to register it as a food supplement (Pordié 2015). 'Reformulating', Pordié asserts, refers both to the product's material content and to the adjusted efficacy claims.

The re-articulation processes also echo processes that occur in pharmaceutical markets (see, for example, Ecks and Basu 2009). Greenslit (2005) describes how Pfizer successfully reformed its blockbuster drug fluoxetine (the active ingredient of Prozac) for treatment of premenstrual dysphoric disorder by giving the pill a pink colour and naming it

Sarafem. Similarly, Hartley (2006) describes how the 'pinking' of Viagra reoriented this potency drug to address female sexual dysfunction, thereby expanding its market. Martin (2006, 282) emphasizes that such reforming of pharmaceuticals involves 'carefully engineered images and concepts with sparse language designed to capture desires and hopes while transposing in minuscule font the potential side effects that are not really meant to be read'.

Sadly, the food supplements marketed by means of impressive efficacy claims may not be as potent and safe as their distributors promise they are. First Vita Plus's nutrition information box reveals that it contains little nutritional value, but who reads (and can understand) the box's small print? Still, as already discussed, the company alleges that the sachet is 'so full of life' and that it contains five plants, though it also contains no fibre and hardly any vitamins. Assertions that the preparations improve metabolic health may cause consumers to believe supplements are viable treatments for chronic diseases – which is not supported by evidence from clinical research, and may have adverse consequences if consumers assume packaged plants' efficacy, and refrain from seeking out medical advice.

Our analysis further suggests that the products, in addition to having questionable nutritional and health value, may not be as safe or as effective as promised. Regulators maintain that the products are, in fact, sometimes adulterated with pharmaceuticals to enhance effects (and consequently sales), while efficacy claims are based on very limited clinical evidence. Food supplement manufacturing and distribution have escaped government regulations globally. Consumers are put at risk of buying products that they not only do not need, but which also may harm them. Pharmacologists (Gurley et al. 2018) warn that supplement manufacturers often provide consumers with inadequate information regarding appropriate consumption and adverse effects. Moreover, when medically untested, multi-ingredient blends may pose greater risks than single-ingredient botanical supplements.

The popularity of the packaged plant products we have reviewed in this chapter indicates that people fall victim to promises of abundant good health. It can also be understood as a reflection of what is at stake in people's everyday lives, including prevailing concerns about metabolic precarity. Although the material contents of the packaged plants range from containing hardly any plant material to being adulterated with pharmaceuticals, they do 'work', by giving consumers a sense of control over their precarious lives. That they are both medicine and food, moreover, fits with Filipino cultural notions of what plants can do. While government authorities try to draw boundaries between the medicinal value of some packaged plants and the dietary role of others, consumers in the Philippines (and elsewhere) see no need for such a delineation. They and their families and communities have a long history of using plants simultaneously as both food and medicine in their quest for a good life.

So how can we understand what the supplements do? The efficacy of plant-based supplements cannot be understood solely in relation to the material effects of the herbs that are selected, packaged, and (mis)labelled by manufacturers. Manufacturers' claims are reinforced by Filipino nutritionists, who advise mothers to use supplements to augment the diets of their children, adding to people's expectations that supplements will be good for them. They are likewise reinforced by the Philippines Department of Science and Technology, which treats herbal products as an industrial growth market and invests in their development; by both the US and Philippines Food and Drug Authorities, which fail to regulate and check for quality (roles they do perform for pharmaceuticals), and by local pharmacists, who allow company agents to promote products to the elderly when they come in to fill their prescriptions, thereby subtly supporting the agents' promises of good health – fuelling nutritionist metabolic shifts.

In the next two chapters, we follow First Vita Plus to the remote island of Palawan where, 10 years after its invention, the supplement is popular among poor and lower-middle-class men and women who aspire for a better life. There, we turn to the question of First Vita Plus's benefits, both as a health-enhancing supplement and as an income-generating scheme, and seek to understand its popularity in an ecological context where vegetables and fruits are abundant. We argue that while positive expectations of beneficial effects can materialize in positive health outcomes (Moerman 2002), exploitative marketing schemes perpetuate inequalities.

Notes

1 As stated in the previous chapter, following the example of the United States, the Philippine FDA's regulations allow a drug to be registered only with proof of efficacy and safety in large scale clinical trials. Likewise following the United States, in the Philippines, manufacturers may register food supplements without needing to prove efficacy. All they need to do is print on the labels for their products that none of the therapeutic claims made have been proven.
2 See https://livetoplant.com/panyawan-plant-benefits/ (Accessed 6 June 2024).
3 See https://atchealthcare.com.ph (Accessed 6 June 2024).
4 See Bhattacharya et al. (2018) for a recent review of phytochemical properties and pharmacological characteristics of Moringa leaves.

5 See http://www.gdetoxplus.com/index.php for more information on this product, which is designed and distributed in Cagayan de Oro on the southern Philippine island of Mindanao. Glomar Herbal Phils. Corp in Metro Manila manufactures GDetoxPlus and promotes itself on Facebook: https://www.facebook.com/glomarherbalphilippines (Accessed 6 June 2024).
6 Ephedra refers to the plant, which has several alkaloids with effects on multiple systems in the body, including serious risks of heart attack and stroke. It has been used in supplements that are promoted for weight loss because of the alkaloids' depressing effect on the appetite. Ephedrine is a derivative of ephedra and is used in nasal decongestants and weight-loss supplements. It is legal in many countries, including the Philippines, but is supposed to be subject to strict regulations because it can be used to manufacture shabu and metamphetamine, which are major drugs of abuse. https://www.webmd.com/vitamins/ai/ingredientmono-847/ephedra (Accessed 20 December 2020).
7 China Welcomes Philippine Approval of Lianhua Qingwen. Xinhua dispatch, http://www.china.org.cn/world/Off_the_Wire/2020-08/12/content_76591831.htm (Accessed 18 December 2020).
8 'Philippine OKs Chinese drug Lianhua Qingwen, but not for Covid-19'. CNN dispatch, 12 August 2020 (no longer found online).

Part II
Socio-metabolic precarity and work in a rural boomtown

5
'Be your product': metabolic precarities in Puerto Princesa

Shortly after arriving in Puerto Princesa, to work with a team from Palawan State University that was researching the chemical lives of young people (Hardon and Tan 2017; Hardon 2021), Anita stumbled upon a product centre for First Vita Plus in the middle of town (described in Chapter 1). It was 2014, 10 years since Dr Jaime Galvez Tan had invented the five 'power herbs' formula for the product. Our colleagues at the Palawan Studies Center, which was hosting our research project, had told us that many young people were selling First Vita Plus in Puerto Princesa through multilevel marketing (MLM). Others, they said, sold C24/7, the plant-based capsules discussed in Chapter 4. Inside the First Vita Plus product centre, the walls displayed many pictures of plants, and a promotional poster showing an attractive, super healthy and athletic looking woman sipping a glass of First Vita Plus (see Figure 5.1).

The poster is crowded with images and text. The Latin names of the five 'power herbs' included in the drink are printed in bold, blue capital letters, with the Tagalog names underneath, in smaller italicized text. The poster also lists 20 diseases that the drink supposedly helps prevent, with the additional claim, 'Anti-cancer breakthrough', in a bright yellow circle that catches the eye. At the bottom of the poster, we find the Philippine FDA logo and the phrase 'halal certified',[1] as further attempts to convince us of the product's credibility.

Curious to understand the appeal of these plant-based supplements in a rural boomtown town where people have access to an abundance of fruits and vegetables, Anita decided to attend the health seminars where distributors receive information about the product's potential health benefits. Along with her team, she also interviewed users and sellers of the products (Hardon, Davatos and Lasco 2019; Hardon 2021).

Figure 5.1 First Vita Plus promotional poster, from the First Vita Plus product centre in Puerto Princesa. Author (Hardon), 2014.

Chapter 4 describes how the manufacturers of supplements make various health claims and exploit interest in and demand for supplements. This chapter employs the idea of distributed agency (among manufacturers, nutritionists, government authorities, pharmacists, and doctors; see also Chen 2009 and Hawkins, Potter and Race 2015) to explain the seduction of supplements in Puerto Princesa. We conducted ethnographic research to examine in depth the promises and health claims of two manufacturers regarding three of their widely used supplements. We studied how face-to-face and social media interactions between consumers and sellers participating in MLM schemes create expectations that the supplements will have health benefits.

We found that the distributors of First Vita Plus and C24/7 used remarkably similar marketing techniques to compete for people's attention. Both were distributed through product centres run by local distributors. The distributors organized regular health symposia that included lectures by doctors and nurses on the products' health impacts and testimonials from people whose health had improved after taking the products. The people we encountered had first started consuming the products because they were worried about their health, and then themselves became distributors, which gave them access to the products at a discount and allowed them to earn some additional income. One of Anita's research assistants, Jaime, attested to the multiple benefits of C24/7, which he took every day, although it ate up around 10 per cent of his earnings. Jaime had a demanding job at the local university and paid his younger siblings' school fees. He needed stamina, he explained to Anita, insisting that C24/7 helped him sleep, supplemented his fast-food diet, and protected him from hangovers. Like many other young men and women in his peri-urban community, Jaime was a member of the Philippine company, Alliance in Motion (AIM) Global, which distributed C24/7 (Hardon, Davatos and Lasco 2019). However, selling the products was hard work. They were relatively expensive and many people in Puerto Princesa were poor and could not really afford them.

Our fieldwork revealed that MLM trainers presented both First Vita Plus and C24/7 to distributors as protective shields and cure-alls, using marketing techniques that bring to mind Dumit's definition of 'surplus health'. In *Drugs for Life*, Dumit (2012, 206) argues that, in the United States, direct-to-consumer advertising of pharmaceuticals on television encourages patients and doctors to 'overvalue [a] pill's benefits relative to its side-effects and costs'. Overvaluing the potential of pharmaceuticals leads consumers to seek 'surplus health'. Something similar seems to be taking place in the selling of plant-based supplements, although the means employed – exploiting multilevel marketeers and social media to generate demand for 'surplus health' – are different.

Reflecting on the promotion of First Vita Plus and C24/7, we wondered why these products were in demand in Puerto Princesa, a city that appears to be lush with plant life. Along her routes from home in a peri-urban community to the Palawan Studies Center, Anita observed numerous fruit trees – mango, banana, papaya, lime – and backyard gardens containing a variety of vegetables and root crops. Mangos fell from the trees, including onto the roof of the office where she and her research assistants worked, and children picked them up on their way to school. Stalls along the sides of the streets and sidewalks sold cheap produce. The city government, moreover, was known for its solid environmental policies, which encouraged people to care for the town's green spaces. Puerto Princesa was not a food desert, where one might expect people to worry about the nutritional value of their diets. Why would people in this town want to buy packaged plants, when fresh fruits and vegetables grew in and around it in abundance?

Metabolic shifts in Puerto Princesa

On a map, the island of Palawan appears isolated on the edge of the Philippines. It is one of the few islands where tropical rainforest, which makes the country a hotspot for biodiversity, still covers most of the territory. The surrounding seas are also known for their abundant diversity, although commercial fishing, including the use of cyanide, has affected the quality of marine life. The island has long been home to six indigenous peoples (the largest groups being the Palawan, Tagbuana and Batak), who live in relative isolation in the forests and on the coasts.[2] They practise shifting cultivation in the forest, clearing small areas, and growing food in them before moving on and allowing the forest to regenerate. Along the coasts, communities rely on fishing and growing vegetables for income and home consumption. People in the municipality harvest cashew nuts, mangoes and other fruits from the many fruit trees that grow there (Eder 1999).

The coastal communities of Puerto Princesa tap the seas for food, not only from fish but also sea vegetables (seaweed). One would think such rich marine reserves would mean that no one goes hungry. However, while the coastal areas draw thousands of tourists who rave about inexpensive seafood and the beaches, fisherfolk are among the most impoverished and their children among those most affected by malnutrition (Capanzana et al. 2018; Fabinyi 2018). The reasons for this impoverishment extend back in history to marginalization of the fishing sector, growing populations and overfishing. Unfortunately, environmental degradation has affected not only terrestrial resources but also those of the seas.

Palawan's population has increased tremendously over the last century: in 1903, it was 35,369 (Eder 1999), but by 2020 had expanded to 1.2 million. Puerto Princesa's population grew by 4% annually between 2015 and 2020 (Laririt 2021). This growth was mainly due to migrants from other parts of the Philippines moving to the island, encouraged by government offers of homestead land. Moreover, in recent decades, commercial investments have poured in at breakneck speed, especially for logging, mining, fisheries and tourism ventures.

Both civil society organizations and the general public see this boom in commercial development as primarily extractive and worry about the loss of biodiversity in the region. Their call for sustainable development found a champion in Puerto Princesa's Mayor Edward Hagedorn, who assumed office in 1992, beginning the first of five terms. Hagedorn made tourism rooted in environmental protection the platform for his economic agenda. His vision was to make Puerto Princesa the greenest, most environmentally and business-friendly city in the Philippines. In 2010, he was successful in getting UNESCO to declare the Saint Paul Subterranean River (on the 'bucket list' to visit for many Filipinos) one of the seven natural wonders of nature.

During our fieldwork (2014–18), daily wages in Puerto Princesa were low, at around $6 US per day. Because of this, families work together to *hanap buhay* (supporting each other financially: literally, 'seek life'), as people do in other locations on the periphery of global capitalism (Besnier 2011; McCormack and Barclay 2013). Relatives working in Manila and abroad help their kin in Puerto Princesa by sending remittances, which the latter invest in education, appliances, land (cheap until recently) and houses. Still, despite pooling resources and remittances, a 2011 report from Community-Based Monitoring System (CBMS), *The Many Faces of Poverty – Palawan*, states that one-fifth of households in 2009 lived below the poverty threshold, meaning they lacked the income to meet their basic needs; moreover, one-tenth of those able to work were unemployed (CBMS 2011). Such high levels of poverty and unemployment have an impact on health: the MIMAROPA (Southwestern Tagalog region), which includes Palawan, has the highest rate in the country of underweight children under five years old, as well as the highest rate of childhood stunting (National Nutrition Survey 2015).

In the past twenty years Puerto Princesa has become a popular tourist destination for Manila's emerging middle class, who fly in and out in a few days to visit attractions such as the underground river or a crocodile farm, or to take a cruise around the Honda Bay Marine Reserve, which is teeming with marine life. Foreign tourists pass through Puerto Princesa on their way to island resorts. In 2009, the city's tourism office recorded 268,942 visitors, with this number increasing to 700,000 in 2014 and 1.2 million in 2018. In 2010, the city featured 99 registered guesthouses and hotels, this number had more than doubled by 2018. Along with tourism, the number of bars and restaurants has increased dramatically (Doblado 2017; Reduble 2019).

To cater to the rapidly growing population and the influx of tourists, two shopping malls opened (Robinson's in 2012 and SM

Hypermarket in 2017), car and motorcycle dealers offering attractive deals launched and the airport expanded. Outside the malls and along the road to the airport, posters of happy people eating fast food, living in gorgeous townhouses and driving shiny new cars and motorcycles attract the attention of young locals. Young people spend their free time in the malls, mingling with the tourists, imagining a middle-class lifestyle where they can afford the goods on display or take a plane to Manila or beyond. The few who find good jobs and achieve middle-class status – often with the help of remittances from family – fuel the aspirations of those left behind.

While investors marvel at Palawan's cheap land, developing it has displaced people, including indigenous peoples, from their subsistence farming plots. Locals' access to land has thus declined due to the development of housing estates, hotels and guesthouses. The establishment of marine reserves has restricted fishing for food (Fabinyi 2018). Since 2000, the city's population has doubled. Meanwhile, the cost of living has increased substantially because locals can rely less on homegrown vegetables and root crops, or fish they catch, than they could before 2000.

In the more rural villages on Palawan, people continue to work in agriculture (on coconut plantations and poultry farms, and harvesting rice, cashew nuts, fruits, corn and vegetables), and in fishing (70 per cent of the fish sold in Manila comes from the sea surrounding Palawan). But in Puerto Princesa, people increasingly work in retail, transportation, construction and tourism – in hotels, guesthouses, restaurants and with tour companies. These transformations in the work people do have changed the rhythms of their everyday lives. Working in the service sector means commuting and spending long hours at work, which cuts into time they could spend gardening, fishing or collecting shellfish to augment their diets.

While Anita at first thought there was a bounty of fresh fruits and vegetables and fish for the taking, it turned out that drastic changes to life in Puerto Princesa since it became a boomtown in the past decade had complicated the social fabric; in socioeconomic terms, the metabolic lives of the people in Puerto Princesa have changed. Agricultural work requires more physical activity than many of the jobs in town, while commuting in heavy traffic means inhaling air pollution. Working long hours to make ends meet results in less time for childcare, cooking, relaxation and sleep, which can create feelings of stress. In Solomon's (2016, 62) analysis of 'metabolic living' in Mumbai, his interlocutors refer to such stress as *tenshun*, which he defines as 'symptoms of absorption between environment and the body'. The multifaceted stress of urban life fuels the demand for First Vita Plus and C24/7.

Many people in Puerto Princesa express concern about the disruptive effects that poverty, stress, changing foodscapes and polluted environments have on their physical metabolisms, as also experienced by people living elsewhere in the Global South (Gálvez 2018; Hardon, Davatos and Lasco 2019; Hardin 2019; Roberts 2017; Solomon 2016; Yates-Doerr 2015). While meals previously consisted of rice with vegetables and fish, diets in the newly monetized economy are heavy on instant noodles, cheap hamburgers, processed breads and packaged juices, which explains why people worry about potential nutritional deficiencies. The nutritional health programmes that warn about vitamin and mineral deficiencies (referred to in Chapter 2) reinforce these worries.

Adults increasingly suffer from metabolic disorders, including obesity, diabetes, cardiovascular disorders and cancer. These diseases often require hospitalization and high out-of-pocket health expenditures. Table 5.1 shows the prevalence of and mortality rates for Palawan's leading infectious diseases, as reported in the most recent Community-Based Monitoring Survey (from 2009; the 2019 data have not yet been analysed), which threaten people's lives. From 2007–9, mortality rates for cardiovascular diseases and accidents have increased dramatically, by 230 per cent and 475 per cent, respectively.[3]

As noted in Chapter 2, when people consume increasing quantities of ultra-processed foods that are low in micronutrients and high in sugar, fat and salt, and engage in less physical activity than previously, rates of cardiovascular diseases surge. This is particularly the case in rapidly developing towns like Puerto Princesa. Also, an upsurge in road accidents occurs in boomtowns, reflecting the increased presence of cars and motorcycles on busy streets, likewise contributing to increased stress in everyday urban life.

Table 5.1 Puerto Princesa statistics for infectious and cardiovascular disease.

Indicator	2007	2009
Prevalence of malaria per 1,000	48	13
Prevalence of TB per 1,000	0.12	0.24
Deaths due to malaria per 100,000	2	4
Deaths due to TB per 100,000	12	25
Deaths due to cardiovascular disorders per 100,000	27	63
Deaths due to accidents per 100,000	4	19

Source: CBMS Survey 2009.

Not reflected in these statistics are the expenses, usually out of pocket, that people incur when health emergencies occur, including payment for ambulances and hospital care. In Puerto Princesa, catastrophic illness often entails being flown to Manila for treatment, costing hundreds of thousands, or even millions, of pesos – if one can afford it (see Xu et al. 2003). Healthcare expenses burden families, deplete their scarce resources, and leave them in debt. All these factors – the rise in cardiometabolic disorders, the stress caused by long hours of service-sector work and economic concerns regarding the costs of living and healthcare – contribute to a strong demand for 'surplus health', which is what distributors of First Vita Plus and C24/7 promise residents, as we saw when observing seminars at the First Vita Plus Product Center.

First Vita Plus

When the seminar started, Ester 'Kim' Venhoff, owner of the First Vita Plus Product Center, entered the room carrying a big yellow bag full of First Vita Plus. She told the attendees – women of various ages, some carrying infants, and a few men – that her engagement with First Vita Plus started when her grandmother had diabetes and suffered a stroke. Previously, she said, she had been cynical about the health benefits of First Vita Plus because it is just juice. But she became convinced of the drink's power when her grandmother's health improved after consuming it, extending her life by five years. 'Isn't that great?!' Ms Venhoff remarked. The audience clapped. Ms Venhoff then said that First Vita Plus is valuable to the people of Palawan because so many cannot afford to go to hospital and so use herbal medicine instead.

A nurse (see Figure 5.2) then took the stage and provided information to the audience about each of the five 'power herbs' in First Vita Plus, emphasizing the nutritional value of the sachets and their healing potential. She explained that the sachets contained vitamin C, which can help a person resist illnesses such as coughs, colds and tuberculosis, and four times as much vitamin A as carrots, which she said improves eyesight and skin. Further, she said, the sachets had four times as much calcium as milk and three times as much iron as spinach; they could be used to treat type 2 diabetes and to reduce blood pressure.

Ms Venhoff attested to the potential health benefits of First Vita Plus, while Nurse Pam pointed to the product's nutritional value by comparing the content of the sachets with carrots, milk and spinach. Nurse Pam's quantitative claims make the product sound scientific.

Figure 5.2 Nurse Pam explaining the potentials of the herbs in First Vita Plus. Source: *Sweet Medicine* documentary (2017).[4]

But the arithmetic is sloppy. To how much milk, carrots and spinach are the sachets compared? As we saw in Chapter 4, scrutiny of the nutritional contents of a sachet shows that the quantities of vitamins A and C and iron it contains are very small. Nevertheless, the audience appeared impressed, even more so when other speakers took the stage and gave testimonials about their cures after they started taking First Vita Plus. Such testimonials were a regular feature at these health symposia. They made use of a before-and-after format, giving the impression that First Vita Plus was what caused the change. The audience seemed convinced. Missing from the accounts of the supplement's efficacy were the other things occurring simultaneously in the lives of the patients. Were they being treated by a doctor or taking medicines that could have caused the cure? Or was the condition self-limiting? After all, bodies have the capacity to self-heal.

During the seminar, a pamphlet with an intriguing header circulated: 'Detoxification = healing crisis' (see Figure 5.3). The pamphlet featured a certain Dr Rolan Mendiola, pictured wearing a white coat, with a list of his credentials. In the pamphlet, he warns that after starting to take First Vita Plus, you may not feel well because First Vita Plus rids the body of superfluous salts ['Tinatangal ang mga sobrang alat ng katawan']. If this happens, he advises drinking more First Vita Plus: if you were taking one

Figure 5.3 Detoxification leaflet, featuring Dr Rolan Mendiola, given to attendees during the seminar. Source: *Sweet Medicine* documentary (2017).

sachet daily, then increase the dosage to two per day; if you were taking two, increase the dosage to three.

After the seminar, attendees lined up to buy boxes of First Vita Plus, either for their own personal use or to distribute (see Figure 5.4). If buying to distribute, they bought a 'Power Pack' containing twelve boxes, of which two were 'free'. This appeared to be a bargain to those who had just learned about the amazing potential health benefits the sachets supposedly possess. An added advantage for those who joined as distributors was that they could earn money both selling the product and recruiting new distributors, to the economics of which we turn in Chapter 6.

After the seminar, we spoke with some of the attendees to learn why they were buying First Vita Plus. Many said that they were convinced of the product's potential health benefits. Many also said the product would be good for their family members. Lina and Dora, two seasoned distributors, agreed to show us how they sold First Vita Plus. They turned out to be quite talented at promoting the surplus health benefits that First Vita Plus is touted to provide. A few days after the seminar, we met them by the harbour, where they circulated and spoke to potential clients. In those conversations, they emphasized the vegetable content

Figure 5.4 Poster advertising Power Pack discount (left) and attendees buying boxes of First Vita Plus (right). Source: *Sweet Medicine* documentary (2017).

of the sachets. Lina, for example, says to a woman selling tickets for a harbour tour, 'We do not eat vegetables daily, so this was made.' She names the vegetable content, 'malunggay, sili, kamote, kulitis, saluyot', emphasizing that the product is 'complete: full of vitamins, minerals, antioxidants, fibre and micronutrients to fight disease'. Dora chimes in, 'If you have high blood [pressure], it lessens your blood pressure … it can also be used for slimming.' The potential client, who is quite chubby, laughs and answers, 'My husband will look for other women if I am too thin.' Dora explains that if you drink it before you eat, you will become thin, but if you eat first and then drink it, then you will become fat. The client is amazed by the versatility of the product. Lina adds information from the leaflet, stating that users of First Vita Plus go through detoxification: 'You can feel heart palpitations … or you will experience stomach pains … That's normal. If you are taking one sachet, drink two. If you still [suffer], you can make it three. There is no overdose because these are vegetable ingredients.'

Dora and Lina then turn to the captain of a boat, who was standing nearby. They told him the sachets are also good for him. 'This is for you, Cap! It's delicious, delicious, and it can help your body … For overfatigue, it can help too.' Suggesting that it will increase his libido, they add, 'It rejuvenates, will boost your—', they giggle. The captain laughs and agrees to buy two sachets. 'My girlfriend will wonder. Hey, you've changed … You could only do it once; now you've changed.' Dora concludes the conversation with another pitch: 'Your girlfriend can buy [some] too. Just contact me' (*Sweet Medicine* 2017, 00:24:30–00:25:00).

Distributors told us that the sachets' high cost (38–40 pesos, or $0.80 US apiece) presents a problem: many people try them out, but few can afford to keep taking them. Leo, one of our research team members, like Ms Venhoff, had his own personal story. Once, his two-year-old child was suffering from fever after travelling home from visiting family in the rural countryside. He gave the child First Vita Plus, and she was better the next day. This was such a relief, he explained, because he and his wife did not like giving modern pharmaceuticals to their child, since they worried about side effects.

Convinced of the supplement's efficacy, Leo bought a Power Pack and embarked on a selling campaign. He visited potential clients, explaining that the sachets can protect their health and are safe because they are just vegetables. He pitched the product to a retired civil servant suffering from arthritis and a fisherman with tuberculosis, tailoring his pitches to their particular ailments. Still, these and other potential clients were poor, and while they were convinced of the likely health benefits of First Vita Plus, they often lacked the money to buy it.

Leo and other distributors often sought out knowledge online regarding the product's potential. They watched supplementary health seminars. Dr Mendiola (of the leaflet mentioned above) had a significant internet presence. He hosted a Zoom presentation during the COVID-19 lockdown, giving a long explanation about the human immune system and encouraging viewers to clean surfaces and use face masks to avoid infection. Dr Mendiola also emphasized the need to eat plenty of vegetables and fruits. Halfway through the one-hour presentation, Mendiola turned to the benefits of taking First Vita Plus, which, he asserted, was perfectly safe because it only contains vegetables (see Figure 5.5).

Mendiola also noted the variety of First Vita Plus flavours. In addition to the dalandan flavour that Galvez Tan had developed, customers could now also buy guyabano, pineapple and melon flavours, with each having their own attributes. The watermelon-flavoured product was, for example, touted as 'natural Viagra'.

We returned for a follow-up interview with Ms Venhoff and learned she was keeping records of people's stories about First Vita Plus to share with the central office in Manila. She had already compiled 100 stories in a booklet she called *Palawan Testimonies*. The first page (Figure 5.6) identifies Ms Venhoff as the 'Palawena who fights for inspired healing and brought success to countless lives' and shows Ms Venhoff in a meeting with the CEO of First Vita Plus, Doyee Tactacan-Tumpulan.

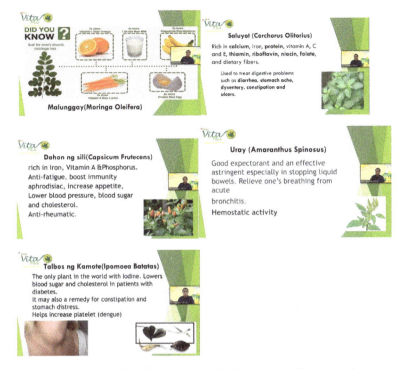

Figure 5.5 The benefits of the five power herbs, presented in a YouTube video of a 2020 First Vita Plus Health Symposium, led by Dr Roland Mendiola. Accessed 6 June 2024. Source: https://www.youtube.com/watch?v=dQMX8sqhjew (from 31:17).

Each testimonial in the booklet is accompanied by a diagnosis, printed in capital letters: 'UTI', 'ASTHMA', 'PSORIASIS', 'BONE CANCER' and so on. The testimonials include before-and-after pictures of patients, close-up images of affected body parts or patient portraits. Some include first-person narratives; these always relate how a family member or neighbour, or sometimes Ms Venhoff herself, suggested First Vita Plus, and they always end with the patient feeling better (see Figure 5.7). Obviously, we do not present them as proof of healing, but rather we analyse them as 'healing narratives' that attribute power to First Vita Plus.

One testimonial, for example, tells the story of Josephine, who suffered from pain in her breasts, for which she went to a doctor. She then asked for help on Facebook to pay for her treatment because she lacked the needed funds. A former classmate offered help by giving her a box of First Vita Plus. She drank it every day and started feeling better, although sometimes she had difficulty sleeping. She went to

Figure 5.6 The front cover of the booklet of testimonials that Ms Venhoff had collected (left) and one of the testimonials (right). Source: Author (Hardon), 2016.

Figure 5.7 Example of a testimonial compiled by Ms Venhoff. Source: Author (Hardon), 2016.

Ms Venhoff's restaurant where she was given a glass of hot First Vita Plus, which made her feel sleepy. She had been scheduled to go to Manila for an operation in August 2001, but the doctor informed her that the operation had been cancelled because she no longer needed it. She cried because she was so happy.

Another testimonial comes from a former vice president at the Palawan State University, who declared that First Vita Plus helped him fight a persistent cold that had left him bedridden. One of his neighbours insisted that he try First Vita Plus and, after drinking three sachets, his phlegm was expelled and he felt much better. He expresses gratitude to his neighbour for suggesting the product to him.

There are dozens of such testimonials. We mention one more here that illustrates how these testimonials cast the product as both a curative and a preventive. Delfina, a 79-year-old woman, states that she was constipated and had blood in her urine. Her doctor diagnosed her with kidney problems. Her daughter said she should try First Vita Plus. Delfina doubted it would help since it is only juice. Her daughter insisted, however, and bought her two boxes of First Vita Plus, instructing her to drink the supplement three times per day. After three days, she no longer had blood in her urine and was sleeping well. Delfina was so pleased with the outcome that she bought another box of First Vita Plus to clean the dirt (*dumi*) from her body.

When we interviewed the CEO of First Vita Plus in Manila about the effects of First Vita Plus, she insisted that she simply conveys the stories of people who take the product, saying, 'There are so many amazing stories in terms of health.' She explained, as well, that she had initially wondered whether people were not just reporting placebo effects and had asked herself, 'Is this really happening?' But the testimonials, such as those Ms Venhoff provided, have convinced her that 'this is for real'. She continued:

> For example, you see cancer patients who have lumps in their breasts, and they will write to me and ask for my assistance, and I will give them support in terms of the product. And then, what I ask from them is just to give me an update, a regular update, on the improvement that the First Vita Plus product has given them. And so, you know, after three months, six months, they send me photos with the lumps totally gone. And these are stage 2, stage 3 cancers. And sometimes, you will see patients with [a] goitre, and you'll see the monthly progress of the goitre disappearing. And you'll see psoriasis patients with marks all over, and you'll see progress after months and months of taking First Vita Plus. So, these are real people with real conditions that have improved through the product. And these are just a few stories, but there are many, many more stories. (Doyee Tactacan-Tumpulan, President First Vita Plus Cooperation. Interview 10 February 2017 in Pasig City)

She added that this is a strength of First Vita Plus: if you give the product to people, they will then spread the word of its beneficial effects. As a consequence, she does not have to waste money on advertising.

C24/7 in Puerto Princesa

AIM Global, the MLM company that distributes C24/7, also has a product centre in Puerto Princesa. Like First Vita Plus, the corporation attracts individuals concerned about their health, who often become distributors. Jaime, Anita's research assistant, referred to at the beginning of this chapter, became a member of AIM Global in order to access C24/7.

In the middle of the image in Figure 5.8 is a sign for the Alliance in Motion Members Lounge, which is somewhat overshadowed by the bold, eye-catching sign for the CardioPulse, a new service the product centre offers which measures people's vascular health to see if they should take AIM's other major supplement Vida! (see Chapter 3 for more on Vida!). On the left is a banner announcing a visit by AIM Global Vice President Sir Arnel Limpin, who will conduct an orientation for new distributors in Puerto Princesa. One can obtain an impression of his training style by viewing his YouTube videos.[5] Limpin gives the training sessions in a mixture of English and Tagalog, lending the promotional clips an aura of modernity.

Figure 5.8 AIM Global Business Center in downtown Puerto Princesa. Source: Author (Hardon), 2014.

On the outskirts of Puerto Princesa, where Anita had rented a house while we were conducting fieldwork, people's backyards provided them food, serving as a source of food security in times when they were short of income. Our neighbours kept chickens and grew papayas, bananas, mangoes and vegetables. Felicia ran a small store there, which she called the Guapa Rich Health Center (see Figure 5.9).

Attracted to its colourful images of herbs, fruit and vegetables, we entered the small shop, not sure what to expect, and discovered that Felicia was also a local distributor of C24/7. In fact, the store only sold AIM Global products. Looking more closely at the storefront, we saw AIM's logo prominently displayed.

Felicia explained that she had learned about C24/7 when her father, a pastor at an evangelical church, became very ill some time earlier. A relative had advised him to take C24/7, so Felicia went to buy it for him at the AIM Global office. When she arrived, she decided also to become a distributor to be able to pay for her father's treatment. She bought three memberships and sold the supplies her father did not need in her shop. Her father initially consumed six capsules a day, which was expensive, given that each capsule costs around $0.80 US. This means she spent $4.80 US a day, which is roughly equivalent to a Filipino's daily earnings. But it was worth it, Felicia insisted. Her father's health improved. After a while, they lowered the dose to two capsules a day. She continued to attend regularly the seminars offered at the AIM Global office. Like First Vita Plus, AIM Global invited medical doctors to explain

Figure 5.9 Guapa Rich Health Center, in a residential Puerto Princesa neighbourhood. Source: Author (Hardon), 2014.

the health values of C24/7, including a Dr Butch Villena, who also authored the 346-page product guide (Villena 2011).

At these seminars, AIM Global trainers strongly advise distributors to use the products they sell so they can provide first-hand testimonials regarding the products' effects. 'The best drug pusher', states one of the trainers, in an ode to the power of personal testimony, 'is a drug user' (Hardon, Davatos and Lasco 2019, 435). Similar to the First Vita Plus seminars, AIM Global trainers also provide time for users to share their stories about the supplement's success. We listened, for example, to Jess, a 28-year-old security guard, sharing his experience. He and his wife took C24/7 when they were trying to conceive a baby. They had been married eight years without conceiving when a friend told them about C24/7. After four months of taking the supplement, he assured the seminar attendees, his wife was pregnant. Another speaker, Ricky, told the audience that his wife recovered from stage 4 breast cancer. 'Before' and 'after' pictures of people who had overcome serious illnesses were also shown to the audience as a kind of visual testimonial. Those attending the seminars seemed to accept the photos as evidence of efficacy.

The trainers invoked prevailing health problems and health risks repeatedly during the seminars: 'Who among you has not gotten sick in the past? Raise your hands,' they said. 'There are many more diseases now than ever before,' they declared, and continued, 'There was no cancer in the past, but there are now all kinds of cancer!' 'We are all prone to illness, and our diets cannot protect us.' Moreover, they reminded the audience of the high cost of modern medicine: 'How much is chemotherapy? How much is kidney dialysis per session? Will you be able to pay for it?' (Hardon, Davatos and Lasco 2019, 435).

The trainers also frequently referred to the WHO's recommendation that everyone should consume six portions of fruits and vegetables each day. Overlooking the fact that many families in Puerto Princesa could grow their own fruits and vegetables in their backyards, they asked the rhetorical question: 'Who among us has the money to buy six different vegetables and fruits every day?' Then, they declared C24/7's multiple ingredients: a blend of 12 whole fruits, a blend of 12 whole vegetables, 12 kinds of mushrooms and numerous other wholesome-sounding ingredients (a selection of these contents were included in the banner on Felicia's store). See Figure 5.10.

These convenient capsules, packed with reconstituted vegetables and fruits, were attractive to people working multiple jobs. The C24/7 package presents the product as a 'Natura-Ceutical' for 'round-the-clock nutrition'. Its 'Supplement Facts' panel (see Figure 5.11) shows the

Supplement Facts

Amount Per Serving	% Daily Value
Amino Acids (from Spirulina, Zinc AAC, Chlorella, Blue Green Algae, Boron AAC) (Glutamine, Asparagine, Leucine, Alanine, Arginine, Lysine, Threonine, Valine, Glycine, Isoleucine, Serine, Proline, Phenylalanine, Tyrosine, Histidine, Methionine, Tryptophan, Cysteine)	225 mg **
Garden Veggies™ Blend: Parsely Juice Powder; Kale Juice Powder; Spinach Juice Powder; Wheat Grass Juice Powder; Brussels Sprout Juice Powder; Asparagus Juice Powder; Broccoli Juice Powder; Cauliflower Juice Powder; Beet Juice Powder Carrot Juice Powder; Cabbage Juice Powder; Garlic Juice Powder	100 mg **
Orchard Fruits™ Blend: Plum Juice Powder; Cranberry Juice Powder; Blueberry Juice Powder; Strawberry Juice Powder; Blackberry Juice Powder, Bilberry Juice Power, Cherry Juice Powder; Apricot Juice Powder; Papaya Juice Powder; Orange Juice Powder; Grape Juice Powder; Pineapple Juice Powder	100 mg **
Myco Defense® Mushroom Blend: Cordyceps Mushroom; Reishi Mushroom; Shitake Mushroom; Hiratake Mushroom; Maitake Mushroom; Yamabushitake Mushroom; Himematsutake Mushroom; Kawaratake Mushroom; Chaga Mushroom; Zhu Ling Mushroom; Agarikon Mushroom; Mesima Mushroom	100 mg **
Digestive Enzyme Blend: Concentrated Enzyme formula: (Protease I, Protease II, Peptizyme SP, Amylase, Lactase, Invertase, Lipase, Cellulase, Alpha Galactosidase); Betaine HCl); Bromelain(from pineapple); Papain(from papaya)	100 mg **
Omega Fatty Acid Seed Blend: Flax Seed Powder(dry, cold pressed); Sunflower Seed Powder (dry, cold pressed) (providing Alpha-Linolenic Acid, Oleic Acid, Linoleic Acid, Palmitic Acid, Stearic Acid, Behenic Acid, Gadoleic Acid, Palmitoleic Acid, Eicosanoic Acid, Lignoceric Acid)	100 mg **
Anti-Aging / Anti-Oxidant Enhancer® Proprietary Phytochemical Blend of Cystein HCl 98%, Quercitin, Concentrated Grape Skin Extract, Green Tea (95% EGCG Polyphenols) and Co-Enzyme Q10	90 mg **
Citrus Bioflavonoid Complex (from lemon, orange, grapefruit, lime and tangerine) providing: Eriocitrin 600mcg; Naringin, Narirutin, other Flavanones 1.8mg; Flavonols 600mcg; Flavones and related phenolic compunds 600mcg	60 mg **

Figure 5.10 C24/7 content, as listed on the product information in the C24/7 welcome pack, bought in 2014 at the AIM Global Business Center. Source: Author (Hardon), 2021.

Supplement Facts
Serving Size : 7 Vcaps®

Amount Per Serving		% Daily Value
Calories	10	
Total Carbohydrate	2 g	1%+
Vitamin A	15,000 IU	300%
(33% [5,000IU] as retinol palmitate and 67% [10,000IU] as beta carotene) providing(typical analysis) : beta carotene 5625mcg, gamma carotene 5.6mcg, trans beta carotene 5.4 mcg, beta zea carotene 1.1mcg		
Vitamin C (as sodium ascorbate)	140 mg	233%
Vitamin D (as ergocalciferol)	400 IU	100%
Vitamin E (as d-alpha tocopheryl succinate)	200 IU	667%
Vitamin K (as phytonadione)	80 mcg	100%
Thiamin (as thiamin mononitrate)	25 mg	1667%
Riboflavin (Vitamin B2)	25 mg	1471%
Niacin (as niacinamide)	125 mg	625%
Vitamin B6 (as pyridoxine HCl/ pyridoxal 5- phosphate)	50 mg	2500%
Folic Acid	400 mcg	100%
Vitamin B12 (as cyanocobalamin)	200 mcg	3333%
Biotin (as biotin triturate)	300 mcg	100%
Pantothenic Acid (as d-calcium pantothenate)	125 mg	1250%
Calcium (as citrate/carbonate)	250 mg	25%
Iron (as amino acid chelate)	18 mg	100%
Iodine (from pacific kelp powder)	150 mcg	100%
Magnesium (as citrate/oxide)	125 mg	31%
Zinc (as amino acid chelate)	15 mg	100%
Selenium (as selenium monomethionine)	70 mcg	100%
Copper (as amino acid chelate)	2 mg	100%
Manganese (as amino acid chelate)	4 mg	200%
Chromium (as polynicotinate)	120 mcg	100%
Molybdenum (as molybdenum triturate)	75 mcg	100%
Sodium	35 mg	1%
Potassium (as amino acid chelate)	50 mg	1%

Figure 5.11 C24/7 product information. Source: Author (Hardon), 2021.

percentages of recommended daily vitamins and minerals in a 'serving size', which is seven capsules.

Some of the facts included in the table are: seven capsules contain 31 per cent of the daily recommended intake of magnesium, 300 per cent of vitamin A, 233 per cent of vitamin C, and as much as 2,500 per cent for vitamin B6. Taking seven capsules daily seems rather a lot, especially considering that each capsule costs 38 pesos, making the total cost 266 pesos (about $5.60 US) per day. Moreover, the recommended high intake of B6 (pyridoxine) is contraindicated as this vitamin can cause nerve damage at high dosages (Dalton and Dalton 1987). We found that most people did not actually take seven capsules per day, which lowers the risk, although Felicia's father's early 'treatment' consisted of taking six capsules daily, which may not have been safe.

Perhaps even more impressive are the multiplicity of cellular actions the capsules promise to effect, listed in Figure 5.12. These efficacy claims originate from Dr Villena's (2011) guide, which begins with a short history of Nature's Way, the American company that produces C24/7, describing how its founder Tom Murdoch developed the product after a Native American shaman recommended a herbal tea to treat Murdoch's wife's recurrent cancer. The guide promotes natural healing and has sections on cells, body systems and free radicals, along with

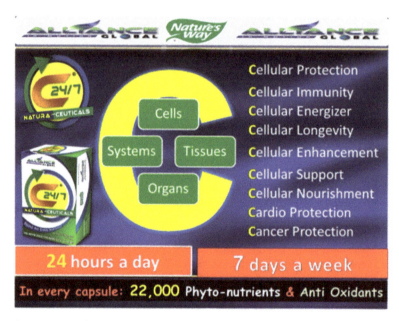

Figure 5.12 The promise of C24/7. Source: Author (Hardon), 2021.

detailed information about the cardiovascular, blood-sugar-moderating, anti-cancer, and stress-reducing potential of the specific phytonutrients in C24/7.

During one of her visits to the AIM Global Business Centre, Anita met an Adventist pastor who was a great fan of C24/7 and promoted its potential health benefits in his sermons and on local radio station broadcasts. The vegetarian capsules had become very popular in Puerto Princesa's Adventist community, whose members adhered to healthy living through heavily plant-based diets. The pastor encouraged Anita to sign up as a member of AIM Global so she could obtain C24/7 at a discounted rate. He said that it was worth a try and that 'at her age', she should 'start looking after herself'. He insisted that C24/7 is full of phytochemicals and that Anita's body would make use of whichever substances it needed. When Anita told him that she was afraid of having an allergic reaction, he reassured her that the contents of the capsules are all natural. When Anita still resisted his sales talk, he asked her how much her iPad cost, suggesting that it was strange for her to invest in technology and not in her body. Anita did not believe the capsules would bestow a magical cure for aging; nor did she intend to become an active distributor. But she wanted the sales pitch to end and giving in seemed to be the only way for that to happen. She was also interested in analysing the contents of the 'welcome pack'.

The kit included five packages of C24/7 (each containing 30 capsules) and pamphlets that make clear why, in contrast to First Vita Plus, so many young people are interested in joining AIM Global and becoming distributors (see Figure 5.13). In addition to the supplements themselves, worth 6,000 pesos, the package gives distributors access to a Banco de Oro ATM card, a webpage, a business kit and a scholarship programme.

Towards the end of our fieldwork period, Anita called in again at the Guapa Rich Health Center, where Felicia told her about the AIM Global Business Center's new diagnostic service, the CardioPulse, and gave Anita a voucher to try the service for free. Anita replied that she had a headache at the moment, but she would think about it. Afterwards, Felicia texted Anita repeatedly to follow up on their conversation and try to convince her to go to AIM Global for a check-up. After receiving several texts from Felicia, Anita gave in and agreed to go to AIM Global the next day. She was curious to find out more about this device AIM Global was using. Felicia met her at the business centre and called in a colleague to perform the test. Anita put her finger in a small gadget

Figure 5.13 The AIM Global welcome pack. Source: Author (Hardon), 2021.

called CardioPulseR, which a leaflet claims is a 'painless, non-invasive alternative angiogram device' from Korea.

Anita's test results included both a stress score and level of arterial health. Reassuringly, her physical stress level was reported to be low. The text in the box below the graph in Figure 5.14 reads: 'Physical stress level is low and its stress resistance is also good. You are mentally stable but you may temporarily feel gloomy, sluggish and unenthusiastic. You need to make yourself refresh with exercise, climbing mountains and traveling.'

Anita was intrigued that the test included an assessment of stress, which she found a frequent complaint among urban dwellers in Puerto Princesa. But how could the device measure stress, or even do so accurately? Her level of arterial health (Figure 5.14) was 5 – 'bad' – on a scale of 1 to 7. Anita asked what this indicated. The graph reported that Anita's 'eccentric constriction' was 'good', but her 'arterial elasticity' and 'remaining blood volume' was 'bad'. The text in the box below the graph reads: 'Your vessel is in the process of growing aged and also blood circulation is not good. Your hands and feet can be sore and cramped. You should try to avoid improper life tendency, smoking and heavy drinking, high calorie, fatty and

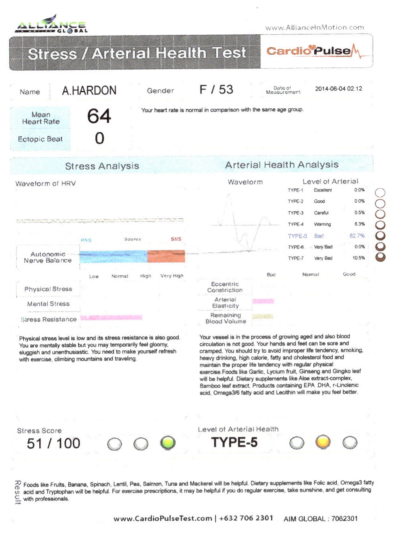

Figure 5.14 Anita Hardon's CardioPulseR test result. Source: Author, 2021.

cholesterol food and maintain the proper life tendency with regular physical exercise.'

While not recognizing any of these complaints, the result nevertheless left Anita feeling a bit worried! The computer programme the AIM representative had used now issued a prescription: three sachets of Vida! along with five capsules of Choleduz – an Omega-3 supplement – daily. The cost was 540 pesos a day (around $11 US), equivalent to two days' wages in Puerto Princesa. Such was Anita's introduction to Vida! a new

AIM Global product.[6] The CardioPulseR test was a key element in its marketing: everyone who took the test was advised to use C24/7, and people who scored 'bad', 'very bad' or 'high risk' were told they should start taking Vida! and Choleduz.

Attributing health benefits to supplements

In Puerto Princesa, First Vita Plus, C24/7 and Vida! were all attributed value through MLM schemes, which relied on local distributors to find clients to whom they could sell the products. Distributors were encouraged to share testimonials about the products' health benefits, to prospect potential clients, and to tailor their pitches about the supplements' merits to the specific health concerns of potential clients. As we have emphasized, these supplements were particularly attractive in the context of recent metabolic shifts occurring in this booming small town, in which families have a hard time making ends meet, where people are confronted with middle-class lifestyles that fuel their desires for an improved future and where everyone knows that becoming ill can throw families into poverty.

These supplements were promoted through seminars, during which trainers referred to the common precarity of everyday life and promoted supplements as both protective shields and cure-alls. The trainers and distributors repeatedly pointed to the safety of the supplements, emphasizing that they are not synthetic, but rather merely conveniently packaged plants. The people attending the seminars were impressed by the seemingly scientific accounts of nutritional value and the before-and-after stories attesting to metabolic efficacies. Many decided to become members and purchased a welcome pack, which they then tried to sell in their communities and to their families.

These marketing techniques may seem like those of pharmaceutical representatives, whose primary goal is to push ever more drugs into healthy people's bodies (Oldani 2004). Pharmaceutical representatives expand the market for drugs by promoting the use of preventive medications, such as anti-hypertension and cholesterol-reducing substances, and by promoting therapies for ever-expanding health indications. Something similar takes place in the distribution of First Vita Plus and C24/7, during which distributors, just like pharmaceutical representatives, amplify products' therapeutic and potentially positive effects for people who are not (yet) sick (Oldani 2004). Both pharmaceuticals and supplements can cause side effects, which pharmaceutical manufacturers are required to list, and refer to in very small letters in package inserts (Martin 2006), but supplement manufacturers tend to ignore. People end up spending a large portion of their meagre incomes on products that have few benefits and may cause harm, based on the promise of improved (future) health.

But in contrast to supplements, food and drug authorities tightly regulate the promotion of pharmaceuticals, demanding clinical evidence of efficacy and safety before allowing a product to enter the market and monitoring pharmaceutical companies' products to ensure that the leaflets accompanying medications list potential side effects. Such regulatory action does not exist for dietary supplements: companies only need to declare the supplement's contents on the label and include a statement that no therapeutic claims are proven.

Aware that the contents of supplements are not routinely checked, we had both First Vita Plus and C24/7 tested at the Philippine Institute of Pure and Applied Chemistry at Ateneo University. Due to limited funding, the capsules were only analysed for their vitamin A, C and E levels and fibre. The laboratory found that the First Vita Plus sample had no vitamin or fibre content and consisted largely of sugar and flavouring. This in fact confirms the nutritional information printed in small letters on the product's packaging, but which alas nobody seems to read closely, perhaps because larger, brighter letters call the drink 'so full of life', as noted in Chapter 4. For C24/7, the laboratory found that the vitamin content was much lower than advertised: instead of 140 mg per serving of vitamin C (20 mg per capsule), the analysis found only 4.4 mg per capsule. The package also states that one serving contains 15,000 IU of vitamin A, or 2,142 IU per capsule, but the laboratory found that one capsule contained less than half of that, only 950 IU.

Reflecting on this fieldwork, we are struck by the similarities in how the two MLM schemes operated, given the supplements' quite different origins. First Vita Plus is a Filipino product, one that emerged out of national R&D, the story of which we outlined in Chapter 3. In contrast, C24/7 is made in the United States by an American manufacturer. But, in both cases, local distributors attributed a similar range of potential health benefits to the products, and the companies used similar techniques when training distributors to expand their markets. Consumers also used these supplements in similar ways. When advised to take them by family members and distributors, they tried them out and monitored their effects. Often the supplements made them feel better, which is somewhat surprising, given their lack of nutritional content.

One explanation for this is that distributors generate positive expectations that the supplements will work by matching their descriptions of the supplements' benefits to their clients' concerns about the lack of nutrients in contemporary diets causing disruption to their metabolism, thus generating powerful placebo effects (Moerman 2002).

MLM as prosperity gospel

MLM orientation sessions and lectures bear many similarities to religious worship: MLM lecturers have the charisma and convincing power of pastors and priests, and audiences are swept up by their zeal, exhortations to do more and the many promises of rewards. Luca (2011) describes the close links between prosperity gospel and MLM, dating back to the 1950s when American Protestant networks associated with the prosperity gospel first put MLM into practice in the United States. These prosperity gospel proponents preached that it is God's wish for all humans to prosper. MLM can be understood as secular versions of prosperity gospel churches. They may not have the Pentecostals' 'laying of the hands' to heal, but their products, with promises of miraculous cures, are sometimes more powerful than the healing-by-prayer.

It is not surprising that MLM appeals to so many Filipinos, in a country where a 2006 survey covering 10 countries found that 44 per cent of Filipinos – the highest percentage among the 10 countries surveyed – identified as charismatic Christians, the term usually defined as those believing in 'gifts' of the Holy Spirit animating worshippers to go into frenzied prayer, healing and speaking in tongues. This 44 per cent of Filipinos includes Pentecostals, as well as Catholics and mainline Protestants (Pew Research Center 2006).

In addition to this magical thinking, the supplements gave users a sense of control over the precarious conditions of everyday life in Puerto Princesa, where people worried about what the future might bring and the economic consequences of falling ill. The MLM schemes offered people the opportunity to earn an income by selling supplements and recruiting new distributors. In the next chapter we show how MLM trainers teach practical financial tools, particularly around selling and marketing. The zeal of the economic messages of the MLM trainers converges with prosperity ethics. If you do not do well with recruiting new sellers, it is because you didn't work hard enough. You lack the zeal and/or the faith to prosper.

Notes

1. This certification signals that the product conforms to Islamic law, containing no pork and that animals are slaughtered using prescribed religious guidelines. Globally, many institutions provide halal certifications.
2. Palawan is known for its archaeological record as well, with the discovery of human bone fragments dating back 47,000 years. Until recently, these remains in the vicinity of Tabon Cave were the oldest known human remains in the Philippines.
3. This table also shows that a campaign to eradicate malaria, which aimed also to clear the way for tourists, has had some success in reducing the disease's prevalence.
4. An ethnographic documentary film that was part of a 5-year research programme by the Chemical Youth Project, funded by the European Research Council. See *Sweet Medicine* (2017).
5. See, for example, https://www.youtube.com/watch?v=aWxq0MZLzFM.
6. This product contains resVida, made by the Dutch company DSM, whose website cites scientific publications that claim that resVida can help in the 'maintenance of a healthy cardiovascular system' (DSM 2014, 1). See also Chapter 3 for more information on the efficacy claims for resVida.

6
Endgame

In Chapter 1, we outlined the metabolic shifts, including a turn to highly processed foods, that led to a deterioration of diets, and, subsequently, culminated in Filipinos seeking out supplements to make up for the deficiencies. In the previous chapter, we described how distributors generate demand for supplements in Puerto Princesa, an environment in which people face multiple forms of urban precarity, including low-paid jobs, loss of access to land, lack of time to home-cooked meals, deficient diets and a rapid increase in the occurrence of metabolic diseases, such as diabetes and cardiovascular disorders. We related that First Vita Plus and C24/7 distributors received trainings to tailor their pitches to potential clients' dietary deficiencies and metabolic concerns.

In the current chapter, we recount how these trainings simultaneously incited distributors to engage in a speculative business practice – multilevel marketing (MLM) – which could, the trainers insisted, substantially augment distributors' family incomes. To do so, they must invest in the products, which often meant borrowing money or selling family assets. They needed to mobilize the people in their social networks to buy supplements from them and to recruit new members. This, we argue, is difficult relational work. It demands that distributors capitalize upon their social networks, embodied in the fact that MLM workers are under pressure to 'be the products', in this case, to present testimonies about the supplements' positive effects, without necessarily experiencing them as beneficial. This intense socio-metabolic labour creates alienation similar to that flight attendants experience when painting fake smiles on their faces (Hochschild 1983). The labour is further 'dislocated' (Harvey and Krohn-Hansen 2018) by the upward movement of capital, which perpetuates existing inequalities. It is tragic that people whose everyday lives have been compromised due to intersecting metabolic rifts are lured into providing cheap labour to enhance sales of plant-based supplements, without much chance of a return on their investment of (social) capital and time – a cynical endgame in the metabolic transitions that we outline in this book.

AIM Global vows to turn ordinary people into millionaires. First Vita Plus offers distributors 'the power of financial freedom' (see Figure 6.1). These were attractive promises for our Puerto Princesa interlocutors, who sought to attain the middle-class lifestyles that had become increasingly visible in their booming provincial town. We conducted participant observation at MLM training sessions, where trainers encourage youth to buy memberships in food supplement companies along with guidance on how to recruit and sell their products. We also followed up with 40 individual distributors (20 selling First Vita Plus and 20 selling C24/7) to learn if they succeeded in fulfilling their dreams of acquiring wealth.

In both the First Vita Plus and C24/7 schemes, distributors earn money by selling supplements and by recruiting new distributors who purchase the product to sell themselves, a business model that originates in the United States. In the 1950s, AMWAY (short for the American Way) emerged as a way of selling consumer goods, including cosmetics and health products. Bromley (1995, 142) who studied AMWAY distributors, explains that they form sect-like social groupings

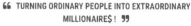

Figure 6.1 The business opportunities offered by AIM Global and First Vita Plus. Source: Author (Hardon), 2016.

that share an ideology that 'one's financial success in life is limited only by ability, imagination, initiative and persistence'. They receive free training from charismatic leaders and value the entrepreneurial skills and abilities they acquire (Wilson 1999). In MLM, years of schooling do not determine success; nor does working fixed hours or following standardized protocols. Instead, one is expected to manifest creativity and flexibility when it comes to developing innovative ways to recruit new clients and distributors. The only demands are 'friendliness, hard work and a plan' (Wilson 1999, 416).

The Direct Selling Association of the Philippines (DSAP) defines this type of marketing activity as 'direct', which they define as 'face-to-face selling to the consumers through independent distributors or salespeople. It is a legitimate marketing medium that is used to sell practically anything.'[1] Krige (2012) distinguishes between schemes that sell products, such as MLM companies, and 'real' pyramid schemes focused on recruiting new members called down-lines. In 2002, the Philippines' Department of Trade and Industry issued Administrative Order No. 8 prohibiting pyramid schemes, which it defines as business endeavours where emphasis is on recruiting new members and the product lacks fair market value. A pyramid scheme, the DSAP states, is 'an illegal money scam often confused with legitimate network marketing plans, where people are convinced to pay money for a chance to profit from the payments of others who might join later'.[2] We would argue that AIM Global and First Vita Plus constitute hybrids of pyramid schemes and network marketing plans; to maintain their reputations, the companies must maintain a balance between recruiting and selling.[3]

The DSAP does not mention multilevel marketing, but it provides a set of warning questions as a guide to caution the public. The test includes the following eight questions:

1. Is there a product?
2. Are commissions paid on the sale of products and not on registration/entry fees?
3. Is the intent to sell a product, not a position?
4. Is there no direct correlation between the number of recruits and compensation?
5. If recruitment were to be stopped today, would the participants still make money?
6. Is there a reasonable product return policy?
7. Do products have fair market value?
8. Is there a compelling reason to buy?[4]

The DSAP states that if the answer to all of the questions is 'yes', then the company is legitimate. But if the answer to any of the questions is 'no', there is a high chance it is a pyramid scheme. Applying this test, neither First Vita Plus nor AIM Global are legitimate because there is a direct correlation between the number of recruits and amount of compensation (Question 4). In addition to a 25 per cent discount on products, members of both companies receive financial rewards for recruiting new members who become their 'down-lines', from whose sales and recruits they receive commissions. The answer is also 'no' to Question 6 – neither scheme has a return policy. We observed many distributors stuck with supplies they could not sell. Beyond this, we would argue, the market value of the products is questionable.

Pyramids

Pyramid schemes are, essentially, simple money-making schemes. People high in the pyramid – those who join the scheme early on (known as up-lines) – benefit from the membership fees paid by those who join later, those who are below them in the pyramid. As long as increasing numbers of down-lines sign up, up-lines receive a return on their investment. But if members fail to recruit new members, or if their down-lines are not active, they earn very little. Engaging in pyramid-based selling is thus risky business, especially for people who, to start with, possess little capital. Krige (2012), studying participation in pyramid schemes in South Africa, suggests that participants are aware of the risks they are taking, but join anyway because they have few other opportunities to accumulate capital and because they are used to taking risks. We also observed this in our fieldwork. These risks are not necessarily acceptable to distributors' social networks, however, as many distributors encountered not only concern, but also criticism from family members and neighbours for engaging in MLM.

Herbalife, an American MLM company, which sells food supplements in the same way as First Vita Plus and AIM Global, albeit with a much bigger global reach, was fined $200 million by the US Federal Trade Commission (FTC), after it found that Herbalife members were mainly earning by recruiting new members. Under United States law, an MLM is only allowed to exist when the company primarily engages in selling products to consumers. The FTC found Herbalife's business operations to be unfair because most dealers, despite their hard work, came nowhere near to recovering their initial investments.

'This settlement', stated FTC Chairwoman Edith Ramirez, 'will require Herbalife to fundamentally restructure its business so that participants are rewarded for what they sell, not how many people they recruit' (Federal Trade Commission 2016). Consumer protection organizations in the United States have been concerned about the pyramid-like characteristics of MLM schemes since the 1990s, including requirements of large up-front purchases and investments and rewards for recruitment (Nat and Keep 2002).

The attraction of MLM

Anthropologists argue that MLM flourishes in contexts where unemployment and underemployment are rampant, and where globalization has led to the increasing flexibilization of labour and the retrenchment of welfare arrangements (Wilson 1999; Cahn 2006; Nelson 2013). In MLM schemes, distributors aid companies by reaching consumers outside established markets and create wealth for higher-ups in the pyramid. Because MLM depends on social networks instead of on conventional marketing, it works well in places with large informal sectors (Krige 2012), which certainly applies to the Philippines (Ofreneo 2008). To this analysis, we would add: MLMs that have food supplements at the core of their business model work well in settings such as the Philippines, where metabolic shifts have challenged people's lives and left them malnourished and impoverished.

Research by ethnographers reveals that people who have few economic opportunities value the income-generating opportunities MLM offers (Nelson 2013; Desclaux 2014). Nelson (2013) who examined participation in Omnilife (a Mexican company that employs food supplements to drive MLM) suggests that making a living as a distributor helps people meet obligations to others disrupted by neoliberal economic reforms. She describes how in Guatemala, Omnilife helped her interlocutors re-establish livelihoods in a post-war environment, in which their needs were no longer met by state welfare services or revolutionary organizations. One of her key informants, for example, was proud that, by selling Omnilife products, he was able to finance his studies himself, without taking money from his parents.

As also noted in Chapter 5, MLM's promises of health and wealth are remarkably similar to the doctrines of some charismatic and evangelical Christian churches, which declare that health and wealth can be attained as long as one believes, spreads the word and takes action to recruit new believers (Coleman 2000; Hunt 2000), a modern-day amalgamation of Weber's Calvinism and capitalist zeitgeist. The rise of prosperity gospel ideas is especially strong in Catholic countries, where cultural emphasis has traditionally been on advocating self-abnegation, charity and sacrifice. Prosperity gospel advocates challenge this ethos, saying it is good to want to and strive to be wealthy, proselytization that dovetails nicely with the neoliberal promotion of entrepreneurship as a solution to poverty, without, however, addressing structural inequities.

The neoliberal subjectivity that distributors embrace when participating in MLM, however, can challenge social norms of reciprocity and family obligations, and threaten intergenerational hierarchies, which are key to survival among poor and middle-class families in the Philippines. Narotzky and Besnier (2014, S12) call on anthropologists to examine 'on-the-ground practices' of how people make a living, without privileging a particular domain of activity or intentionality of action. In a similar vein, social scientists have called for ethnographies of people's connected lives, in which economic transactions and intimate relations are linked in many different ways (Zelizer 2012; Narotzky 2015). These links must be unravelled through participant observation to uncover how people engage in 'relational work' to navigate these complexities. Zelizer gives the example of how women and men in the United States are compensated differently when helping neighbours: women are expected to do chores for neighbours for free, while men can ask for payment for lending a helping hand. Zelizer's main argument is that navigating various social ties, transactions, norms and obligations requires work.

MLM models rely on distributors engaging in intense relational work, navigating the boundaries between intimacy and instrumental economic logics. Distributors receive encouragement to profile their family members as potential customers, to research what their health concerns are in order to match them with food supplements and to recruit their friends as new members or down-lines. This involves establishing rapport and delicately identifying people's needs and putting pressure on friends to become members, too. We refer to this multifaceted set of activities as 'socio-metabolic work' (defined in Chapter 1).

We must understand socio-metabolic labour in the Philippines in relation to the social nature of people's health. When a family member becomes ill, the expectation is that the whole family will contribute to medical costs, which, as we noted in Chapter 5, can be catastrophically high and lead to severe family debts. Children drop out of school to earn extra income to pay for hospital bills. Thus, earning extra income by selling products that can restore health and protect oneself and one's family from chronic disease is merely an extension of pre-existing socio-metabolic labour configurations. People's lives are intertwined.

But in the case of MLM, the socio-metabolic labour is not just for one's family. Our co-researchers in Puerto Princesa have many stories about how their friends attempted to recruit them, and how they resisted. One of our informants shared with us that she was surprised when a classmate from kindergarten contacted her through Facebook and asked, 'How's life going? Can we meet up for coffee?' The coffee date turned out to be an MLM orientation. When we went out for lunch in Puerto Princesa's fast-food restaurants, we often saw distributors sharing their MLM business opportunities with friends, flipping through booklets showing the purported effects of products and calculations of the astronomical earnings to be made. Other clandestine MLM orientations included inviting friends to birthday parties or workshops with free snacks at nice hotels. While many people valued the business opportunities these events presented, others were cynical and worried that the schemes would turn out to be scams. Those people told us they had seen it all before: people do not earn money and end up losing their investments. Moreover, they pointed out, another sad consequence of MLM activities in Puerto Princesa is that people think twice when a friend invites them to a party or an event. This growing cynicism makes it hard for distributors to find new down-lines, the difficulty of which is increased by competition among MLM schemes.

To understand the complexity of working as an MLM distributor, we conducted participant observation of seminars that advise distributors about how to earn a living through MLM (which research also informed Chapter 5) and we interviewed First Vita Plus and AIM Global distributors individually (Hardon, Davatos & Lasco 2019). First Vita Plus attracted middle-aged distributors, the majority of whom were women with children, while AIM Global attracted young women and men. The corporate executives who design MLM schemes target women and youth because they are skilled in the emotional, interpersonal labour MLM requires. Our fieldwork demonstrates that extending this relational work outside the family to earn a living through MLM can be extremely taxing to those relations, and to distributors themselves. Moreover, no amount of effort guarantees success. While it was common for distributors to espouse an ideology that hard work will make a person rich, we found most distributors were struggling just to earn back their initial investments. We turn now to describing the basic economics with which distributors have to work and showing how the schemes deliver riches to some but leave many more behind.

Distributing First Vita Plus

The distributors of First Vita Plus we contacted through the product centre in Puerto Princesa have varied backgrounds and reasons for engaging in the scheme. All were encouraged to join by an up-line person and many were intrigued by the healing testimonials and motivated by the desire for extra income. Over time, some gave up their jobs to concentrate fully on selling supplements. Our informants generally could not afford the initial investment of 7,700 pesos ($137 US) to buy a Power Pack (average daily income is $6 US) and relied on their up-lines to sponsor them by purchasing their initial supplies. Once they had sold one or more Power Packs, their up-lines registered them as distributors.

After they 'earned' distributor status, they could start making money for themselves, by selling sachets and recruiting new down-lines. Each Power Pack contains 12 boxes of 20 sachets each, meaning the wholesale price is 32 pesos per sachet. Distributors then sold the sachets at 40 pesos a piece, accruing a profit of eight pesos per sachet, or 160 ($2.80 US) pesos per box. First Vita Plus distributors earn another 500 pesos if they recruit a new distributor (once the new person buys a Power Pack and is registered in the computer system as a down-line). If they register two down-lines, they receive an additional 'matching bonus' of 1,500 pesos ($26.70 US) for having reached the first level of down-lines. At the First Vita Plus product centre in Puerto Princesa, top-selling distributors explain how this works to those attending the health seminars (see Figure 6.2.)

Leo, one of the researchers on our Puerto Princesa research team, was himself a distributor and contributed auto-ethnographic research to our study. He also interviewed 20 of his peers to find out how well they were able to achieve the astronomical earnings that First Vita Plus promises and he discovered great variation in terms of their success. A few of his informants had long histories of being distributors and reported substantial earnings. For example, a former military officer became a distributor after his sister was healed of a goitre subsequent to drinking First Vita Plus, eight years before he was interviewed. Over time, he amassed 6,000 down-lines in the Philippines, Malaysia and the United States, and reported earning $770 US per week.

Many distributors sold First Vita Plus in their hometowns in remote areas of Palawan. Diosa, for example, lived on an island one day's travel from Puerto Princesa. Her husband was a teacher and had become a distributor of First Vita Plus. Diosa became a distributor when she met a First Vita Plus dealer at the annual Baragatan Festival – an event that

Figure 6.2 A local trainer explaining how distributors can earn money by recruiting down-lines (Source: *Sweet Medicine* documentary 2017).

showcases Palawan's history and culture – in Puerto Princesa. She was able to obtain a microfinance loan in her hometown for the $137 US necessary to buy her first Power Pack. Diosa sold the Power Pack in four days by visiting people in her community, looking for those who were ill. She explained to us that there are many health needs on her island because of its remoteness and lack of access to medicines. People die because they cannot make it to the hospital quickly enough to receive emergency medical care, especially during the rainy season when it is hard to navigate the sea. Diosa was successful in recruiting down-lines on her island and received weekly cheques of $40 US to $60 US at the time of our interview. She was the only distributor there when she signed up in 2015, and within a year she had 20 down-lines. To motivate them, she gave seminars in her house every Wednesday. Having internalized the trainings she received in Puerto Princesa, she emphasized that self-confidence and willingness to sacrifice can turn a person's dreams of having more wealth into reality, adding that, of course, God is always there to guide 'our every move. Just do your best and God will do the rest', she assured us.

By contrast, Grace's story, recorded by Leo, features much less success than Diosa's. In fact, it reinforced the doubts of people who do not 'believe' in First Vita Plus. Grace was a full-time mother of five children, living in a municipality five hours' drive over land from Puerto Princesa. Her family runs a sari-sari store out of their house. When she joined First Vita Plus, the family was in financial trouble because her husband had stopped working as a security guard in Puerto Princesa. After returning to the village, he became a moto-taxi driver, but earned little in comparison to his former income. Grace, who wanted to increase the family earnings, was recruited by a First Vita Plus dealer, who gave her an initial 10 boxes of First Vita Plus to sell. The money she acquired through selling was remitted to him, and eventually she became a distributor. She decided to shut down the sari-sari store to work full time as a distributor, while her mother looked after her children. The first two months went smoothly; she had fun going to neighbouring villages to sell First Vita Plus, and it cost her little to do so because she was able to rely on her friends' hospitality. She also successfully recruited three down-lines. But then she discovered her up-line had not registered her account and was still earning money from her work. She then ran into more trouble. She recommended First Vita Plus to an elderly person with multiple illnesses. Unfortunately, he died after taking the sachet and his family blamed her. The experience left her feeling bad and she decided to stop doing MLM work altogether. While Grace was able to earn back her initial investment, she did not earn much more than that due to her up-line's exploitation of her efforts.

The story of Leo, our research team member who recorded these stories, also merits attention. When we met him, Leo was a valued teacher at the local high school, married, with two young children. As part of our fieldwork, we followed his efforts to sell First Vita Plus in Roxas, a town south of Puerto Princesa, which resulted in *Sweet Medicine*,[5] a documentary film that depicts the difficult relational work distributors perform. Leo recalled that the health seminars had motivated him to become a distributor, and that he and his wife sold the first Power Pack of First Vita Plus sachets quite quickly. But then he started having difficulty making sales. His potential clients were poor, so he lent them sachets to try out. But they had difficulty repaying him. One day, we accompanied him on a visit to a family that made a living by fishing and peeling cashew nuts, both common income-generating activities in the area. The father of the family, who goes out to sea regularly in a small boat to catch fish, had a bad respiratory infection (possibly TB) and was very thin. Leo gave him five sachets of First Vita Plus to try out, at a value of $4 US. The daughter responded, 'We owe you', referring to Leo as the 'medicine man'. Leo gingerly asked them when they would be able to pay, but the father replied that he was ill, so he could not work. Leo left the family with no promise of repayment.

Leo told us that his relatives criticized him for engaging in MLM, saying things like, 'You graduated with your bachelor's degree in philosophy in four years, and then you just go house to house and sell that product.' For them, he explained, this is a 'cheap' activity and continued, 'Somehow it's not normal for a [university] graduate. Because somehow, they are assuming you are in an office. You're just wearing nice clothes, saying nice things, and going to nice places.' But, he said, 'I just ignore what they are saying, and focus on my goals and my aspirations.' He then showed us a plot of land by the sea, where he dreamed of building a house for his family.

Ms Venhoff, Leo's up-line, whom we met in the previous chapter, had encouraged him to think specifically about what he wanted to do with his earnings and told him to ask his wife to help him. A shining example of success, Ms Venhoff was one of the first distributors in Puerto Princesa, signing up as a distributor in 2009. At the time of our research, she estimated she had 5,000 down-lines. She said she earned one million pesos (approximately $20,000 US) in her first year as a distributor, earning in one month what she had earned in a whole year working at her previous job in city government. She gave up her job, purchased a pickup truck, invested in an apartment and, as mentioned in Chapter 5, began running a local restaurant. In her conversations with us, Ms Venhoff underscored that her wealth was not just financial: it included all the people she worked with in her network, all those who believed in First Vita Plus. Moreover, she said, being healthy is such a blessing, one 'that the Lord gave me'.

Ms Venhoff stressed that success required hard work. She asked Leo, 'What is your dream?' and referred to a training manual that depicted a distributor showing off a large car. She then asked Leo if he dreamt of a 'house and lot'. That would cost two million pesos ($40,000 US), she estimated. She went on – a car equals one million, travel equals one million – encouraging him to add up the value of his dreams. 'How will you earn that?' she asked, offering to help him activate his group. Leo explained that when he made a pitch to prospective clients, they dismissed it, saying that the product was just vegetables. Even his wife was cynical about the scheme. Ms Venhoff assured him that she had strategies that would help his group succeed and his income would grow. Again, she showed him pictures of up-lines and their cars. 'Why are they able to achieve this?' she asked, rhetorically, and then answered: 'Because they help each other. Teamwork.' She ended the conversation by instructing him to bring his wife in for more training.

ENDGAME 163

Back home, Leo talked to his wife, who resisted becoming involved. Together they calculated their living costs against the income from Leo's teaching job and what they earned from their small grocery store. Arguing that being a distributor was too time intensive, she suggested that Leo should instead help her sell popcorn in their community, reasoning that it was an easier way to acquire some additional income. Leo maintained that they would earn more through First Vita Plus, if they could inspire their down-lines to increase their activity.

Leo checked in with one of his down-lines, Flor (see Figure 6.3), who told him she was tired of travelling around Palawan to recruit new distributors and sell sachets. She complained that a Power Pack was expensive, and that you had to sell the sachets quickly or the powders become hard. 'I now just get the five vegetables from my own backyard,' she said, 'Or I buy them at the market. I chop them and add them to the rice soup for my mother.' Leo was impressed by her backyard, where she grew chillies, moringa and spinach. Their discussion ended up with the two of them exchanging recipes using the five vegetables.

Leo stopped working for First Vita Plus after we received the results from a laboratory in Manila that indicated that the sachets possessed no nutritional value. The laboratory report stated that the powder had no fibre, which prompted Leo to wonder how it could consist of the five power herbs. We double-checked the laboratory results against a vitamin C testing kit, which also indicated that the sachets did not contain the vitamin. In the end, Leo decided to follow his wife's plan for additional income: selling popcorn.

We now turn to AIM Global, an MLM scheme that appeals especially to youth in Puerto Princesa, who, like Leo, have aspirations for a better life.

Figure 6.3 Leo talking to Flor in her backyard (left), where she grows chillies (right) (Source: *Sweet Medicine* documentary 2017).

Life is hard – AIM Global

'Life is hard nowadays,' lamented Erick, a trainer for AIM Global. A former hotel worker in the Caribbean, Erick had joined AIM Global at his wife's insistence. In his mid-thirties, wearing a polo shirt, jeans, and sandals, he came across as a relaxed and successful businessman. This training session had only seven attendees: four housewives in their late 20s, two young female retail workers, and a gasoline station attendant. Erick asks them about the minimum wage in Puerto Princesa, 'It's just 275 pesos, isn't it?' They nod. 'Do you know how much it costs to start up a business like Jollibee?' Erick continues, referring to the popular Filipino fast-food chain. Answering his own question, he gives the figure of two million pesos. Erick then urges the attendees to join AIM Global so they can have their very own businesses, for an investment of just $160 US. 'Life is hard and jobs such as those at Jollibee do not pay enough,' he declares. The message rings true. Although the national economy has been growing in recent years, there is little inclusive growth: only the rich benefit from it, while employment opportunities remain limited. 'It's simple,' Erick assured them. 'Just talk to your relatives and friends,' he continued, 'and invite them. Once they register as members, you earn 500 pesos. And once you register two down-lines, you can connect them, which earns you another 1,500 pesos. When the down-lines of your down-lines do the same, you earn yet again.' He wrapped up by saying: 'You can earn as much as $430 US a day.' In light of this amazing figure, a start-up investment of $160 US seemed a small sacrifice.

We attended several training seminars in AIM Global's main office in Puerto Princesa. Often the conference room above the office was full of young people invited by active members, like Felicia, who ran the Guapa Rich Health Center that Anita frequented. The speakers at these trainings were often distributors from AIM Global's headquarters in Manila, and they always told stories of people who went from rags to riches. First, the speakers explained how, by becoming a member, one receives a lifelong 25 per cent discount on C24/7. While the retail price for 30 pills was $24 US, members only paid $18 US. Then, they stated that one could earn money by inviting others to become members (see Figure 6.4)

The scheme's simplicity and apparent potential for astronomical earnings appealed to many young people, as did the success stories the trainers recounted. In his session, Erick illustrated how the system works by telling stories of people who had 'made it'. The most compelling story was that of Janvic, who was just 26 years old when he joined AIM Global. Legend had it that he sold some of his personal belongings to buy the

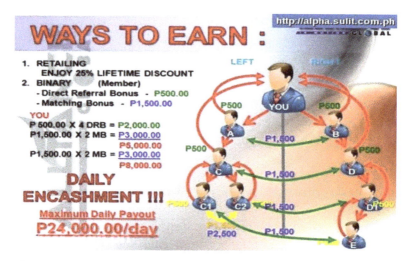

Figure 6.4 Earning by recruiting. Source: Author (Hardon), 2018.

initial membership. He became a 'millionaire', owning a house and a car. His age and personal circumstances made him someone the young attendees could relate to and aspire to emulate.

Felicia's socio-metabolic work

Felicia became an AIM Global distributor, as already noted, in order to obtain discounted C24/7 for her father. Hers was a success story: she initially invested $480 US in three memberships, which gave her a supply of 15 boxes of C24/7, each containing 30 capsules. As this was more than her father required, she sold the surplus in her store. In addition, she recruited down-lines, through whom she earned $300 US per month. She was also successful in that she managed to accumulate wealth without creating overt tensions between her family obligations and her business plans.

Felicia invited Anita to join a training session at the AIM Global office, where she was introduced to Lionel, an 18-year-old moto-taxi driver from the neighbourhood in which she was living. Lionel wanted to join AIM Global to receive a 25 per cent discount on university fees for Palawan Polytechnic College, where he hoped to study marine transportation. He did not have enough money for his own $160 US membership, but Felicia said she would buy it for him. The membership comes with five boxes (30 capsules each) of C24/7. Felicia told him that he could repay her for the membership by selling the capsules at $0.80 US each, which would yield an income of $120 US. He would then only require $40 US to cover repayment of the membership fee. This, she assured him, he could borrow from family members, given that he would be receiving a discount on his university fees. Lionel was doubtful and unsure about his ability to sell dietary supplements. But Felicia assured him it would be easy: 'Whenever you have an older person in your taxi, just start talking about the health benefits and they will be interested.' She gave him some promotional materials that spelled out how to earn through MLM and invited him to another training event that coming weekend.

The brochure states that distributors can earn between $360 US and $700 US each month, impressive sums in a town where most young people had to be content with minimum wage jobs that pay around $120 US per month. The membership includes a business webpage and an ATM card. Lionel did not understand how all this worked so Felicia explained, using the office computer. In addition to the discount in university fees, she said, Lionel also would obtain access to the office spaces of AIM Global in downtown Puerto Princesa, and the opportunity to open a bank account and receive an ATM card, both attractive ingredients of a new lifestyle, which were difficult to obtain for people without regular incomes. Lionel still seemed a bit daunted – but signed up. Felicia promised that, as his up-line, she would help him. By signing up with AIM Global, Lionel gained access to the trappings of a middle-class lifestyle and became embedded in a new hierarchy of social relations.

Rare success stories

Anita was introduced via another member of our research team to Hazel, one of the best-known, most successful distributors in Puerto Princesa. Hazel had joined AIM Global while still working for the city government. Early on, she realized that she would earn more money if she bought more memberships, so she went for the maximum of seven,[6] investing her monthly wages in her new sideline. Like Felicia, she was successful in recruiting new members and selling C24/7. Hazel explained that it is very important to be active: to keep going, even when you face rejection; and to nurture your down-lines, make them feel that they belong to a group. After a period of time, the work of managing all her down-lines became too time-consuming and she gave up her day job. Her husband began helping her, once he noticed that she earned more than he did with his poultry farm. They earn millions, they told Anita. While Anita spoke with Hazel, her husband showed her attractive business plans on his iPad, alongside pictures of bank cheques showing how much the couple has earned. The slides were familiar; they are the same ones used for recruitment at the training seminars. Anita told them she was already a member, and that as an anthropology professor, she was interested in how the MLM scheme works to promote health and wealth, and was not an entrepreneur.

Both Felicia and Hazel were widely touted as successes, examples of people for whom AIM Global met its promises. A key aspect of their success, however, was simply timing: they joined the company early on, when it was still relatively easy to recruit new members, and continued to earn money because they were relatively high up in the sales pyramid.

Facing the challenge

To learn more about the experiences of the rank-and-file members of AIM Global in Puerto Princesa, we used snowball sampling and interviewed 20 young adults. In a setting where few families can afford to pay the $160 US membership fee – more than the average family's entire annual expenditure on health – we wanted to know how they were able to raise this sum and whether they were able to sell the products and recruit new members.

We heard stories of new recruits channelling money earmarked for their educations to buy their memberships and of others requesting cash advances from their regular jobs, borrowing money from their up-lines, or selling or pawning family assets. Inspired by charismatic trainers like Erick and recruiters like Felicia, they believed that they could easily recover their investments and repay their debts. Rose, for example, pawned her mother's necklace; she knew her mother would look for the necklace and worked very hard to earn it back. In the first month she recruited five new distributors and earned $120 US, which she decided to invest in another membership. She borrowed money from her up-line (in exchange for her computer) in order to retrieve the necklace from the pawnshop. When she did not earn enough to repay her up-line, she lost her computer. Ron, who worked in a hotel as a bellboy, borrowed money from his parents and pawned his father's tricycle to join AIM Global. He went house to house selling C24/7 and met up with other distributors to give out flyers in front of the local mall. But he typically only earned about $1 US, of which 60 cents went to gas and the rest to a cheap meal of *arroz caldo* (chicken porridge) with an egg. Eventually, he was able to recruit several down-lines, which helped him increase his income. He told us that his desire to repay his parents led to his success.

Most parents discouraged their children from joining AIM Global, as many had either had experiences with other MLM schemes that did not deliver or had heard about such enterprises, since TV and radio programmes regularly report on scams. Iris, a student at Palawan State University, did not heed her parents' warnings and sold her phone and entered a beauty contest to raise the money for a membership. When her classmates found out, they began teasing her, shouting out the AIM battle cry, 'Power! Power!' when they passed her on campus. While members of her AIM Global group did not see much value in formal education, Iris saw synergies between her studies and her business, and thus continued to study while working as a distributor. She used her foreign language skills for online marketing and her maths skills to develop a profitable business strategy. Her major in human resources helped her to communicate with customers and potential recruits. Having resisted all the pressure from her family and friends to stop, she was eventually successful, and says she earned her first million pesos in 2016.

Many of our interlocutors complained of the difficulties of recruiting new members. Some met this challenge by forming new social groups. Up-lines became godparents to their down-lines, organizing dinners, parties and gatherings (Hardon, Davatos & Lasco 2019, 434). Insiders were referred to as 'Ka-AIM Global', '*ka-*' being a prefix that evokes belonging, as in *kapatid* (brother or sister) and *kapamilya* (family member). 'Becoming family' with fellow members meant up-lines could count on down-lines' support to recruit new members. 'Hindi ka namin iiwanan sa ere' (We will not leave you in the air), one member told us. One such group, called the Knights, frustrated with their many failed attempts to bring prospects to seminars, developed aggressive tactics, which they referred to as 'kidnapping'. This involved inviting prospects to a meal, a birthday party or other social event that then turned out to be a recruiting session, either at someone's home or the AIM Global office. Encouraging each other to work hard and quit their jobs and their *barkadas* (peer groups) to have more time for networking, they helped each other to invest in multiple memberships to increase their joint earnings.

Ges, whom the Knights had recruited, gave us some insight into the group's dynamics. She had been studying mass communication when some friends invited her to a seminar at the AIM Global office. Unlike her classmates, who considered MLM a scam, Ges saw something in it. She brought it up with her mother, who encouraged her to give it a try.

Ges withdrew her membership fee from a savings account her mother had set up for her. Once a member, she attended trainings and invited prospects to recruitment seminars. She was able to recruit seven people, some of them online. Three of them made a good effort, but to her dismay, she earned very little. Then the Knights group dissolved, with its active members poached by a rival group. To make matters worse, her up-line stole a prospect she had introduced to him and advised her to close her AIM Global account. When we met with her, she had not recouped her initial investment.

Others approached the challenge of recruiting online. Jess, a security guard, recruited prospects during his graveyard shift from 3 a.m. to 6 a.m., when it is evening in the Middle East. Pat, trained to be a seaman, compared online networking to catching fish with a net in deep water, and claimed that he had 3,000 down-lines. Peter had a Facebook tagline that read: 'People don't just join [a] business, they join you.' He stressed the importance of establishing personal credibility so people in other parts of the world would trust him. Clay, a call centre worker with a bachelor's degree in business accounting, told us her older brother had tried to recruit her when she was in her fourth year of high school, but she did not join because her parents disapproved of the idea. But while working at the call centre, she participated in an on-the-job training session by an AIM Global member, who was also a co-worker. The promise of a better life and owning her own house lured her. But she did not have the $160 US required to become a member, until two of her office-mates helped her to buy a membership. Although she worked hard and was able to repay her friends, she was able to recruit only two down-lines, neither of whom were successful at selling the product.

Clay followed the advice of her up-line at the office to set up a Facebook account for the business, which she did. He told her to show a car on her page to project an image of success, but she wanted to be honest and just posted images of the products instead. She would stay late at the call centre to take advantage of its high-speed internet, recruiting across time zones. One time, just when an overseas worker was about to purchase a membership, she could not close the deal because her up-line was unavailable and she did not know how to coordinate payment for the membership from abroad. She felt let down by her up-line. 'That's really the problem,' she said, 'You're new and you do not know the tactics or recruitment process.' Feeling deceived, she stopped recruiting. Her co-workers at the call centre spent nights in coffee shops planning their strategies, but, after a while, they gave up as well. Their MLM work was affecting the quality of their work at the call centre.

Romeo, whose friend had been distributing C24/7 for over a year, told us he was initially happy with his sideline. 'You just have to make it work,' he declared. But over time, it became clear that he was nowhere near achieving a return on his investment. 'It's hard,' he sighed during one of our discussions. 'I had this old woman client who was worried about side effects and I really didn't know how to reassure her. I called my up-line, but I couldn't reach him. Someone else demanded a new package the same day, but I was working and was unable to bring a package to her.' Romeo did not feel confident distributing the product and had yet to recoup his investment. When we last talked, he was somewhat ashamed for not having succeeded when it all seemed so easy. Similarly, Rudy only managed to recruit five people in nearly a year and thus barely recovered his investment. Although low-paying, his job at a gasoline station proved more stable. Another young man, Ernest, a pedicab driver, told us that the sales talk convinced him to join, but he did not make a single cent from his membership. 'Who would buy a single tablet for 40 pesos?' he asked. At the market in town, 40 pesos buys a complete meal of rice, vegetables and meat.

While the company's trainers boasted that Palawan had produced 11 millionaires, their highlighting of individual successes did scant justice to the several hundred distributors in Puerto Princesa who had yet to benefit from their investments. This causes one to question the accuracy of the success stories presented during the training seminars. One of our interlocutors complained about members lying in their testimonials, claiming to have reaped much larger sums than they had actually earned. We observed that people were generally reluctant to talk about their failure to earn back their initial investment and the difficulties they had maintaining a steady income. But those who admitted failure also said that they were not sorry for trying. They valued the entrepreneurial skills and mindset that they had acquired through their work for AIM Global.

Once they raised enough money to become members, distributors were encouraged to make a list of prospects that included their family, friends and co-workers, and to then recruit them as members and/or as clients. 'If you are not good at convincing people, your up-lines can help by talking to potential recruits,' the trainers assured them. But seasoned distributors had learned that recruiting new members is no easy task. As one of them said, 'Out of 10 people you invite, you will be lucky to get one or two.' Training manuals and seminars coached them to deal with rejection. 'NO,' the trainers asserted, means 'New Opportunity'.

'Recruit people who wouldn't say "no" to you,' one trainer advised, while another suggested scoping out the elderly in one's family to find out who is ill. This strategy entails piggybacking on already-established networks of obligation among kin. The trainers further encouraged members to take out multiple memberships for themselves: up to seven if one is serious about turning it into a business, they said, which means having yourself as a down-line six times over, expediting the reaping of benefits from the scheme. But purchasing seven memberships cost $1,120 US. Anticipating prospective members' concerns, recruiters assured them that the effort would be worth it. 'Like any other business, the first steps are tough,' Erick stated, and then promised: 'But as long as you work hard, you will be greatly rewarded.'

The trainers at the weekly AIM Global seminars encouraged distributors to recruit not only in the Philippines, but also abroad. 'Our name is AIM *Global* for a reason, after all', said the Adventist pastor whom Anita met in the AIM Global office when she was there to observe a training session. He went on to explain that she could start earning money as a distributor by inviting her friends in the Netherlands to become members. His eyes shone with the prospect of this potential expansion of his business.

Working through the Filipino diaspora, AIM Global networkers have carved out markets in areas with large Filipino populations, such as Hong Kong, the United States, Qatar, Italy and Spain. Ramon, a leading networker who regularly spoke at seminars, stated that he had down-lines in Hong Kong and that he earned between $2,000 US and $4,000 US per month through AIM Global. The remoteness of the income source was an enduring source of fascination. 'Can you imagine?' Ramon marvelled, 'I'm earning from people I've never even met!' Nathalie, one of the self-declared millionaires, moved to Manila, where she ran the business for her husband, a captain on a large container ship. Her husband recruited down-lines among his sailors, who may have felt obliged to buy from their superior. Similar networks of subtle coercion, such as office supervisors pushing their staff to buy into the schemes, exist throughout AIM Global.

AIM Global offered additional rewards to those who succeeded. If you sold a certain amount of food supplements, you became eligible for travel on foreign junkets and additional commissions from your down-lines' sales. Along with an insurance policy and other benefits, new members received a DVD containing clips of overseas trips that top earners had made to Macau, Hong Kong, the United States and France, as an inducement when recruiting. Against backdrops of Europe's most iconic landmarks – the Eiffel Tower and Ancient Roman ruins – global ambassadors invite viewers: 'Join us!' In this heaven of materialism, it appears that one must not even work; money just flows in, thanks to your down-lines. Ending his seminar, Erick asked a rhetorical question: 'Do you want to be rich or very rich?'

Conclusion

Distributors sold First Vita Plus and C24/7 to their clients as protective shields and cure-alls, but perhaps the MLM schemes simultaneously involved distributors in something more important: a new way of earning money in precarious times of rapid socio-metabolic transformations. The MLM schemes are seductive, offering quick, lucrative incomes to meet these precarious times and yet end up exposing people, particularly the poor, to new forms of precarity and risks: financially as well as in terms of health – in other words, metabolic precarities. In Puerto Princesa and its surrounding hinterlands, people's lives have changed. They increasingly confront other people's middle-class lifestyles: family members who work overseas and make salaries that are much higher than those in Palawan, tourists who visit the island to see its scenic hotspots, and people who have found new ways of making a living, including through MLM.

In the past, Filipinos in Palawan relied on their backyards for vegetables, fruits and herbal medicines and on each other when serious disease hit. But in this new time of a booming service sector, most people have diminished access to the land and sea because they are increasingly engaged in a wide range of low-paid jobs: as construction workers on the numerous real estate development projects, as security guards protecting those new properties, or as receptionists, cleaners and sales people serving those enterprises. People often work multiple jobs to make ends meet; living in the city is expensive, coming with high costs for utilities, transportation and rent. Puerto Princesa residents compensate for their lack of time by buying food from stalls on their way home, the quality of which they question, and they compensate for their dietary insecurities by buying supplements that eat up a substantial proportion of their income. Becoming a distributor of food supplement commodities offers them a welcome opportunity to earn extra money.

First Vita Plus and AIM Global build on pre-existing socio-metabolic family ties, relying on the fact that people in the Philippines are used to generating income to contribute to family health. These MLM operate at the three-way intersection of distributors' family obligations, their insecurities in increasingly flexible labour markets and their customers' anxieties about their health. Labour laws provided social protection to a certain extent in the past. However, in today's liberalized economy, First Vita Plus and AIM Global are able to capitalize on people's precarity and their worries about changing diets, polluted environments and the catastrophic cost of poor health. These MLM consequently have the capacity to push Filipinos to perform socio-metabolic work beyond their family networks, by also recruiting new distributors from among their networks of friends and colleagues. The companies appeal to urban residents who hope that selling food supplements will allow them to not only look after their aging family members, but also to obtain access to food supplements at discounted rates, both for themselves and their family members, and (perhaps most importantly) to attain desirable middle-class lifestyles. The unchecked positive health imagery of food supplements disguises the company's exploitative processes, in which distributors higher up in the MLM scheme benefit from the sales generated through the intense socio-metabolic work of the people lower down in the hierarchy.

Finding money to invest in memberships requires interpersonal relational work to divert funds earmarked for schooling, to pawn family assets, or to borrow from families, friends, or up-lines. Distributors negotiate their obligations to pay back loans, while also navigating tensions with family members who believe that MLM companies are scams. Their relational work extends to assessing their connections for possible clients and trying to recruit friends as members. Earning depends on whether down-lines are 'active', which adds the burden of mentoring to their socio-metabolic labour. Sometimes distributors operate in groups, which can create unpleasantly complex relational dynamics, especially when frictions over unequal investments, debts and workloads occur.

Distributors are expected to simultaneously embody the supplement's efficacy and to tailor their supplement pitches to clients' specific health needs. Sharing their own metabolic experiences of taking supplements constitutes another part of their relational work. So do collecting testimonials from their clients and generating evidence that demonstrates the products' merits, while developing trust, in both face-to-face and online interactions, with people nearby and in other time zones. If up-lines can continue to recruit new down-lines, they make money. But if they fail to recruit new members or if their down-lines are inactive, they earn very little (Legara et al. 2008). Entering an MLM scheme is thus risky business, especially for people who, to begin with, have little in the way of financial and social capital. Our ethnography shows that, more often than not, MLM activities disrupt the socio-metabolic fabric of family life in the Philippines. People end up with debts and strained relations with their relatives and friends.

Socio-metabolic work is limited neither to MLM nor to the selling of food supplements; it is also performed in other service sector settings, such as beauty salons, where workers detoxify skin and replenish it with nutrients; gyms, where trainers advise clients regarding the use of protein shakes (often also part of MLM programmes) and design exercise programmes to build muscles; and anti-aging clinics, where health workers seek to slow the processes of metabolic disintegration. In all these service-sector sites, workers are expected to embody metabolic health with glowing skin, radiant energy, toned and muscular bodies and youthful appearances. Consequently, they play a pivotal role in the global expansion of the market for plant-based supplements like First Vita Plus and C24/7, thereby accelerating the metabolic shift that we consider the turn to supplements. But the results of our ethnographic research suggests that this comes at a huge social cost.

Notes

1. See https://www.dsap.ph/the-industry/ (Accessed 12 December 2020).
2. See https://www.dsap.ph/the-industry/, section: Definition of Direct Selling and MLM vs. Pyramiding. Accessed 14 February 2021.
3. Avon, Tupperware, and Herbalife are members of the DSAP (likely as a way to increase the perception of their legitimacy), but AIM Global is not.
4. See https://www.dsap.ph/the-industry/ section: How to differentiate a legitimate direct selling company from pyramiding using the 8-Point Test. Accessed 14 February 2021.
5. This film can be viewed at https://www.chemicalyouth.org/#/projects/sweet-medicine (Accessed 6 June 2024).
6. AIM Global has set seven as the upper limit for memberships by a single individual.

Part III
Proposals for repair

7
Towards plant sovereignty: proposals for repair

Our story of the reconstituting and packaging of plants in the Philippines is one of colonization and capitalist extraction, in which multiple metabolic rifts and shifts ruptured relations between Filipino people and plant resources, causing a loss of plant sovereignty. Negative valuations of indigenous plant-based healing practices by first Spanish (1565–1898) and then US (1898–1946) colonizers dramatically altered Filipinos' everyday relations with plants. Our review of seventeenth-century chronicles by the Spanish friars reveals their ambivalence: on the one hand they were fascinated by the locals' extensive knowledge of so many plants; on the other, they feared that local healers were practising sorcery. Like other Spanish written sources, these contained recognition that Filipino healers enjoyed respect among the population, to such an extent that the colonizers perceived the healers as potential leaders of revolts against Spain.

Like the Spaniards, the American colonizers were ambivalent about indigenous uses of plants, both as food and medicine. Eager to collect voluminous information, they also tended to treat local knowledge and indigenous healers with condescension. This negative stance towards indigenous practices and knowledge had long-term consequences. In the 1950s, after the Philippines regained independence, the government and the Philippine Medical Association launched campaigns against traditional healers, even arresting and imprisoning some of them (Stauffer 1966, 43). Traditional healers were considered a threat to the emerging state, and their practices seen as backward.

However, the most profound ruptures between Filipino people and the plants that once figured as medicines and food in their everyday lives were due to the industrial reformulation of plant materials into ultra-processed, reconstituted and conveniently packaged commodities, including packaged breads, cereals, crackers and chips, candy, vitamin-fortified and sweetened fruit juices, ice cream, instant noodles, sodas and 'reconstructed meals' such as chicken nuggets and, of primary concern here, dietary food supplements. These foods became ubiquitous in the Philippines, purchasable in (super)markets and local 'variety' stores, displacing fresh fruits and vegetables in everyday meals. Their easy accessibility and increased consumption reduced the nutritional value of people's food intake, while increasing their risks for suffering from cardiovascular diseases (Srour et al. 2019) and, more dramatically, of 'all causes of mortality' (Rico-Campà et al. 2019). For growing urban populations of people who lack time to cook and eat at home because they work in the demanding service-sector economy, fast foods are inexpensive and convenient to eat on the run. Consequently, persistent malnutrition has become a serious problem in the Philippines and continues to be so, even as the country experiences economic growth.

With this historical background as context, in Chapter 2, we illustrated how post-independence, government-sponsored nutrition programmes responded to widespread malnutrition by promoting both community gardens and nutritional supplementation. These programmes encouraged people to help their children grow and 'glow' by eating more vegetables and fruits, and also by adding micronutrient powders to pre-schoolers' meals. This dual message further contributed to the loss of plant sovereignty, by perpetuating exaggerated anxieties that ordinary fruits and vegetables do not provide enough nutrients to ensure good health. We explained that this problem emerges from a highly reductionist view of nutrition called nutritionism, which treats food as chemicals and molecules, often visualized in isolation, that act independently of each other. This entails reifying vitamins as solutions to individual deficiencies, through fortification and supplementation introduced in chemical forms, even though these deficiencies occur because industrial processes remove the vitamins from whole foods. We also noted that modern packaging of reprocessed and hyper-processed foods creates new health risks because the packaging materials themselves are toxic substances.

In Chapter 3, we described how, in the 1970s and 1980s, research into the uses of medicinal plants became an important component of a movement towards health self-reliance in the Philippines. The community-based health programmes (CBHPs) valued Filipino plants as remedies for common illnesses. However, this return to plant sovereignty was undermined by the commodification of plants. Emerging research programmes built on the knowledge of plant medicines the CBHPs compiled, resulting in the packaging of plants as medicines, and increasingly also as food supplements. Chapter 4 explored how plants packaged as food supplements now compete on a vibrant market that promises surplus health by means of exaggerated efficacy claims, facilitated by aggressive information technologies, which reinforce the alienating idea that people require plant-based supplements to be healthy and succeed in life.

In Chapter 5, we followed the flow of packaged plants to Puerto Princesa, an urban centre to which people migrate to find jobs in the Philippines' rapidly growing service sector. Our urban ethnography reveals that people there lack the access their parents and grandparents had to water and land, as well as the time to attend to backyard gardens and to cook meals. They need to earn a steady income to cover the costs of rent, drinking water, food, prepaid credits for their mobile phones and transportation. Working long hours, usually at multiple jobs to be able to afford city life, they experience exhaustion and stress. We show that aggressive advertising of supplements that promise to round out diets and protect metabolic health preys upon people's worries about these circumstances. We further demonstrate that, as people shift to buying and consuming reconstituted plants in the form of capsules, tablets and powders, they increase their precarity because they spend scarce resources that they might otherwise use to buy vegetables and fruits at local markets or could save for other purposes, if they were to cultivate plants in their backyards.

Finally, in Chapter 6, we examined how people living in urban precarity find food supplements attractive as a way to engage in multilevel marketing (MLM) schemes to acquire additional income. In order to become distributors and sell supplements, poor people must invest in the products, which often means borrowing money or selling family assets. Beyond this, MLM trainers encourage them to capitalize on their social networks to recruit new members and find customers. If they are persistent, the trainers and up-lines preach, they will earn millions of pesos. However, our fieldwork shows, being a distributor in an MLM scheme involves intense socio-metabolic work, which entails alienation from the self and society. First, MLM workers are under pressure to 'be the product', that is, to present testimonies of the beneficial effects of supplements, without necessarily having experienced any benefits. Second, they are coerced to capitalize on their social networks, which risks alienating them from friends and family. Thus, people whose everyday lives have been compromised by the intersecting metabolic shifts we describe above end up donating labour to promote the sales of supplements, with little chance of recovering their investments of financial and social capital and time. This constitutes a cynical endgame in the metabolic transitions we have portrayed in this book and which we expose in our documentary movie, *Sweet Medicine* (see also Chapter 5).[1] On closer inspection, globalization and capitalist expansion are the true causes of the dysfunctional metabolic shifts and rifts the supplements ostensibly bring about. The dark sides of these systems cause significant problems, particularly under the Philippines' regime of laissez-faire neoliberalism (Hardon 2021; Nestle 2002; Schlosser 2001).

In the Philippines, the supplements industry mirrors social food and nutrition inequities that permit undernutrition and obesity to coexist side by side. The industry has developed parallel markets that cater to this paradoxical situation. To the poor, it peddles vitamins and plant-based products that are supposed to help people manage stress and nutritional deficiencies. For middle- and upper-class people, there are also vitamins, along with weight-loss products that range from Chinese teas to amphetamines. We did not discuss weight-reducing products, but they are a matter for concern because they include potentially toxic drugs banned even in the US, which has been so liberal in deregulating supplements.

Among the most dangerous products are 'nutraceuticals' (nutritional pharmaceuticals), a term coined by marketers but which Aronson (2017) critiques as referring to products that are neither nutritional nor pharmaceutical. They are products that are often not approved as drugs, but which are widely promoted and sold with claims for both nutrition and medical benefits. One popular nutraceutical in the Philippines is administered intravenously – a widespread problem that made it to the front pages of newspapers in the Philippines in the last week of February 2024 (Ramos 2024). Actress Mariel Rodriguez posted on social media photographs of herself receiving an IV drip in the office of her husband, Senator Robin Padilla. Her intention was to show how supporting her husband's work means she has no time to do things, like receive IV infusions. The product in the drip was glutathione, which she said was for beauty and health. Widely consumed in the Philippines as a skin whitener, it is openly sold through online outlets.

Social media exploded with reactions from another senator, as well as a number of netizens, whose main complaints were that government offices, including senators' offices, are not meant to be places where one receives a 'gluta drip'. Lost in the controversy was a more basic issue, which the country's Food and Drug Administration (FDA) finally brought to the fore: glutathione is not approved for use in the Philippines. The FDA warned that there can be adverse side effects. Even the health secretary joined in the fray, warning that a woman had recently died hours after receiving a glutathione injection in a clinic. He also reminded the public that just a month before, in January 2024, he had issued a warning that glutathione is not approved as a skin whitener. Indifferent to all the fuss, Rodriguez insistently posted on social media: 'I never miss a drip because it really helps in so many ways – collagen production, whitening, energy, metabolism, immunity and much more.'

The controversy over glutathione has been going on for several years. Anita and Michael referenced it in their project, Chemical Youth,[2] and in the subsequent book (Hardon 2021) about supplements that, as Mariel Rodriguez claimed, were ingested 'for beauty and health'. The Philippine FDA's warnings about the dangers of glutathione have been sporadic and seem to have had no effect and it is too early to say whether or not the infusion incident in a senator's office will have any long-term repercussions.

Meanwhile, Rodriguez added fuel to the fire by coming out with a clarification on social media, claiming she was not being injected with glutathione in her husband's office but with vitamin C. The FDA then issued another warning, this time against intravenous injections of vitamin C, pointing out that people with G6PD (glucose-6-phosphatase deficiency), a genetic disorder involving a missing enzyme, can suffer adverse effects from high doses of vitamin C, mainly hemolysis – the destruction of red blood cells (La Vieille et al. 2019).

While perceived as a powerful fix, intravenous infusions represent the worst kind of metabolic shift. In China, patients being administered IV drips of vitamins are a common sight in hospital corridors, an ordinary outpatient routine performed to boost immunity. Late in 2023, the practice took another turn, when respiratory infections swept China. Anxious parents brought their children to hospitals for IV drips to boost immunity. The IV drips were administered while pupils did their homework and, in one case, a child practised violin while receiving a drip (McCartney 2023). Comments on social media lamented that Chinese children were being overworked, missing the point that the IV injections have no proven efficacy.

Such extremes have not been reported in the Philippines. Michael, however, has childhood memories of receiving intramuscular injections of calcium for colds, sometimes together with eucalyptus oil injections, if he had a cough. Filipino health professionals now consider these practices outdated, but that does not mean a revival cannot occur. In the US, naturopathic practitioners have begun re-introducing IV therapies for stress, anxiety and immunity.[3] A May 2024 *New York Times* article describes how luxury condos are offering IV drips as part of wellness programmes (Kayzen 2024). In the near future, similar services might well be introduced to the Philippines.

The glutathione and vitamin C infusions not only serve as a dire warning about metabolic rifts but also signal a disturbing loss of autonomy. Instead of preparing a nutritious meal, people become dependent on injectables provided by a health professional, medical clinic, or supplements seller. Such dependencies can exacerbate or even create serious problems.

In the rest of this final chapter, we examine opportunities with the aim of repairing the ruptured relations between Filipinos and the plant resources that grow in their fertile, biodiverse archipelago, with the aim of re-establishing plant sovereignty. We insist that, under today's circumstances, governments, civil society actors, health professionals and social scientists cannot sit back and allow the existing situation to continue. Acknowledging their distributed agency in the loss of plant sovereignty and the persistence of metabolic precarity, we invite these actors to engage in six ways to repair the ruptured relations between people and plants: (1) take stock of the political ecology of malnutrition, (2) resist cultural hegemony, (3) learn to read the scripts, (4) reconnect to plants to promote plant sovereignty,[4] (5) improve planetary health and (6) attempt to achieve social solidarity and justice in food and nutrition.

1. Taking stock: the political ecology of malnutrition

A persistent problem, malnutrition takes many forms. In the Philippines, this includes one of the world's highest rates of stunted growth among children along with other forms of undernutrition. Food security is crucial to combatting stunting (Edelman et al. 2014; Gartaula et al. 2018). One study (Capanzana, Demombynes and Gubbins 2020) calculates that providing adequate food security and diversity to all Filipino children could reduce stunting by 22 per cent.

For too long, studies of malnutrition have focused on deficiency states, without probing socioeconomic circumstances, other than with token references to poverty. The cold statistics show, for example, that the regions where undernutrition is most serious are also the most impoverished ones.[5] A recent article by UNICEF (2019) that focuses on malnutrition calls for action but does not address the issue of the economic and social marginalization of Muslims in the Philippines.

Sceptical of programmes that 'devolve regulatory responsibility to consumers via their dietary choices', Guthman (2007, 264) urges a political-economic approach to alleviating malnutrition. We agree. We must examine nutritional problems not just as chemical deficiencies, but also as products of social inequity. Governments tend to blame the poor for malnutrition, pointing to their unfortunate 'dietary habits' without recognizing how powerful corporations control the production and marketing of unhealthy foods and, in the last few decades, also vitamin and mineral preparations and supplements.

A political ecology of malnutrition must also attend to the particularities of what Heynen (2006, 133) calls the 'urbanization of hunger'. All over the Philippines, people have moved to cities and now face the same challenges consuming healthy meals that our interlocutors in Puerto Princesa shared with us. Enter supplements, touted as solutions not just to malnutrition, but also as panaceas that prevent and treat a host of diseases. Then add pollution and the generic 'stress' of modern living to the equation. Pfizer coined its slogan 'Bawal magkasakit' (Don't fall ill) to advertise its multivitamins because becoming ill in the Philippines' bustling, round-the-clock, urban economies is forbidden. Local distributors of vitamins and supplements have adopted this slogan as well. But the purported 'solutions' themselves often cause problems, either because they have no efficacy when it comes to preventing certain ailments or because, even if they have some efficacy against some of the health problems they allegedly cure, they give consumers a false sense of security, which means those consumers may not seek medical treatment from a doctor when they need it. MLM companies target these same consumers, providing poor people with hope that they can attain a middle-class standard of living by entering into pyramid schemes, but instead leave them indebted. This is a tragic form of accumulation by dispossession – a particularly predatory form of capitalism (Harvey 2004).

We described a double burden in the Philippines' nutritional landscape, of undernutrition existing side by side with obesity. As we noted, the supplements market cashes in on both problems, offering questionable vitamins for malnutrition and an array of weight-reducing products. Reversing the tide of the ever-increasing consumption of ultra-processed foods and reliance on plant-based supplements to boost health is urgent, albeit difficult due to the aggressive barrage of marketing inundating consumers. We are concerned about the use of professional associations, including of physicians and nutritionists, to promote the unscientific claims about vitamin and mineral preparations and supplements. This dates back to the 1950s, when even the *Journal of the Philippine Medical Association* carried advertisements for evaporated milk, commended for being vitamin-fortified. Today, promotions spill over into hospitals and clinics, as well as into convention halls, with free samples and all kinds of marketing literature.

When complemented by larger-than-life billboards intended for the general public, health professionals, even those who are conscious of the manipulations of advertising, sometimes find themselves taking the marketed products and giving them to their children, as illustrated by the billboard for growth hormones along a main highway in Metro Manila (see Figure 2.6 in Chapter 2). For several years, Michael taught a course on health, culture and society to a graduate class at the Ateneo de Manila University, composed of health professionals. Inevitably, they discuss vitamin and mineral preparations and supplements. The professionals acknowledge the hype in advertising, but also admit that the unrelenting promotions sometimes affect them, especially those for children's products.

'Walang mawala', meaning 'Nothing lost', is what the students commonly say when referring to their own use of these products, in particular with regard to giving 'growth stimulants' to their children. 'If my kids end up short, I don't want them to blame me later on because I didn't give them the growth stimulant', they argue. 'Walang mawala' is also the reply they give to their patients who ask for advice about giving vitamins to their children.

Physicians – Filipino, as well as American and Dutch – themselves admit that nutrition is not a strong component of their medical training and say it is a field best left to nutritionists. But nutritionists, too, admit their training is often about isolated nutrients, studied simply as chemicals. Although some universities offer community nutrition programmes, food technology students learn little about the social, cultural and political contexts of food and nutrition. When fast food companies sponsoring scientific conferences are added into the mix, the miseducation problem becomes severe.

Physicians and nutritionists speaking about nutrition employ jargon that means nothing to lay people or speak in ways that may cause confusion (Sanabria 2016; Yates-Doerr 2015). The issue of vitamins is illustrative; more than a century after they were first discovered, medical professionals are still undecided as to what advice to give regarding taking a daily multivitamin. Silence and the lack of consensus among professionals create a vacuum of which companies producing and selling vitamins and supplements take advantage, banking on people's fears that they require vitamins in stressful times and they can never be certain they do not have a deficiency. The COVID-19 pandemic amplified such insecurities, including among physicians. However, health professionals can play a major role with their symbolic capital as 'experts'. By remaining silent, they create a void in which misinformation and disinformation thrive. This is particularly true for vitamins and dietary supplements.

More insidious than the advertisements and health professionals' advice (or lack thereof) are the internet promotions, particularly on social media. Our criticism of social media platforms centres on the way social media companies use algorithms for marketing. This entails assessing which websites users visit and collecting background demographic information to determine what types of products and services might appeal to them and what marketing pitches are likely to meet with success. Additionally, the algorithms direct people with similar interests to particular websites that function as echo chambers, amplifying their pre-existing concerns and anxieties in order to promote particular products (for more on social media algorithms see Trivette 2022 and Metzler and Garcia 2023).

2. Resisting cultural hegemony

As anthropologists, we have been particularly concerned with the cultural hegemony that grants the supplements industry powerful advantages when it comes to marketing their products. By 'cultural hegemony', we mean the pervasive control of information and education around nutrition that includes the very definition of what is nutritious. In the twentieth century, well into the post-independence period, American business interests adopted particularly aggressive tactics to introduce US food products into Filipino diets, through schools, imports and even US military bases that distributed canned foods and K-rations (military meal rations). In the 1980s, the supplements industry followed, using the fiction of 'natural medicine' to promote products, exacerbating people's fears and anxieties about their health by demonizing 'synthetic' drugs as dangerous.

When Michael's mother was diagnosed with dementia in 2010, he was approached by well-meaning friends and relatives pushing 'natural remedies', mainly food supplements. One uncle came to see him and brought written materials warning of Big Pharma's 'plot' to keep the supplements industry at bay. Michael was both amused and saddened; only a few years earlier, when he was a health activist campaigning against large pharmaceutical companies, this uncle and other elders in his clan had chided him for not having outgrown his political activism. Now, they were convinced that the multinational pharmaceutical industry was hatching plots and they viewed manufacturers of supplements as saviours.

Paradoxically, the very supplements promoted as both better than food and as natural alternatives to pharmaceuticals are also largely American or modelled after American products, with the preference among upper- and middle-income Filipinos for the expensive, imported varieties. Physicians in Michael's business administration classes often complained of the 'false economies of scale' among their patients, who lament the high cost of antibiotics and cut short their dosing regimens, yet are willing to pay much more, thousands of pesos, for monthly subscriptions to supplies of Herbalife and Usana, two extremely popular MLM supplements distributors. The cost of these imports is far beyond the reach of the poor, whom MLM schemes like First Vita Plus and AIM Global target with the relatively cheaper supplements discussed in previous chapters. Ultimately though, the popularity of supplements depends on two continuing dynamics: transplantation in the Asian region, with products flowing between countries now further amplified by state-sponsored policies to reformulate and package plants, and Filipinos' embedded preference for US products.

Another form that cultural hegemony takes concerns Filipinos living and working in the United States, that country's fourth-largest immigrant group at two million people, after migrants from China, South Asia and Mexico (Gallardo and Batalora 2020). Filipino-Americans send home money and *balikbayan* ('returning to the homeland') boxes packed with gifts, including snacks and canned foods, as well as medicines, often vitamin and mineral preparations and supplements, along with narratives about the land of milk and honey. It makes no difference if some of the contents of the *balikbayan* boxes are not produced in the United States; the point is that they are packed in boxes and shipped from the United States. Physically unpacking these *balikbayan* boxes simultaneously unpacks powerful ideologies about food, medicines and supplements.

Michael participated in the remote unpacking of such boxes, when some friends asked him about three packaged plants (lagerstroemia, garcinia and bacopa) they received from the US. His response elicited surprise. He explained that the plants contained in these supplements grow in the Philippines: Lagerstroemia is *banaba* (Lagerstroemia indica), a common roadside tree, the leaves of which are used as local traditional medicine; garcinia is *mangosteen,* a popular fruit from the southern

Philippines; and bacopa or *ulasimang-aso* (Bacopa monniera) is another common plant. Of these plants, Michael told his friends, only garcinia has been developed by local supplement producers, with one company doing so well with its MX3 capsules that it can afford to place expensive advertisements, including billboards on EDSA, a main Metro Manila thoroughfare.

All this makes sense in a convoluted way, given the growing alienation from plants we are witnessing throughout the world, and acutely in the Philippines. Colonial cultural hegemony there has also taken the form of a fear of nature, tied to distorted notions of modernization. About 30 years ago, Michael was in a relatively remote town in Mindanao, which is surrounded by forests and a huge lake. He passed through the town centre and saw a sign in front of a cemented empty lot: 'The Future Site of the Parking Lot of XXXX Market'. This was in the era before smartphones so we have no photograph of the sign. If we did, it would capture that people perceive cemented lots as a sign of modernization.

The fear of natural spaces means trees and other vegetation must be cut down and rough ground smoothed and paved over. In the sixteenth century, the Spanish colonizers (1565–1898) started cutting down the forests to build cities and ships, and then cleared the land for plantations – activities for which they conscripted Filipino farmers. The process of destroying vegetation intensified under the Americans (1898–1946), when timber became an important export product. The Marcos regime (1965–86) continued the wholesale commercial exploitation of the Philippines' forests, and, despite more progressive forest policies in the post-Marcos era, an ideology of slash-and-pave modernity continues to prevail (Bankoff 2013). No wonder young Filipinos are hard-pressed to identify living versions of the fruits and vegetables they occasionally consume.

Likewise emerging from a need to subjugate nature are the bans on planting fruits and vegetables in middle- and upper-class subdivisions built to mimic US subdivisions, with their iconic, well-maintained, herbicide-infested lawns (Robbins 2007). Adopting a neocolonial US model necessitates degradation of the local, not just in terms of degrading local plants, but also in terms of degrading the very idea of planting, well exemplified by Michael's chagrin when he realized, not long ago, that the subdivision in which he lived did not allow planting fruits and vegetables. None of the property managers could explain why. They were apologetic when they said, that, given the 'plantdemic' – urban dwellers suddenly embracing gardening – that emerged during the COVID-19 pandemic, they would allow the planting of vegetables, even offering seeds. But they emphasized that this situation was only temporary.

This ban on planting fruits and vegetables in middle- and upper-class subdivisions also reflects a broad disdain for cultivating food crops, exemplified by declining enrolments in agriculture courses. Currently, Philippine state universities and colleges offer these courses mainly because private institutes of higher education do not consider the demand high enough to make them profitable. This dates back to the American colonial period, when agriculture became considered a vocation for the poor; since then, farming households have pushed their children to enter other courses of study, ranging from nursing to tourism, in order to escape the poverty trap of farming. The University of the Philippines, the national university, continues to offer agriculture programmes, but most courses centre around entrepreneurship and tracks related to agribusiness. However, a few universities such as the Benguet State University, located in the Cordillera Region, known for its abundant biodiversity, have started to focus on plant sovereignty by offering courses on agroecology.

3. Learning to read the scripts

When the Philippines won independence in 1946, it copied the political system of the United States, down to the names of government agencies and adopting many identical laws and regulations. When the Hatch Law on dietary supplements was passed in the United States, the Philippines adopted similar deregulatory measures. The US required a warning on product labels to the effect that: 'This statement has not been evaluated by the Food and Drug Administration. This product is not intended to diagnose, treat, cure, or prevent any disease.' The Philippines' FDA adopted a similar warning in a simplified form: 'No Therapeutic Claims Approved', which one health secretary, Dr Esperanza Cabral, herself a pharmacologist, deemed ineffective. When she proposed a blunt alert in Filipino 'Mahalagang Paalala: Ang [name of product] ay hindi gamot at hindi dapat gamiting panggamot sa anumang uri ng sakit' (This [name of product] is not a medicine and should not be used as medicine for any kind of illness), local herbal drug manufacturers sued Cabral and the Health Department, blocking her proposal. Although the 'Hindi gamot' (not medicine) warning is now in effect (Department of Health, Food and Drug Administration 2015), as we saw in Chapter 4, supplement distributors defy the government regulation by still using the less explicit, older version ('No Therapeutic Claims Approved') in English, which is often not understood. Alongside this statement are all kinds of curative and preventive claims, messages reinforced by broadcast media advertisements that end with a rapidly spoken 'disclaimer'. A similar case occurs with promotions of infant formula that include all kinds of claims, including intelligence enhancement, followed by the legally required: 'Breastfeeding is still best for babies.'

However, the word *gamot* not only means 'medicine', but also refers to any chemical the effects of which can be seen or felt. Examples include fertilizers, pesticides and even nail polish remover. Consequently, a warning like 'hindi ito gamot' ('this is not *gamot*') may not convey the message that something is not a therapeutic substance. Ultimately, what impresses people are the testimonials presented during promotional events for supplements, advertisements and packaging. Regulations must therefore address the issue of 'truth in advertising' in its broadest sense. Several countries have started requiring front-of-package nutritional information, an early warning mechanism to alert consumers that a product is high in saturated fats, salt, or sugars.[6] For supplements, it might be time to require language similar to that stipulated in the US: 'These statements (claims of indications) have not been evaluated by the Food and Drug Administration.' Or better, labels could read in Tagalog: 'This product has not been tested to prove it is effective for any kind of illness.'

Because it followed the example of the US in deregulating, it is difficult for the Philippines' FDA to enforce its own rules on supplements. The FDA also sent mixed signals when it endorsed instant noodles fortified by micronutrients a few years ago, with the logo 'Sangkap Pinoy' (Filipino ingredients). The Department of Health likewise has difficulty with enforcement. It recently issued a warning about the proliferation of supplement distributors claiming they have the department's endorsement for their products, when they do not (Cabalza 2024).

One major loophole is the creation of grey categories that neither lay people nor even health professionals understand. The Monthly Index of Medical Specialties (MIMS, formerly distributed as Philippine Index of Medical Specialties or PIMS) exemplifies this problem. Meant to be a guide to pharmaceuticals, it contributes to the growing conflation of drugs and supplements by including an entire section on 'supplements', which in a recent internet edition had 423 entries compared to 107 in 2022 (MIMS 2024). Including supplements in the PIMS is confusing to both doctors and consumers because it implies that the supplements have been approved as drugs. Earlier in this chapter, we discussed the media furore that erupted when a senator's wife boasted about receiving an IV drip of glutathione for beauty and health reasons. This nutraceutical is a popular choice for skin whitening. The Department of Health quickly responded by saying glutathione was not approved and yet 12 products with glutathione appear in MIMS, including a vaginal wash. Each entry includes an ATC (Anatomical Therapeutic Chemical) classification. Most entries are cited as 'general nutrient' and 'tonic'.

Much needs to be done to rationalize the regulatory environment, starting with the creation of separate categories for drugs, supplements and herbal products. The Philippine government should require clear, easy-to-understand labels, teach the public how to read and understand them, particularly the underlying 'scripts' we analysed in Chapter 4 with attention to supplement manufacturers' misuse of environmentalism for marketing. Although the words 'natural' and 'organic' are powerful, there are no regulations for their use on labels and in marketing. Corporations evoking them often engage in 'greenwashing' (derived from 'whitewashing') to hide their unethical marketing by co-opting terms that evoke environmental protection (see Hayes 2024). The US Federal Trade Commission (FTC) (2024) now requires claims that a product is 'green' to be backed by facts and details.

Teaching consumers nutrition literacy will not be easy. However, the Food and Nutrition Research Institute (FNRI) has launched initiatives that may be further developed, such as menu calendars, with monthly recipes and weekly meal planning. The multiplicity of products on the market also poses challenges. The small entrepreneurs renting spaces in Philippine malls and markets sell all kinds of supplements, mainly from the United States and China, many of which are not registered with the Philippines' FDA. Beyond this, there are ethnicity-specific sales circuits, such as those we described in Chapter 4: Lianhua Qiwen sold in Chinese drugstores and Chinese groceries and black seeds (Nigella sativa) to Muslims. One Nigella sativa-derived oil sold in the Philippines, we noted, is actually produced in Indonesia, with seeds imported from the Middle East.

The Philippines' FDA issues regular warnings about product labels carrying 'foreign characters', mostly in Chinese and Arabic. However, rather than simply warning the public against products with foreign characters, the FDA should use international connections to other drug regulatory agencies to establish what these products are and whether or not they are associated with safety problems. In some cases, clarification is possible, simply by consulting Chinese-Filipino people who can read the characters. Especially during the pandemic, journalists at the newspaper for which Michael writes a column asked him on occasion to identify products the police had confiscated. They were always Chinese herbal medicines, including Lianhua Qingwen. As we noted in Chapter 4, this herb was initially rejected by the Philippine FDA and then later approved, but with no warnings about its high ephedra content. Difficulties importers encounter registering supplements stem to some extent from xenophobia, even racism, directed against Arabs and Chinese people. In contrast, 'stateside', that is, US products, however dubious the claims their makers make, are sold with few restrictions.

Selling supplements, whether local or foreign, via MLM taps into another grey area in state regulation. While possessing many of the characteristics of illegal pyramid schemes, MLM has thus far successfully escaped regulatory crackdowns because, unlike pyramid schemes, there are actual products. But promotion of these products often occurs by means of unethical tactics, such as using pseudoscientific jargon and, in the case of MLM, exerting pressure on sales agents to recruit new ones.[7]

A weak state is inevitable when the dominant paradigm for governance is neoliberalism. The United States sets the gold standard for minimal government intervention, which the Philippines then adopts. But what will happen as the tide turns, as awareness about hyper-processed foods and supplements and multilevel marketing grows? Are governments ready to tackle class action lawsuits for neglecting the welfare of their citizens, even as scientific documentation amasses about the health risks of various foods and supplements? We ask, too, will the Philippine government, which already imposes 'sin taxes' to reduce consumption of tobacco and sugars in foods, respond to the growing tide in other countries of imposing even more 'sin taxes' on junk foods and hyper-processed foods?

4. Reconnecting to plants

Plant sovereignty can be restored by bringing back knowledge about plants as food and as medicine. This can begin in schools, with steps as basic as helping children learn what vegetables and fruits look like in their natural habitats and how to appreciate indigenous knowledge. Traditional knowledge is often extensive, including a multisensory approach – smell and taste – to identify plants and their uses. Acknowledging and reinforcing people's traditional uses and understandings of plants can foster their capacity to cultivate plants and encourage plant sovereignty, supporting their right to define their own food and agriculture systems (Nyéléni Forum 2007).[8]

Reconnecting to plants means collecting, or rather recollecting, knowledge that is fast disappearing (Nazarea 1978). Plant sovereignty, in our view, also involves appreciating plants with all the senses, which reveals their phytochemistry. Working with the CBHPs in the 1980s, community members learned that plants with strong odours contained essential oils, often useful for treating coughs and colds, body pains, skin rashes and mild infections (World Neighbors 1983). Cultivating this kind of 'lay' phytochemistry will allow consumers to see through the hype around supplements, including manufacturers' appropriation of scientific terms.

The CBHPs promoted plant sovereignty by countering the ideologies of 'West is best' and 'a pill for every ill'. Yet, their countercultural efforts were co-opted. Governmental research programmes nowadays promote packaging of local plants, which manufacturers subsequently promote using unethical marketing techniques and often baseless claims of efficacy. The rejection of 'a pill for every ill' was co-opted as well, by demonizing pills as synthetic and 'unnatural', as opposed to plant-based supplements, presented as 'natural' and therefore 'safe'. Commodifying plants into substances without smell or texture reduces plant literacy and, hence, plant sovereignty.

Michael finds that Filipinos are often shocked when they realize that lost plant sovereignty likewise means lost economic opportunities. Few Filipinos are aware that two common local plants – champaka (*Magnolia champaca L.*) and ilang-ilang (*Cananga odorata L.*) – yield essential oils that are among the most expensive in the world. Many other plants that produce essential oils likewise grow in the Philippines' tropical climate. These have applications in medicine, fragrances and cosmetics. Indeed, essential oils are developing into an important subsector of supplements. They have appeal precisely because of Filipinos' long, albeit half-forgotten, history of using essential oils in healing practices. Ironically, Filipinos now import synthetic essential oils from China that poorly imitate the scents of local essential oil-rich plants.

Plant sovereignty, inevitably, also requires demystifying not-so-traditional quasi-religious beliefs as pseudoscience. Our choice of the term 'demystification' is deliberate. We seek to target the ideological aspects of current marketing strategies employed to sell packaged plants, whether as supplements or as vitamin and mineral preparations. People need to become aware of how marketing techniques prey upon their fears and anxieties connected to living in fast-moving neoliberal societies by employing tropes of modernity – packaged materials and medical jargon like 'phytochemicals' – to sell their products. The close reading of packaging we performed in Chapter 4 is an attempt to teach readers how to deconstruct such marketing techniques. This deconstruction process must begin now, to counteract 'new' discoveries and formulations peddled as the latest miracles. These include prebiotics, probiotics and adaptogens, all of which are, like other trending health-bestowing descriptors, found in Philippine plants. Even more importantly, there are traditional Filipino processing methods that cause plants to generate prebiotics and probiotics, as well as particular vitamins. Again, it is ironic that imported pre- and probiotic products are pushed heavily while local ones go unrecognized. The latter include *burong mustasa* (fermented mustard leaves), *balao-balao* (fermented rice and shrimp mixture), *suka* (palm sap vinegar), *nata de coco* (coconut-derived cellulose pellicle), *tuba* (palm wine), *basi* (sugarcane wine), *tapuy* (rice wine) and *puto* (fermented rice cakes) (Chinte-Sanchez 2009).

Plant sovereignty, finally, involves valuing local produce. Like many Filipinos of his generation, Michael grew up thinking that oranges grew only in temperate countries, mainly in the US. In recent years, Filipinos in the National Capital Region began to realize that oranges were locally cultivated. Navel oranges, for example, were introduced to Sagada, a town in the north. Demand grew over the years and vendors in Manila and Baguio, an urban centre in the northern region, sold crates of oranges labelled as coming from Sagada. However, in 2018, Michael discovered that the 'Sagada oranges' sold in Manila, and even in northern towns near Sagada, were not from that region. Michael was particularly distressed when he found an entire crate of navel oranges with a label that not only claimed they were 'Sagada', but also contained Chinese characters. An entrepreneur in mainland China had caught on to the popularity of Sagada oranges and was selling Chinese oranges under that label. Michael reported his findings in his newspaper column and received responses from people in Sagada and other northern regions in response, confirming that their oranges had been 'counterfeited'. Low-cost fruits and vegetables from China pose a challenge to plant sovereignty because farmers, unable to compete with cheap imports, scale back the variety of vegetables they grow.

Helping young Filipinos rediscover the plant resources that grow in their backyards and communities can help foster plant sovereignty and literacy. This may entail roundabout methods, including playing into prestige aspects of food, such as those apparent in fine dining. When Michael was chancellor of the University of the Philippines, he encouraged hotel and restaurant management students to prepare special meals for important guests, emphasizing that he wanted to see menus that were local, meaning both grown locally and prepared with local condiments. The students were able to deliver beyond his expectations. In one instance, they sourced local macadamia nuts from the largely unknown small project of an entrepreneurial upper-class farmer, who explained that macadamia nuts are a major product in Thailand, the climate of which is similar to the Philippines'. At a lunch for visiting French gourmet chefs, the students were even able to roll out local craft beers, which one of the chefs, who was also a sommelier, rated favourably.

When Michael retired from being chancellor of the University of the Philippines in 2020, he became the head of Guang Ming College, which provides full scholarships to all students, who are from poor families. Among the courses offered as part of its Life Education mandate are Cultural Heritage, which includes substantial discussion of plants, and Plant-Based Culinary Practice in collaboration with the Manila-based Centre for Culinary Arts. During a culminating event for the latter course entitled Bahay Kubo, the students presented what they had learnt, using the title of the traditional song we referenced in Chapter 1 to celebrate the Philippines' lowly vegetables.

Michael will never forget the students' faces as they received praise from friends and sponsors of the college, which sparked a sense of pride in them. 'You can't eat pride of course,' Michael told the students, while briefing them on the many opportunities for developing the Philippines' food industry linked to agriculture and farmers, downstream and onwards to huge local and foreign markets. While researching this book, we uncovered examples of such opportunities which we shared with the university students. These included an upmarket producer in Hawaii incorporating *malunggay* oil into its cosmetics (Cole 2020) and a reformulation of *palapa*, a spice mix the Muslim Maranao in the southern Philippines traditionally use, now suddenly discovered by gourmet cooks, enhanced with shitake mushrooms (Morocco 2017).

A story that should be told more often is that of the popular Filipino snack, *nata de coco*. In 1949, Teodula Africa, a nutritionist working for the government, came up with the idea of developing a local delicacy in Laguna called *nata de piña*. 'Nata' comes from 'natar', meaning 'to swim' and 'piña' is pineapple. Africa's processing technique extracted bacterial cellulose from pineapple, which, when hardened, made a tasty and nutritious snack. Africa realized *nata de piña* was hard to produce because pineapple was not always available, so she perfected a technique for processing *nata de coco* instead, derived from the ubiquitous coconut. *Nata de coco* has since become an industry, imitated in other Asian countries where producers cash in on strong domestic demands, including in Japan, where it is mixed into drinks (Chinte-Sanchez 2009, 341).[9] Similar reappropriations and reformulations of Filipino plant processing techniques would bolster plant sovereignty, but they require accompanying public information and education campaigns about the systems that push ultra-processed, sweet, salty and fatty foods and an end to regulatory lapses in protecting health as a common good.

The challenges to plant sovereignty – aggressive marketing, cultural hegemony and environmental degradation – are overwhelming but the solutions will not come, if researchers and policymakers keep to their own narrow silos. The reductionism and fragmentation surrounding health, food, diets and nutrition and the attempts to reconfigure plants as packages of powders or pills we have described in this book are problematic not because such reconstitution is 'unnatural', but rather because it disrupts life at its core, food being the basis for kinship, community, survival, reproduction and growth.

When people turn to supplements, the social aspects of food are stripped away, disempowering them, so that they come to believe that they must buy these commodities to remain healthy (Yates-Doerr 2012). What makes the situation worse, however, is casting vitamins and supplements as necessary for health and wellbeing, as they insinuate themselves into our imageries of what makes for a healthy routine, popping that daily pill or making a health drink in the morning. Children watch and imitate their parents, internalizing not just the practice, but also the ideology of 'a pill for every ill' and, in more recent years, a pill, capsule, or sachet to prevent ills. Gone is the conviviality that comes with the leisurely meals the 'slow food' movement embraces (Petrini 2013). Gone too is the social bonding that comes with preparing foods. In 2023, the Philippine government declared that the last week of September is dedicated to the *Kainang Pamilya* (family meal). Government workers can go home at 3 p.m. to eat with their families. But how much bonding can occur if such meals are bought from a fast-food outlet or nutrition amounts to popping a multivitamin or supplement? And what is lost when family cooking is replaced by ultra-processed foods?

The field of neuro-gastronomy (Shepherd 2012) establishes that the flavours of food, while found in food molecules, are generated in brains. It is the brain that 'eats'. It processes not just food, but also a constellation of biological (encapsulated as 'taste' or 'flavour') and social (what makes something 'tasty' or 'flavourful') senses and meanings. Taste, in this analysis, is no longer one of the senses, the gustatory, but a convergence of the visual, the olfactory and the tactile. In Filipino (and in sister languages spoken in Southeast and South Asia), people refer to *lasa* (or *rasa*), a total eating experience that goes beyond sweet, salty, bitter, sour and umami (poorly translated as savoury) and instead invokes combinations of these: the interplay of which produces additional *lasa*. The delight people experience eating Asian cuisines, inter alia, are attributed to their boldness in combining sweet and sour and salty to produce additional flavours. The importance of texture is likewise tantamount. Filipino vegetarians like Michael no longer talk about missing the meatiness of meat, but occasionally missing the crackling of *chicharon*, appropriately called 'pork cracklings' in English, with their texture that is audible – and tasty.

Taste, then, is also social.[10] Here, we refer to the way the sensory attributes combine to deem food good or delicious (Mann and Mol 2019). In many cultures, including in the Philippines and the Netherlands, the word for tasty (*lekker* in Dutch) describes not just food, but also sex. The Tagalog *sarap*, the Ilokano *name*, the Cebuano (and other Visayan languages) *lami* are declared over and over, after a meal and after sex – the verdict regarding not just the meal or the act but the accumulated social experiences and interactions. In the Philippines, 'tasty' may compliment a range of food-related activities, including cultivation, preparation, processing, preservation, fermentation and myriad ways of cooking.

The social dimensions of cooking are well studied and comprise a key component of plant and food sovereignty. Many people have memories of grandmothers, mothers, aunts and great aunts cooking without recipes or measuring devices, their knowledge passed down through the communal cooking itself, while the men and boys were exiled from the kitchen. The pleasure one experiences while eating also depends on the people with whom one dines, which was made painfully apparent during the recent COVID-19 pandemic, when so many ate alone. Moreover, while the joys of eating (and drinking) tend to be tied to family and friends – a group activity – cultural norms define the times one should eat alone, or silently, or not eat at all – a reverence that adds to the appreciation of food.

The 'Mediterranean diet', a term that is inaccurate because it subsumes the very diverse diets consumed around the Mediterranean Sea under one name, is often cited as healthy because of the low incidence of cardiovascular diseases in that region. Some common features of the diet, although still varied, are high consumption of fruits and vegetables, more fish than meat, and, the media's favourite, red wine and olive oil. Less is written about the social aspects of Mediterranean meals that also contribute to it being 'healthy'. The Mayo Clinic website at least acknowledges the social: 'Other important elements of the Mediterranean diet are sharing meals with family and friends, enjoying a glass of red wine and being physically active' (Mayo Clinic 2019). The importance of sharing meals resonates with Filipinos, who routinely greet each other with 'Kumain ka na?' (Have you eaten?) or 'Kain na' (Come and eat with us), if a visitor happens to drop by at mealtime. Meals in the Philippines, too, may be long and animated, and, among traditional families, cannot begin (especially dinners), until all members of the family are present. There are likewise the numerous occasions for celebrations, with even longer meals and festivities.

As mentioned in Chapter 1, we are inspired by visionary government agencies, such as the Ministry of Health in Brazil, which published guidelines that contained as a central message to 'unpack less, and peel and cook more' (Monteiro and Jaime 2020, 95). Peeling and cooking more refers to consuming unprocessed foods, fruits and vegetables and the Brazilian staple, beans and rice with modest amounts of animal protein. The Brazilian Ministry of Health dietary guidelines further called for attention to 'circumstances – time, focus, place and company – which influence how foods are metabolized by the body and also the pleasure afforded by eating' (Secretariat of Health Care 2015, 11). The message to eat unprocessed foods met with fierce opposition from large food corporations.

Eating 'whole foods', that is, mainly plant-based foods: grains, cereals, fruits and vegetables that preferably traverse the shortest possible distance from farm to table, is gaining traction. But there is a danger of reductionism, if we do not couple eating whole foods with an awareness of health as encompassing the physical, the emotional and the social. All of these we must nurture not just with whole foods, but also by eating in a way that embraces an ethos of cultural values, practices, caring and coming together. That means questioning the encroachment of reductionist metabolic shifts, such as vitamins and supplements, and introducing alternatives to them to our daily lives, finding every possible opportunity not just to eat healthily but to think healthily, that is, neuro-gastronomically.

We have to ask, given the sociality of food consumption, if there can be joy in swallowing a capsule, a pill, or a powdered drink. It is a question we ask in hospital settings with regard to nutritional supplements, some lifesaving, life-sustaining ones such as total parenteral nutrition (TPN), which intravenously administers vital nutrients to post-surgical and terminally ill patients. Some of us who have had to sign an advance directive to move a loved one into palliative care have paused at the question of whether to withhold such nutritional supplements at the end of life. Even if we know it is all liquid, or even an intravenous feed, we think twice: is it right to withhold this nutrition? What then with these multivitamins and supplements, tasteless and texture-less, yet packed with promises? There is no joy in taking them. But they raise hopes, and that is what makes them so morally unacceptable because people spend down their very limited budgets. Our fear is that taking vitamins and supplements is becoming naturalized, normalized, when it ought not to be. Consuming a sachet of sugar is not healthy, even if spiced with bits of vegetables. The money spent on glorified pills and sachets could instead feed a child a nutritious meal.

5. Planetary health

The urgency of climate change, now appropriately called the climate emergency, is growing. The situation calls us to lay bare the links between environmental problems and the crises packaged plants and metabolic rifts generate and to seek solutions around One Health, a concept that emphasizes the inter-relationships among human, veterinary and environmental health. Challenges to One Health and plant sovereignty include not just global warming, but also the large number of endangered species. The Philippine government's Department of Environment and Natural Resources (2017) has a list of endangered plants that includes several species Filipinos have historically used as food and medicine. The number is probably significantly higher, considering that so much indigenous knowledge was lost because traditional healers were suppressed. In addition to healers' expert knowledge, general knowledge of plants in families has declined, adversely affecting intergenerational transmission. Moreover, plants are disappearing not just from forests, but from backyards as well. Lately, when Michael asks medicinal plants vendors in the Quiapo Market about certain flora, they reply, 'Mahirap hanapin' ('They are hard to find'). Recognition of the connection between the loss of biodiversity and that of medicinal plants dates back to the late twentieth century. Huxtable's (1992, 1) article, 'Pharmacology of extinction', warns: 'The fact that science will never know what has been lost does not lessen the significance of this loss.'

    Dietary changes can affect the health of populations, notably, their cholesterol levels and risk for cardiovascular disease and metabolic syndrome (Rico-Campà et al. 2019). Beyond the health of individuals though, there is now recognition that dietary changes, especially a shift away from meat products and toward plant-based food, can help address the problems of climate change caused by greenhouse gas emissions. The usual example used is that of cattle, which as ruminants release large amounts of methane, one of the problematic greenhouse gas emissions that contribute to global warming. As early as 2014, Reynolds et al. (2014) employed innovative methods to analyse the impact of hypothetical shifts towards more plant-based diets on greenhouse gas emissions, demonstrating that dietary changes can contribute to reducing the climate emergency.

In 2019, the Intergovernmental Panel on Climate Change (IPCC) issued a report, *Land and Climate Change*, that included a chapter on food security, discussing how existing food production systems are contributing to climate change and food insecurity. Among other recommendations, the report called for 'healthier and more sustainable diets' (Mbow et al. 2019).

The Philippine government's National Academy of Science and Technology (NAST) organized an unprecedented webinar on 8 February 2021, entitled 'Feeding Metro Manila in 2050: Attaining a just, sustainable and healthy food system', with speakers from the fields of agriculture and nutrition. The webinar was notable in its push for a 'planetary health diet', initially proposed by an EAT-*Lancet* Commission, that emphasizes whole grains, fruits and vegetables, but allows for some meat, dairy and fish, and a daily 2,500-calorie intake (see Willett et al. 2019).

During the webinar, representatives of the usually conservative NAST embraced the need for justice and sustainability in eating. The speakers kept returning to the question of what should come first: a change in people's consumption patterns or a change in government policies and structures. Online participants also responded to this question and most said, 'a change in people's consumption patterns'. The speakers also favoured this response, arguing that this transformation could happen slowly over time, between the present and the year 2050. The participants thus devolved the responsibility for non-sustainable foodscapes from governments to consumers via their dietary choices (Guthman 2007; Guthman and DuPuis 2006).

The choice should not be between consumer culture and structural change. The two must go hand in hand. The NAST webinar participants could not have illustrated this point more clearly than they did during an unexpected discussion of mung beans, a food often associated with poor people. Advocates of the planetary health diet advocated wide cultivation of mung beans because they are low in cost and high in protein. Yet, the open forum's older participants – who included the country's most respected scientists – warned against consuming mung beans because they are high in uric acid and aggravate gout. Fortunately, one speaker did a quick internet search and announced that this was a misconception. Mung beans are not high in uric acid.

During the NAST webinar, there was also a prolonged discussion of brown rice. Consumption of brown rice in the Philippines is low because Filipinos tend to consider it less tasty and 'dirtier' than white rice. All the webinar participants seemed to acknowledge that brown rice is healthier than white rice. They also noted that brown rice is more expensive than white, an irony considering that white rice is the product of milling, an additional technological process that entails expense. Yet, brown rice's cost is high because demand is low. However, there was no discussion of the skewing of rice consumption towards imported varieties, each with their own consumer-pleasing qualities. Filipinos like American long-grain rice for its texture or Japanese and Thai rice varieties for their stickiness. Only in recent years has a revival of interest in indigenous upland varieties expanded beyond brown to include purple and red rice. These varieties usually grow organically and have lower yields per hectare than the 'Green Revolution' varieties that produce a high yield but require water irrigation, pesticides and fertilizers. Upland varieties can cost twice as much as regular varieties, but are still cheaper than US, Japanese and Thai imports.

To reinstate plant sovereignty, we require integrated approaches that link health, nutrition and agriculture to each other (DuPuis and Goodman 2005; Guthman 2007). So many structural changes are necessary that both government agencies and the private sector must initiate them. Learning from the past, piecemeal approaches – such as school gardens cultivating vegetables and medicinal plants, even when required by the Department of Education – have only limited impact due to the onslaught of advertisements for ultra-processed foods, vitamins and supplements. Governments should incentivize the production of healthy foods and tightly regulate the promotion of unhealthy ones. If they do not ban such products altogether, then they should at least impose 'sin taxes', as the Philippines has done on sugary soft drinks.

Establishing a planetary health diet and rediscovering indigenous foods are still topics that primarily interest people in upper socioeconomic classes. Even so, the fact that many rural markets still stock local varieties of vegetables and fruits, as well as local spices and condiments, often sold for a pittance, is a source of hope. Ask young Filipinos about these plant varieties, however, and their knowledge of them is likely to be scant, which takes us back to the need for plant literacy.

We have a long way to go to achieve plant sovereignty and literacy among different sectors and age groups in the Philippines. The planetary health concept is useful to our advocacy for plant literacy and sovereignty because it identifies dietary changes as not just concerning individuals, but indeed the entire planet, and the need to reconfigure health, eating and the ways we cultivate food. The inclusion of plant-based diets in environmental conservation campaigns, as outlined in a policy framework the United Nations Food and Agricultural Organization has developed (Burlingame et al. 2010), is encouraging. However, we cannot lose sight of the ways in which cultural hegemony and the political contexts influence peoples' food choices.

For decades, the Philippine government has red-tagged (identified as part of the communist insurgency) environmental conservationists because conservation presents challenges to the continuing expansion of agribusiness, mining and other commercial interests, particularly into the ancestral lands of indigenous peoples. Global Witness (2019), an international environmental advocacy group, labelled the Philippines 'the deadliest country' because of the high number of killings of environmental defenders, with some 118 deaths between 2016 and 2019. A quintessential example of this is the case of Leonardo Co, acknowledged as the country's foremost expert in medicinal botany, gunned down in November 2020 while working in the field by soldiers who claimed they thought he was a guerilla. No member of the military has been brought to trial.

6. Social solidarity and justice in food and nutrition

The COVID-19 pandemic has highlighted the importance of dealing with metabolic rifts, with the lockdown initially causing urban areas in the Philippines to be cut off from fresh food supplies. COVID-19 exposed the fault lines in societies all over the world, with marginalized groups suffering much more from the pandemic than non-marginalized ones. (For an analysis of governance amid social inequities during the pandemic in the Philippines, see Tan 2024.)

Early on, despite the lockdowns, entire upper- and middle-class Filipino neighbourhoods contracted farmers to transport their food directly to the gates of their communities. Residents would send a list of the fruits and vegetables they wanted to the farmer's association.

The farmers would then truck in the produce each weekend, although they were not allowed into the subdivisions.

The poor, meanwhile, found themselves penalized many times over. Lockdown orders were more strictly enforced among the poor than the wealthy. This included food vendors, who took the risk of circulating their produce on pushcarts, only to have the police confiscate both their carts and goods, and then fine them. It was the poor, too, whose mobility was most grossly affected. Public transportation was completely halted during the first six weeks of the lockdown in urban areas and then slowly restored, although, even in 2021, it remained limited. The poor had to walk to work and to buy groceries. The elderly, who were banned from leaving their homes, were also significantly affected, not just in terms of accessing food, but also medicine (although those with cars got around the ban, since enforcers could not stop every vehicle for inspection).

In an extraordinary display of social solidarity, one young woman, Patricia Non, in Quezon City, set up a community pantry that handed out free food. She asked people to take the food on an honour system based on need. The government immediately red-tagged her, that is, labelled her a communist. However, in defiance of the government's threats, other communities followed suit and set up their own community pantries.

Early during the pandemic, people began to do backyard gardening, leading to a coining of the term 'plantdemic'. For the middle and upper classes, gardening was mostly an anti-stress activity. They tended to plant ornamentals and exotic plants, although some began to cultivate vegetables as well. The poor planted mostly vegetables and, we discovered during our research, medicinal plants. The visibility of socio-economic class differentiation increased during the plantdemic, when managers of some of the upper- and middle-class subdivisions reiterated the biased perception of agriculture as déclassé in their reminders, mentioned above, that residents were bound to contracts that prohibited the growing of fruits and vegetables in their backyards. There was no such ban in lower-income residential districts and certainly none in rural areas.

One of our researchers, Aaron Joseph Santos (2021), submitted a comprehensive report on backyard gardening in a semi-urban, semi-rural district in Zamboanga City, about 1,300 kilometres south of Manila. There, people intensified the backyard gardening activities, in which they had already engaged before the pandemic, with some distinct changes. First, residents planted more vegetables for consumption. Some families planted more vegetables to sell or to barter for other essential needs.

Those who increased vegetable production during the pandemic claimed that eating vegetables would boost their resistance to disease. Second, residents planted more medicinal plants, including several touted in the mass media and by neighbours as possibly preventing COVID-19. Some of these plants, primarily those traditionally used for respiratory ailments, like ginger, received frequent mention in media outlets.

Planting ginger and other foods and medicines may seem futile efforts to combat COVID-19, but they have symbolic importance: they are an active response to helplessness and despair. The pandemic brought to light a sense that people must prepare themselves for emergencies, especially in the Philippines, which had 317 climate-related disasters between 2000 and 2019, the highest rate in the world (Eckstein et al. 2021, 13–14). These events include typhoons, earthquakes, volcanic eruptions, and in 2020, COVID-19.[11]

Particularly relevant to our topic, Sta. Maria (2020), a historian who writes about food, published a thought-provoking article (cited in Chapter 1) that urges us to recognize the connections between culinary heritage and disaster risk reduction. She underlines the Philippines' vulnerability to disasters, warning of the need to develop the means for 'meta-feeding for meta-disasters' yet to come. She also laments the nation's dependence on foreign food assistance during emergencies. Examining Filipino culinary heritage, Sta. Maria introduces historical accounts from the sixteenth century onwards that describe local methods of preparing foods for long journeys and military expeditions, including Filipinos' responses to Spanish and American colonial incursions. One such account states: 'The rice [wrapped in banana leaves] can partner with a brined egg brought, raw or roasted fish freshly caught, or whatever is sourced during the journey' (2020, 52). Sta. Maria correctly points to other *binalot* – wrapped staples, including boiled yam, sweet potato, corn in the husk and fresh or boiled banana – as 'Philippine portable sustenance' and expresses concern about the growing difficulty of accessing traditional foods: 'When low forests, mangroves and beach forests were still lush, there was plenty of food for free picking' (2020, 52). She thus calls for integrating botanicals into disaster preparedness planning, including planting vital food 'around evacuation camps and along evacuation routes' (2020, 48). Sta. Maria also highlights that 'palatability' should be considered as part of food security and emergency responses.

We mentioned above the urban agriculture project our colleague Aaron Joseph Santos studied in the southern city of Zamboanga. Launched by a private citizen named Muneer Hines, the project was a collaboration between the Sanguniaang Kabataan (Youth Council), the City Agriculturist and a group called Kids Who Farm, which allocates land to young people to plant vegetables that they can then sell directly from the gardens or online. When the project's relevance to food sovereignty became apparent during the pandemic, the local government began to implement it throughout the city. Santos' research respondents stated that the national government's *ayuda* ('help', the Filipino-Spanish word for food assistance) was inadequate because it was unpalatable, and that their own gardens were a better alternative.

The key to developing sustainable plant sovereignty is community empowerment. This is not just a pipe dream: during COVID-19, many indigenous communities practised self-reliance against overwhelming odds (Banning 2020; Global Environment Facility 2020). In the Philippines, a shining example comes from Sadanga, a town in Mountain Province, 400 kilometres north of Manila. Sadanga turned down aid from the national government. The mayor declared that the community could deal with the pandemic on its own, it had mechanisms for sharing food, and even suggested that the authorities should divert Sadanga's *ayuda* to the poor in urban areas (Arcilla 2020).

Another example involves schools organized by the *lumad* indigenous communities in Mindanao. In these schools, students plant their own fruits and vegetables with the goal of promoting self-reliance. The students spend time learning from and connecting to their elders to acquire plant literacy, knowledge that would otherwise be lost. Michael developed close friendships with many *lumad* students when the University of the Philippines Diliman agreed to provide shelter for them, as they fled militarization in Mindanao (Dino and Sta. Cruz 2020). He observed that the students consciously brought and procured fresh foods when they participated in protests against their displacement. No instant noodles for them. He visited their camps several times at the University of the Philippines Diliman and ate what Filipino upper classes would call gourmet dishes, upland rice and vegetables in which the meat was a condiment, the reverse of dishes in the lowlands, where the vegetables are almost decorative. The difference from how the upper classes eat is that these *lumad* students were not engaging in 'healthy eating', but rather survival eating and preservation of their heritage, while they pursued social justice. The students complained that, at the University of the Philippines, their diets became less diverse because there were so many ingredients they had at home that they were unable to procure there. They spoke of how they missed running around their villages and picking up food from the side of the road or plucking it from the trees.

We move from the Philippines to the other side of the Pacific Ocean to view another example that shows how the pandemic presented opportunities to rethink our metabolic shifts and our policies around food, nutrition and health. In late 2020, *The New Yorker*[12] and the nongovernmental organization, Amazon Frontlines[13] collaborated on a film project documenting the response of the Siekopai indigenous community in Ecuador to COVID-19. The film depicts village elders recounting oral histories dating back to the fifteenth century that include accounts of the intrusion of Western colonialism. Diseases decimated their community and now they number only 1,500. Their natural resources have also been exhausted. The Siekopai's forests were exploited for their rubber and other tree gums, their perfumes and essential oils, their wildlife that yielded furs, their timber, their petroleum and gold and, recently, the monocrop cultivation of palm oil. They are disappearing into historical accounts as just another region in the Americas with exotic and valuable plant resources.

Even before the pandemic, Siekopai filmmaker Jimmy Piaguaje and his cousin Ribaldo had launched a social media project to document his nation's use of medicinal plants. A decade earlier, Ecuadorian university researchers (Cerón et al. 2011) confirmed that the Siekopai still use more than 1,000 plant species for various purposes, including 181 for medicines. In a series of videos, the two young men rediscover their community's medicinal plants from elders' accounts of plant selection (including gendered descriptions of the same plant species), proper harvesting times and techniques, preparation, and consumption, all of which activities are communal and vested with a multitude of social meanings.

This film project became integrated into a large community gardening project focusing on medicinal flora, with Amazonian elders transmitting knowledge to the young about plants, both forest plants and cultivars their ancestors had domesticated. The young people's initial fascination with medicinal plants was only the beginning. They developed interest in other aspects of their indigenous culture as well. Although all this took place in the Amazon, it was communicated with the outside world via videos and discussions on Facebook. The importance of this rediscovery of botanical knowledge became more dramatic during the pandemic, which did reach the Siekopai's villages. Citing government inaction with regard to stopping COVID-19's spread, the Siekopai returned to their shamans and local knowledge. They made a long trip along the Amazon River to their heartland, near the Ecuadorian–Peruvian border, where they found medicinal plants that tackle fever. The plants had grown scarce, but the Siekopai were able to find enough to bring back to their home village, prepare communally, and distribute not just to fellow Siekopai, but also to members of four other indigenous communities. They had no illusions that the medicine would cure COVID-19; instead, the long journey and preparation and distribution of the resulting medicine symbolized a quest for plant sovereignty – an effort to regain control over the group's lives and future.

It is striking that people in these video clips consumed the medicinal plant fresh. No processing of it into pills and, so far, no entrepreneurs trying to obtain the plant and sell it, perhaps capitalizing on its Amazon River provenance to market and exoticize the product. The Siekopai prepared and consumed the plant in a way that reclaimed their heritage, serving as a reminder to the world of the importance, in COVID-19 times, of sovereignty over food, medicines, plants and land. This video project made us realize that supplement promoters are particularly aggressive in the way they capitalize on exoticism and potentially fictionalized provenance. By stripping the plants of their contexts and reconstituting them, repackaging them into sugary sachets, manufacturers deprive communities and nations of their heritage, propagating false hopes and dependence on placebos and pills.

In our first chapter, we recounted that, in the 1930s, the National Federation of Women's Clubs promoted backyard gardening in tandem with various government agencies. Given the threat of war, the sense of urgency was strong. The women's federation had a stern admonition: 'Remember the wasting of foodstuffs today is as dastardly a crime as treason' (Sta. Maria 2020, 59). Some 90 years later, that admonition still resonates. We have seen the adverse effects of 'packaged plants' – as vitamins, supplements and ultra-processed foods – on human nutrition, on the welfare of communities and on the natural environment. Valuable food is indeed wasted when fresh whole fruits and vegetables, together with knowledge of and skills for maintaining food security and sovereignty, are devalued, even squandered. It is treason indeed, sometimes even disguised as nationalism, in calls for Filipinos to patronize their own plants, repackaged of course. It is treason, too, in its exploitation of Filipinos' fears and hopes.

Our book describes a centuries-old planetary journey of various cultures in the elusive quest for food, spices and medicines from a treasure trove of thousands of botanicals. The journey continues. But the planet's botanical bounties will best serve humanity as a common heritage, linked to ecosystems and cultures and framed by social solidarity and social justice, not just in terms of how we eat, but also in the very ways we think about food and health.

Notes

1. This documentary follows Leo, a dealer of First Vita Plus, who tried to convince people to buy his supplements, the marketing for which proclaims it will 'treat and prevent all health conditions and make for a better life'. It features charismatic company officials who suggest that Leo can become a millionaire, if he works relentlessly to recruit new dealers and sell the product, while the government warns that the food supplements have no proven therapeutic value. It also presents Flor, who stopped being a distributor for First Vita Plus. She embraced plant sovereignty by growing vegetables and fruits in her backyard and by sharing recipes with Leo. The film can be viewed for classroom use at https://www.chemicalyouth.org/#/projects/sweet-medicine.
2. See www.chemicalyouth.org.
3. See, for instance, The Clara Clinic (2024), 'Benefits of IV vitamin therapy for this cold flu season'. https://theclaraclinic.com/blog-home/benefits-of-iv-vitamin-therapy-for-this-cold-flu-season (Accessed 5 June 2024).
4. This term features in the title of an event the Indigenous Initiatives Office of Queens University, Canada organized in 2020, Indigenous Plant Sovereignty, an annual indigenous knowledge and research-focused symposium. See https://www.queensu.ca/eventscalendar/calendar/events/22nd-annual-indigenous-symposium-indigenous-plant-sovereignty (Accessed 5 June 2024).
5. Joel Abiong was one of many children of seasonal hacienda workers in Negros who, amid the global depression of sugar prices in 1985, went hungry. He and many others died of starvation.
6. See Health Canada (2022) (https://www.canada.ca/en/health-canada/news/2022/06/government-of-canada-unveils-new-front-of-package-nutrition-symbol.html) for a lay version of the government's new labelling policies.
7. This has caused companies such as Avon and Tupperware in several countries, including the US and the Philippines, to distance and differentiate themselves from multilevel schemes by calling themselves direct sellers, with their own organizations and ethical criteria. The Philippine government should incorporate these ethical criteria into its legislation.
8. Edelman at al. (2014) show that food sovereignty is a fluid concept, which may be variously defined. Food sovereignty is often contrasted with food security. The latter emphasizes access to adequate nutrition for all, regardless of the food's origin (Gartaula et al. 2018).
9. Besides serving as a snack food, *nata de coco* alerted researchers to the possibility of developing cellulose for wound dressings.
10. Anthropologists of food have long documented what we eat, how we eat, and why we eat, in the process eliciting the symbolism of food, its relation to social status and prestige, and the socialization behind each meal or snack (Mintz and Du Bois 2002).
11. The Philippines is often hit by natural disasters. In January 2020, Taal Volcano, just south of Metro Manila, had a major eruption. Two months later, the World Health Organization declared COVID-19 a pandemic.
12. 'Fighting COVID-19 with Ancestral Wisdom in the Amazon', a transcript of a film in *The New Yorker*, 11 December 2020. See https://www.newyorker.com/video/watch/coronavirus-threatens-the-people-of-the-amazon.
13. 'The Siekopai's Ancestral Remedy to the Pandemic in the Amazon: Behind-the-scenes of the Siekopai's *New Yorker* video', December 2020. See https://amazonfrontlines.org/chronicles/siekopai-plants-medicine-covid-amazon/.

Photo Essay 2:
Bringing plant sovereignty to town

Co-written with Denice Salvacion
and Francesca Mauricio

We end this book with a second photo essay, which illustrates how women's groups are collectively taking up urban gardening – the plantdemic we refer to in Chapter 7. Michael and Anita have embarked on a new research project called Embodied Ecologies, which involves fieldwork among two groups of urban farmers: Taga-Marikina Ako (TMA), a plot adjacent to the communities where Anita conducted fieldwork in the 1980s, and the Loakan-Apugan Sustainability and Livelihood Association (LASLA) in Baguio City, a town in the Cordillera Mountains 400 kilometres north of Marikina.

In summer 2023, after the COVID-19 lockdowns, Anita visited the gardens with project research assistants Francesca Mauricio (TMA) and Denice Salvacion (LASLA), who are engaged in long-term, collaborative ethnography with these women's groups in the context of Embodied Ecologies.

Photo 1 shows the TMA garden, a narrow stretch of rocky land, longer than it is wide, that makes room for itself behind a large concrete building and a creek. Anita recognizes the creek from when she did fieldwork in the 1980s. It has not changed – the water still has an unpleasant smell.

The garden itself hosts a variety of plants. Different shades of green sprouting from the soil or hanging from the walls grab our attention. The TMA members show us around, pointing out common Philippines vegetables: *sitaw* (beans), *ampalaya* (bitter gourd), *kamote* (cassava), *talong* (eggplant), *sili* (chilli pepper) and okra – note how many of

Photo 1. The TMA Garden grows along a heavily polluted creek. Source: Anita Hardon.

Photo 2. *Ampalaya* (bitter gourd), a common Filipino vegetable. Source: Anita Hardon.

these vegetables are in the lyrics of the 'Bahay Kubo' song we quoted in Chapter 1 of this book. Our interlocutors use the adjective *masarap* (delicious) frequently, while enthusiastically showing us their produce and sharing their methods for cooking the vegetables. See Photos 2 and 3.

Photo 3. *Sitaw* (beans), a common Filipino vegetable. Source: Anita Hardon.

Photo 4 shows a TMA member harvesting the leaves of *camote*, a green leafy vegetable that nutritionists in the Philippines value for its high iron content. Another woman who is harvesting tells us the garden is more than *just* a garden. It is a form of stress relief. She recently lost her husband and the garden serves as a quiet place. Here, even for a short while, she can be just a gardener, not a mother with four hungry mouths to feed.

Photo 4. Harvesting *camote* tops. Source: Anita Hardon.

Photo 5 shows the tall mango tree that marks the border of the garden. The TMA members value the tree for the cool shade it offers. The dense urban community where they live can become suffocatingly hot, much hotter than Anita remembers. The photo also depicts two active TMA members posing for us.

Photo 5. The mango tree provides coolness and shade. Source: Anita Hardon.

Photo 6. Planting vegetables together in fresh soil beds. Source: Francesca Mauricio.

In Photo 6, several women are busy tending to small, freshly planted vegetables. They are all wearing their TMA t-shirts. Having started during the pandemic, the TMA urban farming project was formally launched in March 2023 with the support of the mayor through the Department of Social Welfare and Development's Cash-for-Work Program. The women used their own money to make t-shirts to promote their association. While the land was granted to them free of charge, it is not exactly the most arable soil. Most of it is gravel. The gardeners have no choice but to provide fertile soil themselves. But soil costs money, something not always readily available. So sometimes the gardeners take soil from the banks of the creek beside their garden, braving the unpleasant smell and less-than-clean water.

The women tell us they want to produce a crop free from harmful chemicals, something they would not be afraid to feed their children. Further probing revealed that this was a decision also influenced by precarity. The women make natural fertilizers from food scraps – usually banana peels left to soak in water and then used to water the plants. This is more cost effective than buying chemical fertilizers, which they cannot afford. The water from the creek is considered too dirty. Photo 7 shows two TMA members watering plants with this fertilizer.

Photo 7. Watering vegetables with a fertilizer made from banana peels. Source: Anita Hardon.

The women have more to learn about natural forms of pest control. While most of their vegetables do well, they complain that snails have eaten the *petchay* (a variety of Chinese cabbage). They will look up what to do on the internet. Most of what the women know about the garden and gardening comes from trial and error: testing out things they find on YouTube or techniques they learn by word of mouth and seeing if they work.

LASLA is the second group with which we are collaborating in the Embodied Ecologies project. Their urban garden is 400 kilometres north of Marikina in the mountainous Cordillera Region of the Philippines. In Chapter 1 we referred to ethnobotanical studies that reveal this region's extreme biodiversity.

LASLA has much more experience cultivating vegetables than TMA. The image below (Photo 8) is an artistic rendering of the impressive home garden (*baeng* in the local Ibaloi language) of a woman named Claire. She started LASLA during the COVID pandemic, creating a network of urban gardeners from among her close friends and neighbours. The association has at least 30 household members. When we visited, Claire welcomed us to her place, introducing it to us as a '*probinsya sa loob ng Baguio*' (province – a term Filipinos use to refer to rural living – inside Baguio city). Proud of her rural roots as a farmer's daughter, Claire learned how to farm by observing when she was growing up in villages in the Cordillera Mountains.

Her *baeng* is an eclectic mix of plants ranging from herbs to trees to crops and ornamental vegetation.

Photo 8. A creative cartography of Claire's baeng. Illustration by Denice Salvacion.

Before, Claire said, there were 'no cash crops' and farmers practised *ub-ubo*, a distinctively Kankanaey term that roughly translates to 'working together'. LASLA hosts a Facebook group, through which the gardeners share knowledge and experiences with various gardening techniques (see Photo 9). LASLA members frequently post images and stories online to share their gardening experiences with each other. They exchange tips and sell and trade plants, seeds, and produce and promote alternative practices like supporting blue peas with thread instead of sticks. Through this network and during seminars and seed exchanges, LASLA also share free traditional seeds with other urban gardeners interested in growing their own. LASLA's Facebook page also serves as a learning site for less experienced gardeners, such as the TMA group members.

Photo 9. Screenshots of posts in LASLA's Facebook group. Source: Corazon Loste.

Claire gives us a tour of her *baeng* while picking vegetables and herbs to make up our lunch (see Photo 10). Her garden, as she describes it, is 'sari-sari' (mix-mix). Anita reflects on how different this 'sari-sari' is from the products sold in sari-sari stores.

Photo 10. Sari-sari vegetables harvested from Claire's garden. Source: Denice Salvacion.

As we walk through her garden, Claire mentions several times ways in which she makes a conscious effort to move particular plants from one area to another, whether for partial shading, placing them closer to a water source or pairing plants in certain ways to protect vulnerable plants from onslaughts of insects.

In her garden, she has some 30 herbs, around 40 fruits, and hundreds of ornamental plants, which she has detailed and keeps track of in a small catalogue made up of a stack of index cards neatly tied together with a ribbon. See Photo 11.

Photo 11. The notes where Claire lists the plants growing in her garden. Source: Denice Salvacion.

While we stroll through the garden, Claire encourages us to use our senses 'tignan mo' (look here) or 'amuyin mo' (smell it). See Photo 12. The plants she grows cleanse her body, she says, which, as a breast cancer survivor, she values. The plants also are free, she says. She spends much less than before on groceries.

Photo 12. Close-ups of the plants Claire shows us. Source: Denice Salvacion and Claire.

Her organic practice involves using fermented fruit juice, vermiculture, chicken manure, composting, and a fungus called trichoderma to improve the quality of the soil (see Photo 13). She also carefully observes her plants to know which ones need to be combined with anti-pest plants and which ones are in need of spraying.

Photo 13. Organic practices included fertilizers made using fermented fruits and plants from the garden. Source: Denice Salvacion.

Claire would like it if the garden not only supported daily meals, but also provided for the livelihood needs of the community. How can the young mothers of LASLA become more involved in cultivating their gardens, when they have to grapple with hunger on a daily basis? She is exploring the possibility of manufacturing organic foods out of their produce to serve as a source of income. The first project is to make sayote cupcakes (no sugar added) to sell at the Baguio Market. See Photos 14–16.

Photo 14. LASLA members cut up sayote aka chayote, that belongs to the gourd family and is a popular vegetable. Source: Claire.

In the future, the women hope also to sell the cupcakes to schools as healthy *meriendas* (snacks) for children. See Photo 15.

Photo 15. Cupcakes ready for packaging. Source: Claire.

Photo 16. Cupcakes sold at the Baguio Market. Source: Claire.

Collaborative learning

To support the efforts of these two urban farmers' groups, Michael and Anita allotted funding from the Embodied Ecologies project budget for a training session on agro-ecology in the organic garden of Guang Ming College, which Michael directs. The garden is run by an experienced 'nanay' (mother) whom Michael met at a field school of agro-ecological farmers. He invited her to become a teacher at the college to teach university students about agro-ecology.

We organized transport for TMA and LASLA members to visit the garden. Our interlocutors deeply valued the field trip since they rarely get a chance to leave their home turf. During the training sessions, Nanay Rose first shared the principles of agro-ecology: 'Everything is connected to everything else. Each meal is the result of labour: from the yeast, the egg, the sugar – each ingredient was worked on; a process that involves tilling the land, while grappling with the elements: heat, rain, dirt, and all. The ingredients are then processed in assembly lines and transported through expressways connecting the peripheries to the urban centre in large trucks; then, to the marketplace and onto our plates.'

She differentiated agro-ecological farming from this large-scale, ultra-processing food chains. We heard agreements from around the room during her lecture, whispers of 'tama [yan]' (that's right). Occasionally, someone pulled out a cell phone to take a photo of a slide, but generally, the room was quiet. The participants were attentive, their eyes fixed on the presentation.

The lectures were followed by hands-on-learning about how to make organic fertilizer. In Guang Ming's garden, Nanay Rose and one of her Guang Ming students pulled out tubs of fish and plant scraps and explained that scraps like these could easily be obtained from the public market for free or for a low price. The parts of a plant that grow quickly, such as the body of a banana tree or bamboo shoots, and overripe fruits are ideal for making fermented juices. She instructed the urban farmers to add molasses because it contains a healthy amount of sugar and other necessary minerals like calcium, magnesium, iron, and potassium. She then demonstrated how to mix the ingredients in a container, making sure to coat the fish or plant scraps in an even layer of molasses. After her demonstration, the rest of the gardeners took turns mixing, while others volunteered to prepare another batch of fertilizer. See Photos 17 and 18.

Nanay Rose explained that once the fermentation was finished, the mixture would be filtered, leaving behind a dark and slightly runny liquid. The organic fertilizers would then be useable. Two tablespoons

Photo 17. Making organic fertilizers. Source: Denice Salvacion.

Photo 18.   Making organic fertilizers. Source: Denice Salvacion.

per litre of water, sprayed onto the ground near the plant and on its stems and leaves. She encouraged the LASLA and TMA members to take the containers home and even handed out already-fermented bottled fertilizers for the groups to try out immediately.

After the workshop, some of the leaders reached out to us on Facebook, expressing their appreciation for connecting them with Nanay Rose. The participants in the agro-ecological training session shared that they had learned a lot and were eager to try out their new knowledge in their gardens. Both groups periodically shared photos of their gardens' progress through the group chat that emerged from the workshop. Some members signalled interest in having another get-together to visit each other's gardens and see their collaborative efforts to reclaim plant sovereignty.

References

Abe, Reika and Kazuhiro Ohtani. 2013. 'An ethnobotanical study of medicinal plants and traditional therapies on Batan Island, the Philippines'. *Journal of Ethnopharmacology* 145 (2): 554–65. https://doi.org/10.1016/j.jep.2012.11.029.

Adair, Linda S. and Barry Popkin. 2001. 'The CEBU Longitudinal Health and Nutrition Survey: History and major contributions of the project'. *Philippine Quarterly of Culture and Society* 29 (1/2): 5–3.

Afdhal, A. F. and R. L. Welsch. 1988. 'The rise of the modern jamu industry in Indonesia: A preliminary review'. In *The Context of Medicines in Developing Countries: Studies in pharmaceutical anthropology*, edited by S. van der Geest and S. Reynolds Whyte, 149–72. Dordrecht: Kulwer Academic Publishers.

Aguilar, Filomeno V. 2017. 'Colonial sugar production in the Spanish Philippines: Calamba and Negros compared'. *Journal of Southeast Asian Studies* 48: 237–61. https://doi.org/10.1017/S0022463417000066.

Alcina, Francisco Ignacio. 2005. *History of the Bisayan People in the Philippine Islands*. Lucio Gutierrez and Cantius J. Kobak (eds). Manila: University of Santo Tomas.

Ammakiw, Christina and Marymina Odiem. 2014. 'Availability, preparation and uses of herbal plants in Kalinga, Philippines'. *European Scientific Journal* 4. https://core.ac.uk/reader/328024040.

Ang, Monica. 2017. 'Korea and the Philippines: A comparative study of political leadership'. *Review of Korean Studies* 20 (1): 63–91.

Angeles-Agdeppa, Imelda, Yvonne M. Lenighan, Emma F. Jacquier, Marvin B. Toledo and Mario V. Capanzana. 2019. 'The impact of wealth status on food intake patterns in Filipino school-aged children and adolescents'. *Nutrients* 11 (12): 2910–16.

Arcilla, Gigie. 2020. 'Waiving relief food packs meant to give way to most needy: Mayor'. *Philippine News Agency*, 3 May. Accessed 6 June 2024. https://www.pna.gov.ph/articles/1101732.

Aronson, Jeffrey. 2017. 'Defining "nutraceuticals": Neither nutritious nor pharmaceutical'. *British Journal of Clinical Pharmacology* 83 (1): 8–19. https://doi.org/10.1111/bcp.12935.

Baker, P. and S. Friel. 2014. 'Processed foods and nutrition transition: Evidence from Asia'. *Obesity Review* 15 (7): 564–77.

Bankoff, Greg. 2013. 'Deep forestry: Shapers of the Philippine forest'. *Environmental History* 18 (3): 523–56.

Banning, Jolene. 2020. 'Why are Indigenous communities seeing so few cases of COVID-19?'. *Canadian Medical Association Journal* 192 (34): E993–4. https://doi.org/10.1503/cmaj.1095891.

Bauch, Nicholas. 2017. *A Geography of Digestion: Biotechnology and the Kellogg cereal enterprise*. Oakland: University of California Press.

Benosa, Sherma. 2020. 'Did Filipino "tingi" culture pave the way for plastic sachets in the Philippines?'. Break Free From Plastic. Accessed 11 December 2020. https://www.breakfreefromplastic.org/2020/07/14/did-filipino-tingi-culture-pave-the-way-for-plastic-sachets-in-the-philippines/.

Besnier, Niko. 2011. *On the Edge of the Global: Modern anxieties in a Pacific Island state*. Stanford, CA: Stanford University Press.

Bhattacharya, Ayon, Prashant Tiwari, Pratap K. Sahu and Sanjay Kumar. 2018. 'A review of the phytochemical and pharmacological characteristics of moringa oleifera'. *Journal of Pharmacy and Bioallied Sciences* 10 (4): 181–91. https://doi.org/10.4103/JPBS.JPBS_126_18.

Biehl, Joao. 2006. 'Global pharmaceuticals'. In *Global Pharmaceuticals: Ethics, markets, practices*, edited by A. Petryna, A. Lakoff and A. Kleinman, 206–39. Durham, NC: Duke University Press.

Blanco, Manuel Francisco. 1837. *Flora de Filipinas: Según el sistema sexual de Linneo*. Manila: Impr. de M. Sanchez.

Bown, Stephen. 2003. *Scurvy: How a surgeon, a mariner, and a gentlemen solved the greatest medical mystery of the Age of Sail*. New York: Thomas Dunne Books.

Briones, Roehlano, Ella Antonio, Celestino Habito, Emma Porio and Danilo Songco. 2017. 'Food security and nutrition: Strategic review in the Philippines'. Brain Trust Inc. (Study commissioned by the World Food Program). Accessed 6 June 2024. https://vdocuments.mx/strategic-review-food-security-and-nutrition-in-the-.html?page=2.

Bromley, D. G. 1995. 'Quasi-religious corporations: a new integration of religion and capitalism?'. In *Religion and the Transformations of Capitalism: Comparative approaches*, edited by R. Roberts, 135–60. London: Routledge.

Brooks, S. 2012. *Rice Biofortification: Lessons for global science and development*. London: Earthscan.

Brown, William. 1950. *Useful Plants of the Philippines*. 3 vols. Manila: Bureau of Print.

Burlingame, B., S. Dernini and Nutrition and Consumer Protection Division, FAO. 2010. *Sustainable Diets and Biodiversity: Directions and solutions for policy, research and action*. Proceedings of the International Scientific Symposium *Biodiversity and Sustainable Diets United Against Hunger*, 3–5 November, Rome. Accessed 6 June 2024. https://cgspace.cgiar.org/server/api/core/bitstreams/5c0d9ff8-44e1-4db6-af10-ef9c61d5fa80/content.

Burnby, J. and A. Bierman. 1996. 'The incidence of scurvy at sea and its treatment'. *Revue d'Histoire de la Pharmacie* 44 (312): 339–46. https://doi.org/10.3406/pharm.1996.6343.

Cabalza, Dexter. 2024. 'Public cautioned vs buying DOH-endorsed products'. *Philippine Daily Inquirer*, 20 February. Accessed 6 June 2024. https://www.pressreader.com/philippines/philippine-daily-inquirer-1109/20240220/281646785064987.

Cahn, Peter. 2006. 'Building down and dreaming up'. *American Ethnologist* 33 (1): 126–42. https://doi.org/10.1525/ae.2006.33.1.126.

Canfield, Matthew. 2022. 'The ideology of innovation: Philanthropy and racial capitalism in global food governance'. *Journal of Peasant Studies* 50 (6): 2381–405. https://doi.org/10.1080/03066150.2022.2099739.

Cantor, S. M. and M. B. Cantor. 1977. 'Socioeconomic factors in fat and sugar consumption'. In *The Chemical Senses and Nutrition*, edited by R. K. Morley and O. Maller, 429–46. https://doi.org/10.1016/B978-0-12-397850-9.50029-4.

Capanzana, Mario V., Divorah V. Aguila, Glen Melvin P. Gironella and Kristine V. Montecillo. 2018. 'Nutritional status of children ages 0–5 and 5–10 years old in households headed by fisherfolks in the Philippines'. *Archives of Public Health* 76 (24). https://doi.org/10.1186/s13690-018-0267-3.

Capanzana, Mario V., Gabriel Demombynes and Paul Gubbins. 2020. 'Why are so many children stunted in the Philippines?'. Policy Research Working Paper 9294. Washington, DC: World Bank.

Cerón, Carlos, Carmita Reyes and Pablo Yépez. 2011. 'Mil y más plantas de la Amazonia ecuatoriana utilizadas por los Secoyas'. *CINCHONIA* 11. https://revistadigital.uce.edu.ec/index.php/CINCHONIA/article/view/2363.

Chen, Nancy. 2009. *Food, Medicine and the Quest for Good Health: Nutrition, medicine and culture*. New York: Columbia University Press.

Chiang, Shun Nan. 2020. 'Transecting the fall and rise of brown rice – the historic encounters of the global food system, nutrition science, and malnutrition in the Philippines'. *Food, Culture and Society* 23 (2): 229–48. https://doi.org/10.1080/15528014.2019.1682889.

Chinte-Sanchez, Priscilla. 2009. *Philippine Fermented Foods: Principles and technology*. Quezon City: University of the Philippines Press.

Chua, Charlene, Chelsea Rae Mercadillo, Dana Kriselli Munoz and Ray John Salud. 2018. 'The perceived impacts of alternative food source (pagpag): Selected families in an urban poor community in the Philippines'. *Journal of Social Health* 1 (1):103–15. https://socialhealthjournal.ust.edu.ph/wp-content/uploads/2018/09/103-115-Chua-et-al.pdf.

Chua-Barcelo, Racquel Tan. 2014. 'Ethno-botanical survey of edible wild fruits in Benguet, Cordillera Administrative Region, the Philippines'. *Asian Pacific Journal of Tropical Biomedicine* 4 (1): S525–38. https://doi.org/10.12980/APJTB.4.201414B36.

Co, Leonard. 1977. *Manual on Some Philippine Medicinal Plants*. Quezon City: University of the Philippines Botanical Society.

Co, Leonard. 1989. *Common Medicinal Plants of the Cordillera Region: A trainor's [sic] manual for community-based health programs*. Baguio City: Chestcore.

Cohen, P. A. 2016. 'The supplement paradox: Negligible benefits, robust consumption'. *Journal of the American Medical Association* 316 (115): 1453–4. https://doi.org/10.1001/jama.2016.14252.

Cole, Jess. 2020. 'Hawaii's next wave of natural skin-care products'. *New York Times*, 11 December. Accessed 6 June 2024. https://www.nytimes.com/2020/12/11/t-magazine/hawaii-skincare-beauty.html.

Coleman, Simon. 2000. *The Globalisation of Charismatic Christianity*. Cambridge: Cambridge University Press.

Colin, Francisco. 2018. *Labor Evangelica, Ministerios Apostólicos de los Obreros de la Compañía de Jesús, Fundacion, y Progressos de Su Provincia en las Islas Filipinas*, vol 1. London: Forgotten Books (originally published in 1663).

Combs Jr, Gerald F. and James P. McClung. 2018. *The Vitamins: Fundamental aspects in nutrition and health*. 5th ed. Amsterdam: Academic Press.

Community-Based Monitoring System (CBMS). 2011. *The many faces of poverty*, vol. 2: *Palawan*. Accessed 6 June 2024. https://www.slideshare.net/slideshow/the-many-faces-of-poverty-palawan-volume-2-7865402/7865402.

Corazon, M. and D. Licyayo. 2018. 'Gathering practices and actual use of wild edible mushrooms among ethnic groups in the Cordilleras, Philippines'. In *Diversity and Change in Food Wellbeing: Cases from Southeast Asia and Nepal*, edited by A. Niehof, H. N. Gartaula and M. Quetulio-Navarra, 71–86. Wageningen: Wageningen Academic Publishers.

Coté, C. 2016. '"Indigenizing" food sovereignty: Revitalizing Indigenous food practices and ecological knowledges in Canada and the United States'. *Humanities* 5 (3): 57. https://doi.org/10.3390/h5030057.

Cruz, Arsenia J., Celeste C. Tanchoco and Consuelo L. Orense. 2011. 'Awareness, usage and perception of food supplements among adult residents in Metro Manila'. *Philippine Journal of Internal Medicine* 49 (1): 30–7.

Dalton, K. and M. J. Dalton. 1987. 'Characteristics of pyridoxine overdose neuropathy syndrome'. *Acta Neurologica Scandinavica* 76 (1): 8–11.

Daniels, M. C., Adair, L. S., Popkin B. M. and Truong, Y. K. 2009. 'Dietary diversity scores can be improved through the use of portion requirements: An analysis in young Filipino children'. *European Journal of Clinical Nutrition* 63: 199–208. https://doi.org/10.1038/sj.ejcn.1602927.

David, Lawrence and 12 others. 2014. 'Diet rapidly and reproducibly alters the human gut microbiome'. *Nature* 505 (7484): 559–63. https://doi.org/10.1038/nature12820.

Dayrit Manuel M., Liezel P. Lagrada, Oscar F. Picazo, Melahi C. Pons, Mario C. Villaverde, Walaiporn Patcharanarumol and Viroj Tangcharoensathien. 2018. *The Philippines Health System Review*. New Delhi: World Health Organization. https://www.jstor.org/stable/resrep28462.

Department of Environment and Natural Resources (Philippines). 2017. *Updated National List of Threatened Philippine Plants and their Categories*. DENR Administrative Order 2017–11. https://www.philippineplants.org/Resources/dao-2017-11.pdf.

Department of Health (Philippines). 1995. 'Department Circular No. 50-A, 1995'. Accessed 6 June 2024. https://www.officialgazette.gov.ph/1995/03/20/department-circular-no-50-a-1995/.

Department of Health (Philippines). 2017. 'Philippine Plan of Action for Nutrition 2017–2022. A Call to Urgent Action for Filipinos and Its Leadership'. Manila: National Nutrition Council. Accessed 6 June 2024. https://scalingupnutrition.org/sites/default/files/2022-06/national-nutrition-plan-philippines.pdf.

Department of Health, Food and Drug Administration (Philippines). 2015. 'FDA Memorandum Circular 2015-003. Reiteration of the FDA requirement for the change in the use of message/phrase "no approved therapeutic claim"'. Manila: Department of Health.

Department of Health, Food and Drug Administration (Philippines). 2020. FDA Advisory. Accessed 15 May 2024. https://www.fda.gov.ph/wp-content/uploads/2020/05/FDA-Advisory-No.2020-824.pdf.

Department of Science and Technology, Food and Nutrition Research Institute (Philippines). 2013. 8th National Nutrition Survey. Manila: Department of Science and Technology. Accessed 6 June 2024. https://yp.sg/wp-content/uploads/2017/06/8thNNS.pdf.

Desclaux, Alice. 2014. 'Ambivalence in cultural framing of cosmopolitan alternative "medicines" in Senegal'. *Curare* 37 (2): 53–69.

Dino, Nina and Maxine Sta. Cruz. 2020. 'Dwindling numbers: Lumad schools continue to suffer closures, attack during pandemic'. *Rappler*, 18 September. Accessed 21 February

2021. https://www.rappler.com/moveph/lumad-schools-continue-to-suffer-closures-attacks-coronavirus-pandemic.

Dixon, Jane. 2009. 'From the imperial to the empty calorie: How nutrition relations underpin food regime transitions'. *Agriculture and Human Values* 26: 321–33. https://doi.org/10.1007/s10460-009-9217-6.

Doblado, Michael Angelo. 2017. 'Context: Palawan and Puerto Princesa then and now'. In *Modernizing Frontier: Chemical transformations of young people's minds and bodies in Puerto Princesa*, edited by Anita Hardon and Michael L. Tan, 13–23. Amsterdam: Amsterdam Institute for Social Science Research, University of Amsterdam; Quezon City: Anthropology Department, University of the Philippines; and Puerto Princesa: Palawan Studies Center, Palawan State University.

DSM Nutritional Products. 2014. 'resVida: Health benefit solution'. Accessed 30 July 2024. https://www.dsm.com/content/dam/dsm/human-nutrition/pdfs/resVida_A4_2pp_leaflet_08_09_2014_Final.pdf.

Dumit, Joseph. 2012. *Drugs for Life: How pharmaceutical companies define our health*. Durham, NC: Duke University Press.

DuPuis, E. Melanie. 2015. *Dangerous Digestion: The politics of American dietary advice*. Oakland: University of California Press.

DuPuis, E. Melanie and David Goodman. 2005. 'Should we go "home" to eat? Toward a reflexive politics of localism'. *Journal of Rural Studies* 21 (3): 359–71. https://doi.org/10.1016/j.jrurstud.2005.05.011.

Dwyer, Johanna T., Paul M. Coates and Michael J. Smith. 2018. 'Dietary supplements: Regulatory challenges and research resources'. *Nutrients* 10 (1): 41. https://doi.org/10.3390/nu10010041.

Ecks, Stefan and Soumita Basu. 2009. 'The unlicensed lives of antidepressants in India: Generic drugs, unqualified practitioners and floating prescriptions'. *Transcultural Psychiatry* 46 (1): 86–106. https://doi.org/10.1177/1363461509102289.

Eckstein, David, Vera Künzel and Laura Schäfer. 2021. *Global Climate Risk Index 2021*. Bonn: Germanwatch.

Edelman, Mark, Tony Weis, Amita Baviskar, Saturnino M. Borras Jr, Eric Holt Giménez, Deniz Kandiyoti and Wendy Wolford. 2014. 'Introduction: Critical perspectives on food sovereignty'. *Journal of Peasant Studies* 41 (6): 911–31. https://doi.org/10.1080/03066150.2014.963568.

Eder, J. F. 1999. *A Generation Later: Household strategies and economic change in the rural Philippines*. Honolulu: University of Hawai'i Press.

Education Policy and Data Center. 'Philippines National Education Profile 2018 Update'. Accessed 6 June 2024. https://www.epdc.org/sites/default/files/documents/EPDC_NEP_2018_Philippines.pdf.

Errington, Frederick, Tatsuro Fujikura and Deborah Gewertz. 2013. *The Noodle Narratives: The global rise of an industrial food into the twenty-first century*. Berkeley: University of California Press.

Espina-Varona, Inday. 2020. 'Under Marcos, the lush sugar lands of Negros Island turned red'. *Light for the Voiceless News (LICAS)*, 22 September. Accessed 6 June 2024. https://www.licas.news/2020/09/22/under-marcos-the-lush-sugar-lands-of-negros-island-turned-red/.

Etkin, Nina L. 2006. *Edible Medicines: An ethnopharmacology of food*. Tucson: University of Arizona Press.

Etkin, N. L. and P. J. Ross. 1983. 'Malaria, medicine and meals: Plant use and its impact on disease'. In *The Anthropology of Medicine*, edited by L. Romanucci, D. E Moerman and L. R Tancredi, 231–59. New York: Praeger Publishers.

Euromonitor International. 2016. 'Passport: Vitamins and dietary supplements in the Philippines'. London: Euromonitor.

Euromonitor International. 2019. 'Vitamins and dietary supplements in Asia Pacific'. Accessed 30 July 2024. https://web.archive.org/web/20210115173938/https://www.euromonitor.com/vitamins-and-dietary-supplements-in-asia-pacific/report.

Euromonitor International. 2020. 'Energy drinks in the Philippines'. Accessed 6 June 2024. https://web.archive.org/web/20210515144226/https://www.euromonitor.com/energy-drinks-in-the-philippines/report.

Eussen, Simone, Hans Verhagen, Olaf H. Klungel, Johan Garssen, Henk van Loveren, Henk J. van Karnen and Cathy J. M. Rompelberg. 2011. 'Functional foods and dietary supplements:

Products at the interface between pharma and nutrition'. *European Journal of Pharmacology* 668 (Supplement 1): S2–9. https://doi.org/10.1016/j.ejphar.2011.07.008.

Fabinyi, Michael. 2018. 'Food and water insecurity in specalised fishing communities: Evidence from the Philippines'. *Natural Resources Forum* 42 (4): 243–53. https://doi.org/10.1111/1477-8947.12148.

Federal Trade Commission (US). 2016. 'Herbalife will restructure its multilevel marketing operations and pay $200 million for consumer redress to settle FTC charges'. Press release, 15 July. https://www.ftc.gov/news-events/news/press-releases/2016/07/herbalife-will-restructure-its-multi-level-marketing-operations-pay-200-million-consumer-redress.

Federal Trade Commission (US). 2024. 'Title 16—Commercial Practices: Chapter I, Subchapter B, Part 260, § 260.3'. Code of Federal Regulations. https://www.ecfr.gov/current/title-16/chapter-I/subchapter-B/part-260/section-260.3.

Fleuret, A. 1986. 'Dietary and therapeutic uses of fruits in three Taita communities'. In *Plants in Indigenous Medicine and Diet: Biobehavioral approaches*, edited by N. L. Etkin, 151–71. New York: Routledge.

Foster, John Bellamy. 2000. *Marx's Ecology: Materialism and nature*. New York: Monthly Review Press.

Freire, Paulo. 1970. *Pedagogy of the Oppressed*. New York: Bloomsbury.

Gallardo, Luis Hassan and Jeanne Batalora. 2020. 'Filipino immigrants in the United States'. Migration Policy Institute. Accessed 6 June 2024. https://www.migrationpolicy.org/article/filipino-immigrants-united-states.

Gálvez, Alyshia. 2018. *Eating NAFTA: Trade, food policies, and the destruction of Mexico*. Oakland: University of California Press.

Galvez Tan, Jaime. 1987. 'Primary health care: Health in the hands of the people'. In *Restoring Health Care in the Hands of the People*, edited by Michael L. Tan and Jacqueline Co, 84–117. Quezon City: Health Action Information Network.

Gartaula, H. N., A. Niehof and M. Quetulio Navarra. 2018. 'Introduction'. In *Diversity and Change in Food Wellbeing: Cases from Southeast Asia and Nepal*, edited by A. Niehof, H. N. Gartaula and M. Quetulio Navarra, 15–35. Wageningen: Wageningen University Press.

Gay, Paloma and Huon Wardle. 2019. 'Informants, interlocutors, collaborators'. In *How to read ethnography*, by Paloma Gay and Huon Wardle, 168–91. 2nd ed. London: Routledge.

Gayao, B. T., D. T. Meldoz and G. S. Backian. 2018. 'Indigenous knowledge and household food security: The role of root and tuber crops among indigenous peoples in the Northern Philippines'. In *Diversity and Change in Food Wellbeing: Cases from Southeast Asia and Nepal*, edited by A. Niehof, H. N. Gartaula and M. Quetulio-Navarra, 43–70. Wageningen: Wageningen Academic Publishers.

Global Environment Facility. 2020. 'Indigenous peoples and COVID-19: Response and resilience'. GEF Communications. https://www.thegef.org/newsroom/blog/indigenous-peoples-and-covid-19-response-and-resilience.

Global Witness. 2019. 'Defending the Philippines'. *Global Witness*, 24 September. https://www.globalwitness.org/en/campaigns/environmental-activists/defending-philippines/.

Glover, D. and D. G. Stone. 2020. 'The Philippines has rated "Golden Rice" safe, but farmers might not plant it'. *The Conversation*, 7 February. Accessed 6 June 2024. https://theconversation.com/the-philippines-has-rated-golden-rice-safe-but-farmers-might-not-plant-it-129956.

Gollin, Lisa. 2004. 'Subtle and profound sensory attributes of medicinal plants among the Kenyah Leppo'ke of East Kalimantan, Borneo'. *Journal of Ethnobiology and Ethnomedicine* 24 (2): 173–201.

González Molina, Manuel de and Victor Toledo. 2014. *The Social Metabolism: A socio-ecological theory of historical change*. Heidelberg: Springer.

Gopalan, C. 2001. 'Prevention of "micronutrient malnutrition"'. *NFI Bulletin* 22: 1–7.

Government Accounting Office (US). 2010. 'Herbal dietary supplements: Examples of deceptive and questionable marketing practices and potentially dangerous advice'. GAO-10-662T, Congressional testimony to the US Senate Special Committee on Aging.

Greenslit, Nathan. 2005. 'Depression and consumption: Psychopharmaceuticals, branding, and new identity practices'. *Culture, Medicine and Psychiatry* 29 (4): 477–502. https://doi.org/10.1007/s11013-006-9005-3.

Gregory, Andrew. 2024. 'Ultra-processed food linked to 32 harmful effects to health, review finds'. *The Guardian*, 28 February. Accessed 6 June 2024. https://www.theguardian.com/society/2024/feb/28/ultra-processed-food-32-harmful-effects-health-review.

Gurley, Bill J., Charles R. Yates and John S. Markowitz. 2018. '"… Not intended to diagnose, treat, cure or prevent any disease": 25 years of botanical dietary supplement research and the lessons learned'. *Clinical Pharmacology and Therapeutics* 104 (3): 470–83. https://doi.org/10.1002/cpt.1131.

Guthman, Julie. 2007. 'Commentary on teaching food: Why I am fed up with Michael Pollan et al.' *Agriculture and Human Values* 24: 261–4. https://doi.org/10.1007/s10460-006-9053-x.

Guthman, Julie. 2009. 'Neoliberalism and the constitution of contemporary bodies'. In *The Fat Studies Reader*, edited by Esther D. Rothblum and Sondra Solovay, 187–206. New York: New York University Press.

Guthman, Julie and Melanie DuPuis. 2006. 'Embodying neoliberalism: Economy, culture, and the politics of fat'. *Environment and Planning Society and Space* 24 (3): 427–48. https://doi.org/10.1068/d3904.

Hardin, Jessica. 2019. *Faith and the Pursuit of Health: Cardiometabolic disorders in Samoa*. New Brunswick: Rutgers University Press.

Hardon, Anita. 1987. 'The use of modern pharmaceuticals in a Filipino Village: Doctors' prescription and self medication'. *Social Science and Medicine* 25 (3): 277–92. https://doi.org/10.1016/0277-9536(87)90231-0.

Hardon, Anita. 1991. *Confronting Ill Health: Medicines, self-care and the poor in Manila*. Quezon City: Health Action Information Network.

Hardon, Anita. 2021. *Chemical Youth: Navigating uncertainty in search of the good life*. London: Palgrave Macmillan.

Hardon, Anita, Ian Anthony Davatos and Gideon Lasco. 2019. 'Be your product: On youth, multilevel market, and nutritional cure-alls in Puerto Princesa, Philippines'. *American Ethnologist* 46 (4): 429–43. https://doi.org/10.1111/amet.12830.

Hardon, Anita, Alice Desclaux, Marc Egrot, Emmanuelle Simon, Evelyne Micollier and Margaret Kyakuwa. 2008. 'Alternative medicines for AIDS in resource-poor settings: Insights from exploratory anthropological studies in Asia and Africa'. *Journal of Ethnobiology and Ethnomedicine* 4: 10–19 https://doi.org/10.1186/1746-4269-4-16.

Hardon, Anita and Emilia Sanabria. 2017. 'Fluid drugs: Revisiting the anthropology of pharmaceuticals'. *Annual Review of Anthropology* 46 (1): 117–32. https://doi.org/10.1146/annurev-anthro-102116-041539.

Hardon, Anita and Michael Lim Tan. 2017. *Modernizing Frontier: Chemical transformations of young people's minds and bodies in Puerto Princesa*. Amsterdam: Amsterdam Institute for Social Science Research, University of Amsterdam; Quezon City: Anthropology Department, University of the Philippines; and Puerto Princesa: Palawan Studies Center, Palawan State University.

Hartley, Heather. 2006. 'The "pinking" of Viagra culture: Drug industry efforts to create and repackage sex drugs for women'. *Sexualities* 9 (3): 363–78. https://doi.org/10.1177/1363460706065058.

Harvey, David. 2004. 'The "new" imperialism: Accumulation by dispossession'. *Socialist Register* 40: 63–87.

Harvey, Penny and Christian Krohn-Hansen. 2018. 'Introduction. Dislocating labour: Anthropological reconfigurations'. *Journal of the Royal Anthropological Institute* 24 (S1): 10–28. https://doi.org/10.1111/1467-9655.12796.

Hawkins, Gay, Emily Potter and Kane Race. 2015. 'Plastic water: The social and material life of bottled water'. Cambridge, MA: MIT Press.

Hayes, Adam. 2024. 'What is greenwashing? How it works, examples, and statistics'. Accessed 1 April 2024. *Investopedia*. https://www.investopedia.com/terms/g/greenwashing.asp#citation-2.

Health Action International. 1986. *Problem Drugs*. Amsterdam: Health Action International.

Health Canada. 2022. 'Front of package nutrition labelling. Government of Canada'. Accessed 1 April 2024. https://www.canada.ca/en/health-canada/news/2022/06/front-of-package-nutrition-labelling.html.

Henley, David. 2015. 'Ages of commerce in Southeast Asian history'. In *Environment, Trade and Society in Southeast Asia*, edited by David Henley and Henk Schulte Nordholt, 120–32. Leiden: Brill.

Heynen, Nik. 2006. 'Justice of eating in the city: The political ecology of urban hunger'. In *In the Nature of Cities: Urban political ecology and the politics of urban metabolism*, edited by Nik Heynen, Maria Kaika and Erik Swyngedouw, 129–42. New York: Routledge.

Hochschild, A. R. 1983. *The Managed Heart: Commercialization of human feeling*. Berkeley: University of California Press.

Hollnsteiner, M. and J. Ick. 2001. *Bearers of Benevolence: The Thomasites and public education in the Philippines*. Pasig City: Anvil Publishers.

Huguet-Termes, Teresa. 2001. 'New World materia medica in Spanish renaissance medicine: From scholarly reception to practical impact'. *Medical History* 45 (3): 359–76. https://doi.org/10.1017/s0025727300068046.

Hunt, Shelby D. 2000. *A General Theory of Competition: Resources, competences, productivity, economic growth*. Thousand Oaks, CA: Sage Publications.

Huse, Oliver, Erica Reeve, Paul Zambrano, Colin Bell, Anna Peeters, Gary Sacks, Phillip Baker and Kathryn Backholer. 2023. 'Understanding the corporate political activity of the ultra-processed food industry in East Asia: A Philippines case study'. *Globalization and Health* 19: 16. https://doi.org/10.1186/s12992-023-00916-x.

Huxtable, Ryan J. 1992. 'The pharmacology of extinction'. *Journal of Ethnopharmacology* 37 (1): 1–11. https://doi.org/10.1016/0378-8741(92)90002-9.

Idrus, Ilmi Nurul and Anita Hardon. 2015. 'Chemicals, biocapital and the everyday lives of sex workers and waitresses in South Sulawesi'. In *Sex and Sexualities in Contemporary Indonesia: Sexual politics, health, diversity and representations*, edited by Linda Rae Bennett and Sharyn Graham Davies, 129–47. London: Routledge.

Jacobs, David R., Myron D. Gross and Linda C. Tapsell. 2009. 'Food synergy: An operational concept for understanding nutrition'. *American Journal of Clinical Nutrition* 89 (5): 1543S–1548S. https://doi.org/10.3945/ajcn.2009.26736B.

Javier, E. Q. 2004. 'Let's promote brown rice to combat hidden hunger'. *Rice Today* 3 (1): 38.

Kayzen, Ronda. 2024. 'At-home IV drips are the latest luxury building amenity'. Accessed 1 June 2024. *New York Times*, 14 May. https://www.nytimes.com/2024/05/14/realestate/iv-drip-therapy-luxury-building.html.

Kelly, B., and 13 others. 2015. 'Density of outdoor food and beverage advertising around schools in Ulaanbaatar (Mongolia) and Manila (The Philippines) and implications for policy'. *Critical Public Health* 25 (3): 280–90. https://doi.org/10.1080/09581596.2014.940850.

Kennedy, Gina L., Maria Regina Pedro, Chiara Seghieri, Guy Nantel and Inge Brouwer. 2007. 'Dietary diversity score is a useful indicator of micronutrient intake in non-breast-feeding Filipino children'. *Journal of Nutrition* 137 (2): 472–7. https://doi.org/10.1093/jn/137.2.472.

Kian, Kwee Hui. 2013. 'Chinese economic dominance in Southeast Asia: A *longue durée* perspective'. *Comparative Studies in Society and History* 55 (1): 5–34. https://doi.org/10.1017/S0010417512000564.

Kim, Soowon, Soojae Moon and Barry Popkin. 2000. 'The nutrition transition in South Korea'. *American Journal of Clinical Nutrition* 71 (1): 44–53.

Kimura, Aya Hirata. 2013. *Hidden Hunger: Gender and the politics of smarter foods*. Ithaca, NY: Cornell University Press.

King, Anya. 2015. 'The new materia medica of the Islamicate tradition: The pre-Islamic context'. *Journal of the American Oriental Society* 135 (3): 499–528.

Kraft, Thomas S., Jonathan Stieglitz, Benjamin C. Trumble, Melanie Martin, Hillard Kaplan and Michael Gurven. 2018. 'Nutrition transition in 2 lowland Bolivian subsistence populations'. *American Journal of Clinical Nutrition* 108 (6): 1183–95. https://doi.org/10.1093/ajcn/nqy250.

Krige, Detlev. 2012. 'Fields of dreams, fields of schemes: Ponzi finance and multilevel marketing in South Africa'. *Africa* 82 (1): 69–92.

Laderman, Carol. 1983. *Wives and Midwives: Childbirth and nutrition in rural Malaysia*. Berkeley: University of California Press.

Ladia, Mary Ann J. 2024. *Frailty of Growing Old*. Quezon City: Bughaw.

Landecker, Hannah. 2013. 'Postindustrial metabolism: Fat knowledge'. *Public Culture* 25 (3): 495–522. https://doi.org/10.1215/08992363-2144625.

Lane, Melissa M., and 10 others. 2021. 'Ultraprocessed food and chronic noncommunicable diseases: A systematic review and meta-analysis of 43 observational studies'. *Obesity Reviews* 22 (3): e13146. https://doi.org/10.1111/obr.13146.

Lane, Melissa M. and 14 others. 2024. 'Ultra-processed food exposure and adverse health outcomes: Umbrella review of epidemiological meta-analyses'. *British Medical Journal* 384: e077310. https://doi.org/10.1136/bmj-2023-077310.

Laririt, Patricia. 2021. 'Total population in PPC and Palawan, now more than 1.2 million – PSA'. *Palawan News*, 11 August. Accessed 6 June 2024. https://palawan-news.com/total-population-in-ppc-and-palawan-now-more-than-1-2-million-psa/.

Lasco, Gideon. 2017. 'Height Matters: The making, meanings and materialities of human stature in the Philippines' (Doctoral dissertation). University of Amsterdam, Anthropology Department.

La Vieille, Sebastien, David E. Lefebvre, Ahmad Firas Khalid, Matthew R. Decan and Samuel Godefroy. 2019. 'Dietary restrictions for people with glucose-6-phosphate dehydrogenase deficiency'. *Nutritional Reviews* 77 (2): 96–106. https://doi.org/10.1093/nutrit/nuy053.

Lee Mendoza, Roger. 2009. 'Is it really medicine? The Traditional and Alternative Medicine Act and informal health economy in the Philippines'. *Asia-Pacific Journal of Public Health* 21 (3). https://doi.org/10.1177/1010539509336570.

Lefebvre, Henri. 2004. *Rhythmanalysis: Space, time and everyday life*. London: Continuum.

Legara, E., C. Monterola, L. M. Dranreb and S. Caesar. 2008. 'Earning potential in multilevel marketing enterprises'. *Physica A* 387 (19–20): 4889–95.

Li, Hui Lin. 1969. 'The vegetables of Ancient China'. *Economic Botany* 23 (3): 253–60. https://doi.org/10.1007/BF02860457.

Liebig, Justus von. 1863. *The Natural Laws of Husbandry*. New York: D. Appleton.

Lind, James. 1757. *Treatise on the Scurvy*. Edinburgh: Sands, Murray and Cochran.

Lipton, E. 2011. 'Hatch a "natural ally" of supplements industry'. *New York Times*, 21 June. Accessed 1 April 2024. https://www.nytimes.com/2011/06/21/us/politics/21hatch.html.

Loftus, A. 2012. *Every-Day Environmentalism: Creating an urban political ecology*. Minneapolis: University of Minnesota Press.

Loftus, A. 2019. 'Political Ecology I: Where is political ecology?'. *Progress in Human Geography* 43 (1): 172–82.

Luca, N. 2011. 'Multi-level marketing: At the crossroads of economy and religion'. In *The Economics of Religion: Anthropological approaches*, edited by L. Obadia and D. C. Wood, 217–39. Leeds: Emerald Group Publishing. https://doi.org/10.1108/S0190-1281(2011)0000031012.

Lyon, Margot. 2005. 'Technologies of feeling and being: Medicines in contemporary Indonesia'. *IIAS Newsletter* 37: 14. Accessed 6 June 2024. https://www.iias.asia/sites/default/files/2020-11/IIAS_NL37_14.pdf.

Ma, Z. F., J. Ahmad, H. Zhang, I. Khan and S. Muhammad. 2020. 'Evaluation of phytochemical and medicinal properties of Moringa (*Moringa oleifera*) as a potential functional food'. *South African Journal of Botany* 129: 40–6.

Mackay Foundation. 2018. 'Manna Plus'. Accessed 5 June 2024. https://www.jamesmackayfoundationinc.com/mannaplus/.

MacKendrick, Norah. 2018. *Better Safe than Sorry: How consumers navigate exposure to everyday toxics*. Oakland: University of California Press.

Madjos, Genelyn and Kay Piocnancia Ramos. 2021. 'Ethnobotany, systematic review and field mapping on folkloric medicinal plants in the Zamboanga Peninsula, Mindanao, Philippines'. *Journal of Complementary Medicine Research* 12 (1). https://doi.org/10.5455/jcmr.2021.12.01.05.

Malabad, Cristina G. 2019. 'Food security status of Filipino households'. Alabang: Food and Nutrition Research Institute (FNRI).

Mann, Anna and Annemarie Mol. 2019. 'Talking pleasures, writing dialects: Outlining research on Schmecka'. *Ethnos* 84 (5): 772–88. https://doi.org/10.1080/00141844.2018.1486334.

Martin, Emily. 2006. 'The pharmaceutical person'. *BioSocieties* 1 (3): 273–87. https://doi.org/10.1017/s1745855206003012.

Martinez, Edlynne. 2021. 'The tirtir economy: An ethnography of food recycling among older adults in an urban informal settlement'. *Journal of Social Health* 4 (1): 38–53.

Marx, Karl. 1977. *Capital: A critique of political economy*, vol. 1. Harmondsworth: Penguin.

Mayer, Robert N., Debra L. Scammon and Orrin G. Hatch. 1994. 'Congress versus the Food and Drug Administration: How one government health agency harms the public health'. *Journal of Public Policy & Marketing* 13 (1): 151–2. https://doi.org/10.1177/074391569401300112.

Mayo Clinic. 2019. 'Mediterranean diet for heart health'. Mayo Clinic. Accessed 6 June 2024. https://www.mayoclinic.org/healthy-lifestyle/nutrition-and-healthy-eating/in-depth/mediterranean-diet/art-20047801.

Mbow, Cheikh, Rosenzweig, Cynthia and 24 others. 2019. 'Food security'. In *Climate Change and Land. Intergovernmental Panel on Climate Change*, edited by P. R. Shukla, J. Skea, E. Calvo Buendia, V. Masson-Delmotte, H. O. Pörtner, P. Zhai and D. Roberts. Cambridge: Cambridge University Press. https://doi.org/10.1017/9781009157988.007.

McCartney, Micah. 2023. 'Kids in China receive treatment while doing homework during outbreak'. *Newsweek*, 28 November. Accessed 6 June 2024. https://www.newsweek.com/china-children-homework-hospital-iv-drip-disease-outbreak-1847440.

McCormack, Fiona and Kate Barclay. 2013. 'Insights on capitalism from Oceania'. In *Engaging with Capitalism: Cases from Oceania*, edited by Fiona McCormack and Kate Barclay, 1–28. Leeds: Emerald House Publishing.

McNamara, K. E. and S. S. Adair. Prasad. 2013. 'Valuing indigenous knowledge for climate change adaptation planning in Fiji and Vanuatu'. *Traditional Knowledge Bulletin*, 28 August. https://tkbulletin.wordpress.com/2013/08/28/guest-article-valuing-indigenous-knowledge-in-fiji-and-vanuatu-2/.

Mendez, M. A. and L. S. Adair. 1999. 'Severity and timing of stunting in the first two years of life affect performance on cognitive tests in late childhood'. *Journal of Nutrition* 129: 1555–62.

Mercado, J. L. 2003. '"Bitter melon war" roils health front'. *Sun Star Cebu*, 17 August.

Metzler, Hannah and David Garcia. 2023. 'Social drivers and algorithmic mechanisms on digital media'. *Perspectives on Psychological Sciences*: 1–14. https://doi.org/10.1177/17456916231185057.

Minet, Laura, Zhanyun Wang, Anna Shalin, Thomas A. Bruton, Arlene Blum, Graham F. Peaslee, Heather Schwartz-Narbonne, Marta Venier, Heather Whitehead, Yan Wu and Miriam L. Diamond. 2022. 'Use and release of per- and polyfluoroalkyl substances (PFASs) in consumer food packaging in US and Canada'. *Environmental Science: Processes & Impacts* 24: 2032–42.

Ministry of the Environment (Japan). 2003. Accessed 1 April 2024. 'Water Environment Partnership in Asia: Sharing knowledge for improving the water environment in Asia'. https://www.env.go.jp/en/water/wq/wepa_broc.pdf.

Mintz, Sidney. 1985. *Sweetness and Power*. New York: Penguin.

Mintz, Sidney W. and Christine M. Du Bois. 2002. 'The anthropology of food and eating'. *Annual Review of Anthropology* 31 (1): 99–119. https://doi.org/10.1146/annurev.anthro.32.032702.131011.

Moerman, Daniel. 2002. *Meaning, Medicine and the Placebo Effect*. Cambridge: Cambridge University Press.

Monteiro, Carlos. 2009. 'Nutrition and health: The issue is not food, nor nutrients, so much as processing'. *Public Health Nutrition* 12 (5): 729–31. https://doi.org/10.1017/S1368980009005291.

Monteiro, Carlos, Geoffrey Cannon, Mark Lawrence, Maria Laura da Costa Louzada and Priscila Pereira Machado. 2019. *Ultra-Processed Foods, Diet Quality, and Health Using the NOVA Classification System*. Rome: FAO.

Monteiro, Carlos and Patrícia Jaime. 2020. 'Brazilian Food Guide attacked: Now, overwhelming support for the Guide in Brazil and worldwide'. *World Nutrition* 11 (4): 94–9.

Monteiro, Carlos and 12 others. 2015. 'Dietary guidelines to nourish humanity and the planet in the twenty-first century: A blueprint from Brazil'. *Public Health Nutrition* 18 (13): 2311–22.

Monthly Index of Medical Specialties (MIMS). 2024. Home page. Accessed 12 March 2024. https://www.mims.com.

Moore, Jason. 2015. *Capitalism in the Web of Life: Ecology and the accumulation of capital*. London: Verso Books.

Moore, Jason W. 2017. 'Metabolic rift or metabolic shift? Dialectics, nature, and the world-historical method'. *Theory and Society* 46 (4): 285–318.

Morocco, Chris. 2017. 'This condiment is sweet, garlicky and just ridiculously good'. Bon Appétit. Accessed 6 June 2024. https://www.bonappetit.com/story/this-condiment-is-sweet-spicy-garlicky-and-just-ridiculously-good.

Muller, Carina, Claire Chabanet, Gertrude G. Zeinstra, Gerry Jager, Camille Schwartz and Sophie Nicklaus. 2023. 'The sweet tooth of infancy: Is sweetness exposure related to sweetness liking in infants up to 12 months of age?'. *British Journal of Nutrition* 129 (8): 1462–72. https://doi.org/10.1017/S0007114522002628.

Municipality of Mina. 2016. 'First 1000 days ni baby pahalagahan para sa malusog na kinabukasan'. Accessed 6 June 2024. https://lgu-minailoilo.com/index.php/2016/07/26/latest-updates-143.

Narotzky, Susana. 2015. 'The payoff of love and the traffic of favours: Reciprocity, social capital and the blurring of value realms in flexible capitalism'. *Flexible Capitalism: Exchange and ambiguity at work*, edited by Jens Kjaerulff, 268–310. Oxford: Berghahn Books.

Narotzky, Susana and Niko Besnier. 2014. 'Crisis, value and hope: Rethinking the economy: An introduction to Supplement 9'. *Current Anthropology* 55 (S9): s4–16.

Nat, Peter J. Vander and William W. Keep. 2002. 'Marketing fraud: An approach for differentiating multilevel marketing from pyramid schemes'. *Journal of Public Policy & Marketing* 21 (1): 139–51. https://doi.org/10.1509/jppm.21.1.139.17603.

National Nutrition Survey. 2015. *National Nutrition Survey 2015*. Accessed 6 June 2024. https://www.fnri.dost.gov.ph/index.php/019df8617pdxGojKRVZtb10178czs_s/asbLxKFXx-orhge8.

Nazarea, Virginia D. 1978. *Cultural Memory and Biodiversity*. Tucson: University of Arizona Press.

Nelson, D. 2013. '100 Percent Omnilife: Health, Economy, and the End/s of War'. In *War by Other Means: Aftermath in post-genocide Guatemala*, edited by C. McAllister and D. Nelson, 178–231. Durham, NC: Duke University Press.

Nestle, M. 2002. *Food Politics: How the food industry influences nutrition and health*. Berkeley: University of California Press.

Newell, Kenneth W. 1988. 'Selective primary health care: The counter revolution'. *Social Science and Medicine* 26 (9): 903–6. https://doi.org/10.1016/0277-9536(88)90409-1.

Newson, Linda. 2011. *Conquest and Pestilence in the Early Spanish Philippines*. O'ahu: University of Hawai'i Press.

Non-Communicable Disease Risk Factor Collaboration (NCD-RisC). 2016. 'A century of trends in adult human height'. *ELife* 5 (July). https://doi.org/10.7554/eLife.13410.001.

Nyéléni Forum. 2007. 'Nyéléni 2007: Forum for food sovereignty'. Sélingué, Mali, February. Accessed 6 June 2024. https://nyeleni.org/DOWNLOADS/Nyelni_EN.pdf.

Ofreneo, Rene E. 2008. 'Neo-liberalism and the working people of Southeast Asia'. *Asian Journal of Social Science* 36:170–86. https://doi.org/10.1163/156853108X298734.

Oldani, Michael. 2004. 'Thick prescriptions: Toward an interpretation of pharmaceutical sales practices'. *Medical Anthropology Quarterly* 18 (3): 325–56. https://doi.org/10.1525/maq.2004.18.3.325.

Ong, Homervergel G. and Young Dong Kim. 2016. 'The role of wild edible plants in household food security among transitioning hunter-gatherers: Evidence from the Philippines'. *Food Security* 9 (1): 11–24. https://doi.org/10.1007/s12571-016-0630-6.

Pagliai, G., M. Dinu, M. P. Madarena, M. Bonaccio, L. Lacoviello and F. Sofi. 2021. 'Consumption of ultra-processed foods and health status: A systematic review and meta-analysis'. *British Journal of Nutrition* 125 (3): 308–18.

Pant, A., S. Gribbin, P. Machado, A. Hodge, L. Moran, S. Marschner and S. Zaman. 2023. 'Association of ultra-processed foods with cardiovascular disease and hypertension in Australian women'. *European Heart Journal* 44 (S2). https://doi.org/10.1093/eurheartj/ehad655.2388.

Pauling, Linus. 1970. *Vitamin C and the Common Cold*. New York: W. H. Freeman.

Pauling, Linus. 1986. *How to Live Longer and Feel Better*. Corvallis: Oregon State University Press.

Payumo, Jane, Zheng Gang, Elizabeth Pulumbarit, Keith Jones, Karim Maredia and Howard Grimes. 2012. 'Managing intellectual property and technology commercialization: Comparison and analysis of practices, success stories and lessons learned from public research universities in developing Asia'. *Innovation: Management, Policy and Practice* 14 (4): 478–94. https://doi.org/10.5172/impp.2012.14.4.478.

Pedro, R., R. Benavides and C. Barba. 2006. 'Dietary changes and health implications: An emerging double burden of under and over nutrition'. Manila: Food and Nutrition Research Institute.

Petrini, Carlo. 2013. *Slow Food Nation: Why our food should be good, clean, and fair*. New York: Rizzoli International Publications.

Pew Research Center. 2006. 'Spirit and power: A 10-country survey of pentecostals'. Accessed 6 June 2024. https://www.pewresearch.org/religion/2006/10/05/spirit-and-power/.

PhilStar Global. 2008. 'DOST, UP-MSI link up for "Pharmaseas"'. *PhilStar Global*, 23 October. Accessed 6 June 2024. https://www.philstar.com/business/science-and-environment/2008/10/23/409233/dost-msi-link-pharmaseas.

Popkin, Barry M. 2003. 'The nutrition transition in the developing world'. *Development Policy Review* 21 (5–6): 581–97. https://doi.org/10.1111/j.1467-8659.2003.00225.x.

Pordié, Laurent. 2015. 'Hangover free! The social and material trajectories of PartySmart'. *Anthropology and Medicine* 22: 34–48. https://doi.org/10.1080/13648470.2015.1004773.

Pordié, Laurent and Jean Paul Gaudillière. 2014. 'The reformulation regime in drug discovery: Revisiting polyherbals and property rights in the ayurvedic industry'. *East Asian Science, Technology and Society* 8 (1): 57–79. https://doi.org/10.1215/18752160-2406053.

Pordié, Laurent and Anita Hardon. 2015. 'Drugs' stories and itineraries: On the making of Asian industrial medicines'. *Anthropology & Medicine* 22 (1): 1–6. https://doi.org/10.1080/13648470.2015.1020745.

Pozon, Vincent. 2019. 'Negative versus positive advertising'. *Manila Times*, 5 September. Accessed 1 April 2024. https://www.manilatimes.net/2019/09/05/business/columnists-business/negative-versus-positive-advertising/611555/.

Price, Catherine. 2016. *Vitamania: How vitamins revolutionized the way we think about food*. New York: Penguin.

Price, Catherine. 2017. 'The age of scurvy'. *Distillations Magazine*. Philadelphia: Science History Institute. https://www.sciencehistory.org/stories/magazine/the-age-of-scurvy/.

Ramos, Marlon. 2024. 'Mariel Padilla's "gluta drip" session at Senate draws flak'. *Philippine Daily Inquirer*, 25 February. Accessed 6 June 2024. https://cebudailynews.inquirer.net/558534/mariel-padillas-gluta-drip-session-at-senate-draws-flak.

Reduble, Rich. 2019. 'Palawan's tourist arrivals reaches 1.8 million in 2018'. *Palawan Daily News*, 14 April. Accessed 6 June 2024. https://palawandailynews.com/provincial-news/palawans-tourist-arrival-reaches-1-8-million-in-2018/.

Reid, Anthony. 1995. *Southeast Asia in the Age of Commerce, 1450–1680*. Vol. 2: *Expansion and Crisis*. New Haven: Yale University Press.

Reynolds, Christian John, Jonathan David Buckley, Philip Weinstein and John Boland. 2014. 'Are the dietary guidelines for meat, fat, fruit and vegetable consumption appropriate for environmental sustainability? A review of the literature'. *Nutrients* 6 (6): 2251–65. https://doi.org/10.3390/nu6062251.

Rico-Campà, Anaïs, Miguel A. Martínez-González, Ismael Alvarez-Alvarez, Raquel De Deus Mendonça, Carmen De La Fuente-Arrillaga, Clara Gómez-Donoso and Maira Bes-Rastrollo. 2019. 'Association between consumption of ultra-processed foods and all cause mortality: SUN prospective cohort study'. *BMJ* 365: I1949. https://doi.org/10.1136/bmj.l1949.

Rizal, Jose. 1890. 'The indolence of the Filipino', translated by Charles Derbyshire. Madrid: La Solidaridad. Accessed 23 July 2024. https://www.gutenberg,org/ebooks/6885.

Robbins, Paul. 2007. *Lawn People: How grasses, weeds, and chemicals make us who we are*. Philadelphia: Temple University Press.

Roberts, Elizabeth F. S. 2017. 'What gets inside: Violent entanglements and toxic boundaries in Mexico City'. *Cultural Anthropology* 32 (4): 592–619. https://doi.org/10.14506/ca32.4.07.

Rocha, Tiago, Joana S. Amaral and Maria Beatriz P. P. Oliveira. 2016. 'Adulteration of dietary supplements by the illegal addition of synthetic drugs: A review'. *Comprehensive Reviews in Food Science and Food Safety* 15 (1): 43–62. https://doi.org/10.1111/1541-4337.12173.

Rutten, Rosanne. 2010. 'Who shall benefit? Conflicts among the landless poor in a Philippine agrarian reform programme'. *Asian Journal of Social Science* 38 (2): 204–19. https://doi.org/10.1163/156853110X490908.

Saldaña-Tejeda, Abril and Peter Wade. 2019. 'Eugenics, epigenetics and obesity predisposition among Mexican Mestizos'. *Medical Anthropology* 38 (8): 664–79. https://doi.org/10.1080/01459740.2019.1589466.

Sanabria, Emilia. 2016. 'Circulating ignorance: Complexity and agnogenesis in the obesity "epidemic"'. *Cultural Anthropology* 31 (1): 131–58. https://doi.org/10.14506/ca31.1.07.

Sta. Maria, Felice Prudente. 2020. 'Fitting food to circumstances: Potential contributions of Philippine culinary heritage to disaster risk reduction'. *Budhi* 24: 37–84.

Santos, Aaron Joseph. 2021. 'Analysis of interviews with Zamboanga city residents on backyard gardening during Covid-19'. Unpublished research report, Department of Anthropology, University of the Philippines.

Sartika, Arindah Nur, Meirina Khoirunnisa, Eflita Meiyetriani, Evi Ermayani, Indriya Laras Pramesthi and Aziz Jati Nur Ananda. 2021. 'Prenatal and postnatal determinants of stunting at age 0–11 months: A cross-sectional study in Indonesia'. *PLoS ONE.* https://doi.org/10.1371/journal.pone.0254662.

Schlosser, E. 2001. *Fast Food Nation: The dark side of the American meal.* Boston, MA: Houghton Mifflin Company.

Scrinis, Gyorgy. 2013. *Nutritionism: The science and politics of dietary advice.* New York: Columbia University Press.

Secretariat of Health Care (Brazil). 2015. 'Dietary guidelines for the Brazilian population'. Accessed 1 April 2024. Ministry of Health of Brazil. Secretariat of Health Care. Primary Health Care Department. 2015, translated by Carlos Augusto Monteiro. Brasília: Ministry of Health of Brazil. https://bvsms.saude.gov.br/bvs/publicacoes/dietary_guidelines_brazilian_population.pdf.

Shepherd, Gordon. 2012. *Neurogastronomy: How the brain creates flavor and why it matters.* New York: Columbia University Press.

Singy, Patrick. 2010. 'The popularization of medicine in the eighteenth century: Writing, reading, and rewriting Samuel Auguste Tissot's Avis Au Peuple Sur Sa Santé'. *Journal of Modern History* 82 (4): 769–800. https://doi.org/10.1086/656073.

Sobreira, L. B., M. Garavello and G. B. Nardoto. 2018. 'Anthropology of food: An essay on food transition and transformations in Brazil'. *Journal of Food, Nutrition, and Population Health* 2 (1): 9.

Solomon, Harris. 2016. *Metabolic Living: Food, fat, and the absorption of illness in India.* Durham, NC: Duke University Press.

Spengler, Robert. 2019. *Fruit from the Sands: The Silk Road origins of the foods we eat.* Berkeley: University of California Press.

Srour, Bernard and 13 others. 2019. 'Ultra-processed food intake and risk of cardiovascular disease: Prospective cohort study (NutriNet-Santé)'. *British Medical Journal* 365: l1451. https://doi.org/10.1136/bmj.l1451.

Stauffer, Robert. 1966. *The Development of an Interest Group: The Philippine Medical Association.* Quezon City: University of the Philippines Press.

Sweet Medicine. 2017 [video]. Producers, Anita Hardon and Madeline Landico; Directors, Juul Op den Kamp and Ralph Pulanco. https://www.chemicalyouth.org/#/projects/sweet-medicine.

Sy-Changco, Joseph A., Chanthika Pornpitakpan, Ramendra Singh and Celia M. Bonilla. 2011. 'Managerial insights into sachet marketing strategies and popularity in the Philippines'. *Asia Pacific Journal of Marketing and Logistics* 23: 755–72. https://doi.org/10.1108/13555851111183129.

Tan, Michael L. 1977. *Philippine Medicinal Plants in Common Use: Their phytochemistry and pharmacology.* Quezon City: Luzon Secretariat of Social Action.

Tan, Michael L. 1980. *Medicinal Plants in Common Use: Their phytochemistry and pharmacology.* Quezon City: AKAP.

Tan, Michael L. 1986. 'The chronic crisis of the health care system'. In *Caring Enough to Cure Manila,* edited by Erlinda Senturia and Carolina Araullo, 15–51. Manila: Council for Primary Health Care.

Tan, Michael L. 1999. *Good Medicine.* Amsterdam: Het Spinhuis.

Tan, Michael L. 2024. 'Viral times and governance: The Philippines'. In *Viral Times: Reflection on the COVID-19 and HIV pandemics,* edited by Jaime García-Iglesias, Maurice Nagington and Peter Aggleton, 135–48. London: Routledge.

Taqueban, E. M. 2010. 'Aborted Stories: Maternal health crisis in Eden'. MA thesis, University of the Philippines Anthropology Department.

Thursby, Elizabeth and Nathalie Juge. 2017. 'Introduction to the human gut microbiota'. *Biochemical Journal* 474 (11): 1823–36. https://doi.org/10.1042/BCJ20160510.

Timmers, Silvie and 16 others. 2011. 'Calorie restriction-like effects of 30 days of resveratrol supplementation on energy metabolism and metabolic profile in obese humans'. *Cell Metabolism* 14 (5): 612–22. https://doi.org/10.1016/j.cmet.2011.10.002.

Tissot, Samuel. 1761. *Avis au people sur sa sante*. Lausanne: J. Zimmerly.

Tofoya, Heriberto Ruiz. 2023. *Packaged Food, Packaged Life: Corporate food in Metro Manila slums*. Quezon City: Ateneo de Manila University Press and Kyoto: Kyoto University Press.

Trivette, Hannah. 2022. 'A guide to social media algorithms and SEOs'. *Forbes*, 14 October. Accessed 6 June 2024. https://www.forbes.com/sites/forbesagencycouncil/2022/10/14/a-guide-to-social-media-algorithms-and-seo/?sh=67546a3a52a0.

Tsing, Anna Lowenhaupt. 2004. *Friction: An ethnography of global connection*. Princeton: Princeton University Press.

Tuklas Lunas. 2017. The Tukas Lunas Program Framework of the DOST. Accessed 13 December 2020. https://www.researchgate.net/figure/The-Tuklas-Lunas-Program-Framework-of-the-DOST_fig1_351383793.

Tzaninis, Yannis, Tait Mandler, Maria Kaika and Roger Keil. 2020. 'Moving urban political ecology beyond the 'urbanization of nature'. *Progress in Human Geography* 45 (2): 229–52. https://doi.org/10.1177/0309132520903350.

UNICEF Philippines. 2019. 'Stunting and malnutrition pose health and economic burden in Bangsamoro'. https://www.unicef.org/philippines/stories/stunting-and-malnutrition-pose-health-and-economic-burden-bangsamoro.

Van Tulleken, Chris. 2023. *Ultra-Processed People: The science behind food that isn't food*. New York: W. W. Norton and Company.

Vargas, M. B. 2017. 'The obesogenic food environment: Are we there?' Presentation given to the Philippines Association of Nutrition, 70th Anniversary and Annual Convention, Quezon City, 14–15 July 2017.

Villena, Butch. 2011. *Complete 24/7: The natural healers*. Quezon City: AIM Global.

Watson, Andrew. 1983. *Agricultural Innovation: The diffusion of crops and farming technologies 700–1100*. Cambridge: Cambridge University Press.

Werner, D. 1977. *Where There is No Doctor: A village health care handbook*. Berkeley: Hesperian Health Guides.

Whyte, Susan Reynolds, Sjaak van der Geest, and Anita Hardon. 2002. *Social Lives of Medicines*. New York: Cambridge University Press. https://doi.org/10.1086/424649.

Wickramasinghe, K., Joao Breda, Nino Berdzuli, Holly Rippin, Clare Farrand and Afton Halloran. 2021. 'The shift to plant-based diets: Are we missing the point?'. *Global Food Security* 29: 100530. https://doi.org/10.1016/J.GFS.2021.100530.

Willett, Walter and 36 others. 2019. 'Food in the Anthropocene: The EAT–*Lancet* Commission on healthy diets from sustainable food systems'. *The Lancet* 393 (10170): 447–92. https://doi.org/10.1016/S0140-6736(18)31788-4.

Wilson, Ara. 1999. 'The empire of direct sales and the making of Thai entrepreneurs'. *Critique of Anthropology* 19 (4): 401–22. https://doi.org/10.1177/0308275X9901900406.

Wittman, H., A. Desmarais and N. Wiebe (eds). 2010. *Food Sovereignty: Reconnecting food, nature and community*. Winnipeg: Fernwood Publishing; Oakland: Food First; Oxford: Pambuzuka Press.

Wong, R. H. X., P. R. C. Howe, J. D. Buckley, A. M. Coates, I. Kunz and N. M. Berry. 2011. 'Acute resveratrol supplementation improves flow-mediated dilatation in overweight/obese individuals with mildly elevated blood pressure'. *Nutrition, Metabolism and Cardiovascular Diseases* 21 (11): 851–6. https://doi.org/10.1016/j.numecd.2010.03.003.

World Health Organization. 2014. 'Stunting policy brief: Global nutrition targets 2025'. Accessed 1 April 2024. Geneva: World Health Organization. https://www.who.int/publications/i/item/WHO-NMH-NHD-14.3.

World Neighbors. 1983. 'Understanding medicinal plants' [Filmstrip with booklet]. Oklahoma City: World Neighbors.

World Synod of Catholic Bishops. 1971. *Justicia in Mundo* [Justice in the World]. Rome: 1971 Synod of Bishops.

Wright, Melecia J., Margaret E. Bentley, Michelle A. Mendez and Linda S. Adair. 2015. 'The interactive association of dietary diversity scores and breast-feeding status with weight and length in Filipino infants aged 6–24 months'. *Public Health Nutrition* 18 (10): 1762–73. https://doi.org/10.1017/S1368980015000427.

Xu, Ke, David B. Evans, Kei Kawabata, Riadh Zeramdini, Jan Klavus and Christopher J. L. Murray. 2003. 'Household catastrophic health expenditure: A multicountry analysis'. *Lancet* 362 (9378): 111–17. https://doi.org/10.1016/S0140-6736(03)13861-5.

Yates-Doerr, Emily. 2012. 'The opacity of reduction: Nutritional black-boxing and the meanings of nourishment'. *Food, Culture & Society* 15 (2): 293–313.

Yates-Doerr, Emily. 2015. *The Weight of Obesity: Hunger and global health in postwar Guatemala*. Oakland: University of California Press.

Zelizer, Viviana A. 2012. 'How I became a relational economic sociologist and what does that mean?'. *Politics & Society* 40 (2): 145–74. https://doi.org/10.1177/0032329212441591.

Index

Please note that page numbers in *italics* refer the reader to photographs or other images, while page numbers in **bold** refer the reader to tables, and the suffix 'n' denotes endnotes.

accidents 131, *131*
additives 24, 113
advertising *see* marketing
Africa, Teodula 196–7
agriculture, cultivation and gardening
　agricultural revolution 3
　community gardening 11, 17, 27–9, 35, 43–4, 55, 68, 77, 81, 141, 164, *164*, 180, 204–7, 211–25
　cultivation, shifting 128
　cultivation, of vegetables and fruits banned in residential subdivisions 189–90
　fertilizer, herbicides and pesticides 26, 40, 92, 117, 202, 215
　foraging *see* foraging
　knowledge of (education in) 11, 35, 190, 193, 196, 202, 206, 211–25
　organic (agro-ecology) 215–16, *221*, 223–5, *224, 225*
Alcina, Ignacio 15
alcohol (beer, wine) 36, 118, 146, 195–6
altanghap (single meal per day) 63
Aquino Jnr, Benigno 4, 20
Ateneo de Manila University 149, 186

'Bahay Kubo' (folk song naming various plant foods) **13**, 213
balikbayan boxes 188
baeng (Ibaloi home gardens) 216
basil (*Ocimum basilicum*) 10

Benguet State University 190
Besa, Amy 54–5
Blanco, Fr Manuel 15–16
Borneo 10–11
Brazil 57, 199
bread 19, 23

C24/7
　distributors 125–6, 140–2, 148, 154, 165–7, *166*, 171–3, 185; *see also* marketing, MLM
　health claims 107–8, *107*, 144, *144*, 148–9
　marketing 28, 127, *143*
　price 126, 131, 144, 165–6, 171
Cabral, Esperanza 190
caffeine 98, 121n6
caffeinated tonic drink
　Cobra 98, *100*
　Extra Joss 98, 99
carinderias (small eateries) 63, *65*
cashews 13, 54, 128, 162
Cebu Longitudinal Health and Nutrition Survey 39
charities *see* NGOs and charities
Chemical Youth project 8, 183
Christian groups (Adventists, Charismatics, Evangelicals) 145, 150, 157–8, 172
Chinese immigrants 13, 110
cigarettes
　as breakfast 68
　promotions through sari-sari stores 60
　supplement claims to detoxify tobacco 108
climate change 200–1

Co, Leonard 73, 203
coconuts (Cocos nucifera, *nata de coco*, coconut sugar) 9, 84, 195–6
Colin, Francisco 15
Community-based health programs (CBHP) 1, 6–7, 71–9, 82, 86, 180, 194
Community-based monitoring system (CBMS) 129–131
Cordillera 6, 9, *45*, 190, 211
corporate food 58
corporations
   Alliance in Motion (AIM) Global 127, 140–2, *140*, 145–7, *146*, 154–5, *154*, 159, 164–74, 188
   ATC Healthcare Corporation 100
   Big Pharma 7
   DSM 88–91, *90*, 151n6
   Glomar Herbal Philippines Corporation 108
   Herbafarm 79
   Herbalife 156–7, 188
   Himalaya Drug Company 118
   Monde 41, 48
   Nature's Way 144
   Nissin 42–3
   Nutri-Foods 51–2
   Omnilife 157
   Pascual Laboratories 79–81
   Pfizer 50, 118–19, 185
   Unilever 52–5, *53*
   Usana 188
COVID-19 pandemic
   community pantries 204
   disruption caused by 36, 187, 206–7
   food supplements as 'protection' against 51, 110–14, *112*, 118, 187, 192, 205–8
   lockdown 8, 136, 198, 203, 211
cultural history xvii, 8
cupcakes 221, *222, 223*

Dayrit, Conrado 78–9
diet, local 6, 9, 26, 30, 35, 44, 53–5, 196

Direct Selling Association of the Philippines (DSAP) 155–6
drugs *see* medical treatment
disaster preparedness and food 205
Dumit, Joseph 127

Embodied Ecologies project 211–25
employment, earnings and working culture 50, 129–30, 150, 157, 162–7, 181
Ethnographic conversations 6
eucalyptus (*Eucalyptus globulus*) 183

fermented food 18, 195, 224
First Vita Plus
   demand for 11, 162
   distributors 126–7, 154–6, *154*, 159–64, *161, 164*, 169, 173–5; *see also* marketing; multi-level marketing
   health claims 28, 48, 91–2, 102, 119–20, 125, 132–40, *133, 137*, 149
   invention 9, 82–6
   marketing 51, 84, *84, 85*, 103, *126*, 127, *134, 135*, 138
   price 2, 136, 160–4, 188
fishing, destruction of 128–30, 162
flavour 11, 43, 197–200
Flavier, Juan 47, 81–2
food fortification 47–8, 58, 62
   Araw ng Sangkap Pinoy (Day of Filipino Ingredients, Micronutrients Day promoting fortification) 47
food packaging
   as advertising 6
   forever chemicals 60
   plastics 59
food supplements *see also* metabolic rifts and shifts; vitamins, minerals and trace elements
   Antangin 113
   ASCOF 80–1, *80*
   'black-seed' (Nigella sativa, black caraway, black cumin) 110–11, *112*, 118, 192
   C24/7 *see* C24/7

Cherifer 49, *49*, 94, 106
Choleduz 147–8
Clusivol 50
D-C Calcium 23
demand for 5–7, 25, 87, 91, 95–7, 186–7
First Vita Plus *see* First Vita Plus
GDetoxPlus 108, *109*
Generally Recognized As Safe (GRAS) 88
halal certification 125
health claims 87, 91, 95–108, 114–20, 120n1, 185–6
Lianhua Qingwen 110–11, 117, 192–3
Lola Remedios 111–14, *112, 114*
Mangosteen + Malunggay 104–5
Manna Plus 104–6, *105, 106*
marketing 20, 23, 76, 87, 96–104, *100, 105, 107*, 114, 127; *see also* marketing
micronutrients (micronutrient powder, (MNP) 27, 51–2, *52*, 85
MX3 189
Partysmart 118
price 127, 147–9
regulation and registration, lack of 115–16, *116*, 120n1, 149, 182–3
regulations on labelling, including use of the term 'gamot' 190–1
Robust 99–100, *100, 101*
spirulina 75, 108
Tolak Angin 112, *113*
Tuklas Lunas 92, *93*
Vida! and resVida 88–92, *89, 90*, 140, 147–8
vitamin C preparations *see* vitamins, minerals and trace elements, vitamin C
food, ultra-processed (UPF)
artificially flavored drinks (Tang) 18, 53, 65, 84, 131
biscuits, crackers and cookies 25, 39, 180
bread, white 25, 39, 53, 131, 180
breakfast cereals (cornflakes, sweetened) 18, 21, 25–6, 50, 180

canning 18, 187–8
carbonated drinks (sodas, soft drinks) 37, 44, 53–4, 65, 67, 180, 202
chips (crisps) 25, 54, 180
chocolate bars 18
coffee, instant 54, 68, *69*
definitions of xvi
fat content (trans, saturated) 26, 37, 44, 63, 131
fruit juice (fortified, sweetened) 21, 26, 53, 131, 180
hot dogs and burgers xiv–xv, 18, 47, 131
ice cream 180
instant noodles 25–6, 37–43, **40,** *41, 42,* 47–50, 53–4, 63, *64*, 131, 180, 191; *see also* WINA
introduction of *see* Philippines, colonial rule, American
margarine 21, *22*, 49
milk, evaporated 186
Muncher Green Peas 44, *44*, 57
nuggets 25, 180
packaging *see* packaging
salt content 26, 37, 41, 44, 52–3, 63, 131
soft drinks *see* carbonated drinks
Spam 18
sugar content 26, 37, 44, 52, 102, 193, 200
sweets and candies 37, 180
Foster, John Bellamy 3
foraging 10–11, 30n2, 206
Freire, Paolo 72
fruit, vegetables and root crops
ampalaya (*Momordica charantia*, bitter gourd, bitter melon) 9, 15, 50, 82, 136, 211, *212*
arrowroot (flour derived from *Manihot esculenta* in the Philippines) 9
attitudes to 39–40, 48, 54, 58
avocado *(Persea americana)* 75
banana (*Musa sapientum*) 9–10, 15, 64, 106, 127, 141, 205, *216*

fruit, vegetables and root crops (*cont.*)
  beans (*sigadilyas, sitaw*, mung beans) 10, **13**, 15, 40, 113, 199–202, 211, *213*
  cabbage 15
  carrot (*Daucus carota*) 46, 132–3
  cassava (*Manihot esculenta, kamoteng kahoy*) 10, 68, *68*, 211
  chlorella (a type of seaweed, *Chlorella* spp., used as a vegetable) 104
  corchorus (*Chorchorus olitorus*, jute, *sayote*) 83–5, 102
  corn (*Zea mays*) 10, 164, 205
  cucumber (*Cucumis sativus*) 15
  dalandan (*Citrus aurantium*, local citrus fruit) 50, 83–5, 102, *103*, 136
  eggplant (*Solanum melongena, talong,* aubergine) 10, **13**, 211
  fennel (*Foeniculum vulgare*) 108, 113
  guava (*Psidium guajava, bayabas*) 9, 75–6
  Indian screw tree (*Helicteres isora*) 113
  Job's tears (*Coix lachrymal jobi*) 10
  kalamansi (*Citrus x macrocarpa,* calamondin, local lime) 41, 50, 75–7, 127
  kamatsili (Pithecellobium dulce) 17
  kangkong (*Ipomea aquatica*, water spinach) 68
  katuray (*Sesbania grandiflora*) 17
  kamote (*Ipomea batatas,* sweet potato) 10, 50, 68, 83–4, 102, 135, 205, 213, 214
  kondol (*Benincasa hispida*) **13**
  kulitis (*Amaranthus spinosus*) 83–5, 102, 135
  lagundi (*Vitex negundo*) 15, *16*, 75–81, *78, 80*
  lentils **13**
  mango (*Mangifera indica*) 10, 13, 127–8, 141, 214, *214*
  mangosteen (*Garcinia mangostena*) 87, 92, *105*, 188
  millet (*Panicum milliaceum, kabog*) 10
  moringa (Moringa oleifera, *malunggay*) 9, 17, 46, *47*, 50, 83–5, 101–4, *104, 105*, 135, 164, 196
  mustard (*Brassica integrifolia, burong mustasa*) **13**, 108, 195
  mushrooms (Various species and types) 9, 108, 196
  okra (*Abelmoschus esculentus*) 211
  onion (*Allium cepa, sibuyas*) **13**, 65
  orange (various cultivars) 106, 195
  papaya (Carica papaya, used as a fruit and vegetable) 9–10, 46, 127, 141
  patola (*Luffa aegyptica*) **13**
  peas **13**
  petchay (*Brassica rapa*, Chinese cabbage) 216
  pineapple (*Ananas comosus*) 136
  plantain (*Musa paradisiaca*) 15
  radish (*Raphanus sativus*) **13**
  saluyot (*Corchorus olitorius*, jute mallow) 83–5, 135
  sayote (*Sechium edule*, chayote) *222*
  seaweed 92, 128
  spinach (*alugabati*) 40, 106, 132–3, 164
  squash and pumpkin 10, **13**, 15
  star apple (*Chyrosophyllum caimito, kaimito/caimito*) 13
  stevia 84
  taro (*Colocasia esculenta*, gabi) 10
  tamarind (*Tamarindus indica, sampalok*) 75–77
  tomato (*Solanum lycopersicum, kamatis*) **13**, 65
  turnip (*Brassica rapa*, subsp *rapa*) **13**
  upo (*Lagenaria siceraria*, bottle gourd) **13**
  yam (*Dioscorea* spp, *ube*) 205

glutathione 182–3
greenwashing 192
Guang Ming College 196, 223
Guatemala 57, 158
Guimaras 10

honey 54, 84, 113
Hagedorn, Edward 129
Hatch, Orrin 87, 190
Hines, Muneer 205–6
Hong Kong 172

illness and disease *see also* motherhood, childbirth, mental health problems
    allergies 145
    anaemia 23, 36–8, 50, 83–5
    angin (*hangin*) 114
    arthritis 85, 114, 136
    asthma 1, 30n4, 74–81, 137
    beri-beri (thiamine deficiency) 23, 48
    blindness 46, 86
    cancer xiv–xvi, 1, 18, 48, 59, 115, 125, 131, 137–9, 142–5, 219
    cardio-vascular conditions 18, 24, 39, 59, 117, 121n6, 131, *131*, 145, 180, 200
    cholera 15
    colic 74
    coughs and colds 24, 30n4, 75–81, 113–14, 132, 139, 183, 195
    COVID-19 *see* COVID-19 pandemic
    dementia 187
    dental caries 11
    diabetes 1, 4–5, 35–9, 59, 83, 87, 91, 115–17, 131–2, 145
    dysentery 15, 23
    dysmenorrhea 108
    endocrine disruption 59
    fever 76, 113, 136, 208
    gastrointestinal disorders 11, 15, 24, 75–6, 86, 113
    goitre 139, 160
    gout 202
    growth, stunted 38–40, **39**, 106, 115, 184
    headaches 15
    hemolysis 183
    hypertension 24, 35–9, 83–4, 88–91, 121n6, 132, 135
    infections 11, 15
    influenza (avian) 30n4, 75–7, 94n3
    iodine deficiency 36
    jaundice 23
    kidney disease 139
    lamig 114
    liver disease 108
    malaria 23, 74, *131*
    malnutrition 20, 23, 26, 35–6, 42, 46, 49, *49*, 57–8, 83, 128, 157, 180, 184–5
    masuk angin 98
    metabolic disorders 95, 106–9, 200
    obesity 5, 24, 35–8, 42, 59, 90, 131, 185
    over-nutrition 36
    premenstrual dysphoric disorder 118–19
    psoriasis 1, 137
    rheumatism 15, 85, 114
    rickets 23
    scurvy 23, 30–1n7
    sexual problems 94n3, 98–101, *100, 101*, 108, 117–19, 135–6, 142
    stroke 24, 39, 132
    tuberculosis 23, 74, *131*, 132, 136, 162
    ulcers 15
    urinary tract infection (UTI) 137
    vitamin deficiency 23–4, 36
India 5, 94n2
indigenous peoples and communities 8, 12, 202–3
    rice 45
    Palawan 128
    self-reliance 206
Indonesia 48, 98, 112–4, 118

Intergovernmental Panel on Climate Change (IPCC) 201
International Rice Research Institute 46

Japan 42
Javier, Emil 45

Kalinga 9, 83
Kellogg, John 20–3
Kimura, Aya Hirata 48
knowledge about plants, reconnecting and recollecting 74, 193

labour, forced 14–7
Landecker, Hannah 5
languages (Filipino, Tagalog) 77, 84, 94n3, 113–14, 125, 140, 190, 197
land
  lack of access to (appropriation) 4–5, 12, 16–17, 26, 130, 181
  ancestral 203
Leyte 86n
lifeboat ethics 68
Limpin, Arnel 140
Loakan-Apugan Sustainability and Livelihood Association (LASLA) 211–23, *218*
longue durée 26, 233n

macadamia nuts 196
Makati City 36
malnutrition *see* illness and disease, malnutrition
malt and chocolate-based drinks
  Hemo 22, 23
  Ovaltine 23
Manila, metropolitan 6, 14, 26, 54, 58–60, 63, 75–7, 96, 132, 138, 186
Manila galleon 14
Marcos (Ferdinand Marcos) regime, the 20, 62n3, 72, 83, 189
Marikina 64, 76
  community-based health programmes 77, 211–15

urban farming 216–24
organic farming 220–5
marketing
  AMWAY 154
  elderly people 172
  'nutraceuticals' 182
  packaging *see* packaging
  pyramid schemes 155–7, 168
Marx, Karl 2–3, 107
Maryknoll Sisters, the 75–7
meat, fish and dairy
  attitudes to 37, *41*, 205
  balao-balao (rice and shrimp) 195
  beef 23, 41
  butter 18, 21–2
  chicharon (pork crackling) 198
  chicken (*arroz caldo*, chicken porridge) 18, 141, 168
  eggs (chicken, quail or *kwek kwek*) 23, 64, 106, 205
  milk, cow 50, 106, 132–3
  milk, evaporated *see* food, ultra-processed, evaporated milk
  milk, formula 37, 191
medical treatment
  ayurvedic 94n2, 118
  CardioPulse 145–8, *147*
  Chinese (Traditional Chinese Medicine) 73–4, 110
  community health workers (CHWs) 72, 76
  cough syrups 7
  emergency 132, 161
  ephedra 110, 117, 193
  Galenic 15–16
  growth hormones 186; *see also* illness and disease, growth, stunted
  health, commodification of 8, 76
  intravenous infusions 183–4, 191–2, 199
  pharmaceuticals, Western 7
  price 132, 142, 158, 188
  selective primary healthcare (SPHC) 86
  self-medication 7, 16, 75

semaglutide (Ozempic, Wegovy) 5
Serafem (fluoxetine) 118–19
side effects of 136, 148, 171
total parenteral nutrition (TPN) 199–200
traditional practitioners (*albularyo*, 'barefoot', herbalists, shamans) 15, 18, 25, 71–9, 97, 179, 200–1, 207
Viagra 119, 136
medicinal plants
  angelica 99
  champaka (*Magnolia champaca* L.) 194
  Cnidium monnieri 99
  bacopa (*ulasimang-aso*) 188–9
  banaba (*Lagerstroemia speciosa*) 87, 188
  danshen (*Salvia miltiorrhiza*) 99
  endorsed by Philippine government (10 plants) 81–2
  Gingko biloba 99
  ginseng (Panax ginseng) 98–9, 99
  gotu cola (Centella asiatica, takip kohol) 113
  ilang-ilang (Cananga odorata L.) 194
  jamu (Indonesian compounded preparations) 98, 111–14
  panyawan (Tinospora rumphii, makabuhay) 96
Mendiola, Rolan, 133–6, *134, 137*
mental health problems
  depression 24
  anxiety, 183
  fatigue, 108, 113
  stress, 5, 24, 50, 85, 96, 130–2, 145–7, 181–3, 185, 187, 213
  nervousness 23–4, 86
metabolic rifts and shifts
  definitions 3–5, 14, 19
  diet, post-independence 18, 60, 180
  IV drips *see* medical treatments, intravenous infusions
  malnutrition *see* illness and disease, malnutrition
  plant sovereignty, loss of *see* plant sovereignty
  socio-metabolic work 157–8, 166, 173–5, 181
stoffwechsel 3
MIMAROPA 129
Mindanao 6, 19, 38, 108, 121n5, 189, 206
mint 113
Mintz, Sidney 19; *see also* sugar
Mongolia 118
Monteiro, Carlos 24, 199
Monthly Index of Medical Specialties (MIMS, formerly Philippine Index of Medical Specialties (PIMS)) 48–9, 191
Moore, Jason 3–4
motherhood
  childhood nutrition, maternal responsibility for (breastfeeding) 37–9, 51, 61, 75–7, 191
  pregnancy and childbirth 11, 39, 69, 74, 213
multi-level marketing (MLM) 28–9, 95, 125–7, 140, 148–50, 153–9, 166–70, 173–5, 181, 185, 188, 193; *see also* corporations, AIM Global
  recruitment 161–4
  and religion 157–8
  and social reciprocity 158
  as socio-metabolic labour 158
Muñoz 77
Muslims 110, 184, 192, 196

nata de coco 195–96
nata de piña 196
National Integrated Research Program on Medicinal Plants (NIRPROMP) 78–81
National Nutrition Survey (NNS) 36–7, 96
Negros 19–20, 209n5
neoliberalism 14, 48, 95, 158, 182, 193
neurogastronomy *see* flavour

non-communicable disease risk factor collaboration (NCD-RisC) 38
non-governmental organizations (NGOs) and charities
  Amazon Frontlines 207
  Global Witness 203
  Health Action Information Network (HAIN) 7, 75
  Health Action International 59
  LASLA *see* agriculture, cultivation and gardening
  Via Campesina 12
  World Neighbors 74
nutritionism 5, 20–5, 39, 57, 107, 128–32, 180

One Health 200
over-nutrition *see* illness and disease: over-nutrition
overseas workers, Filipino 172–3

packaging
  discarded 58, *58*
  forever chemicals (Per- and polyfluoroalkyl substances or PFAS) 60
  labels 95, *99, 100, 101, 103, 105, 112, 113, 114*
  plastics in (e.g. bisophenol) 59
palapa (condiments mixture) 196
Palawan 19, 120, 128, 160, 164, 171
Palawan State University 1–2, 125, 139, 169
panciteros 13
Papua New Guinea 43
Pauling, Linus 24
Pharmaseas project 92
Phlippine Plan of Action for Nutrition (PPAN) 51
Philippines
  biodiversity 9
  colonial rule, American 16–18, 71–3, 179, 189–90, 205
  colonial rule, Spanish 14–18, 25, 41, 71–3, 179, 189, 205
  Cordillera 6, 9, *45*, 190, 211
  Dangerous Drugs Board (DDB) 110
  Department of Education (DOE) 81
  Department of Environment and Natural Resources 200
  Department of Health 115–16
  Department of Science and Technology (DOST) 78, 86, 92, 120
  Department of Social Welfare and Development 215
  Department of Trade and Industry 155
  Department of Trade and Industry Administrative Order No. 8 155
  Federation of Natural Health and Environment Associations 82
  Food and Drug Administration (FDA) xvi, 27, 79, 91, 95, 110, 115–16, *116*, 120, 125, 182–3, 190–3
  Food and Nutrition Research Institute (FNRI) 36, 39, 44, 55, 192
  independence 18, 35, 179, 190
  National Academy of Science and Technology (NAST) 201–2
  National Federation of Women's Clubs 17, 208
  Philippine Institute of Traditional and Alternative Health Care (PITAHC) 81
  Philippine Medical Association 73, 82
  Philippine Society of Nutritionists and Dieticians 51, 53
phytochemicals 48, 78, 83–5, 88, 95, 102, 145
phytochemistry, lay 194
Pinggang Pinoy (go, grow, glow) 55, 56
planetary health 200
plant sovereignty 4, 8, 11, 197
  definitions 11–12, 209n8
  erosion of 4, 9, 29, 35, 54–7, 179–80, 184, 203
  reclamation of 211–25

'plantdemic' 29, 189, 204, 211, 215–16
plants, endangered 200
political ecology 184–7
pollution
  air 77, 108, 130–1
  concern about 5, 131, 185
  heavy metals 87, 117–18
  pesticides and fertilizers (soil) 87, 108, 117–18
  water 76, 108, 131, *212*, 215
prosperity gospel 157–8, 188
protein 23, 44, 61n3, 106
Puerto Princesa 1–4, 26, 51, 54, 88, 125–32, *131*, 140–8, *140, 141*, 159, 181

Quezon City 55, 204
Quiapo 6, 200

Ramos, President Fidel 82
re-articulation 118–19
red-tagging of environment groups 203
rice *see also* International Rice Research Institute
  brown 10, 44, *45*, 202
  puto (rice cakes) 195
  tapuy (rice wine) 195
  golden 46
  milling (white rice) 44–5, *45*, 202
  purple 202
  red 202
  trade in 13–15
Rice Enrichment Act (1952) 45
Rizal, Jose 14
Rodriguez, Mariel 182–3
Roxas (city) 162
royal jelly *99*

Sadanga 206
Sagada oranges, mislabeling of Chinese oranges 195
Saint Paul Subterranean River (Palawan) 129
Samar 86
San Jose 40

sari-sari stores (variety stores) 7, 44, *44*, 59–60, 64, *66*, 75–7, 218, *218*
sesame 13
'sin tax' 36, 68, *69*, 146, 193
Siekopai (indigenous people of Ecuador) 207
social media (Facebook, Instagram) xvi, 5, 170, 182–3, 187, 207, 217, *218*, 225; *see also* food supplements: demand for
social solidarity and justice 203–9
socio-metabolic framework, 2–5
Solomon, Harris 5
South Korea 38, 43
spices
  cardamom (*Elettaria cardamomum*) 113
  cinnamon (*Cinnamomum* spp.) 113
  clove (*Syzygium aromaticum*) 113
  chilli peppers (*Capsicum* spp. *sili*) 10, 41, *65*, 83–5, 102, 164, *164*, 211
  garlic (*Allium sativum*, bawang) 9, 13, 75, 108
  ginger (*luya*) 7, 10, 13, 15, 75–7, 108, 113, 205
  nutmeg (*moskada, Myristica fragrans*) 113
Sta. Maria, Felice Prudente 205
stevia 84
sugar
  basi (sugar cane wine) 195
  cane 10, 84, 102
  coconut sugar 84
  consumption of 19, 68, 77; *see also* food, ultra-processed, sugar content
  cultivation of (plantations) 16, 209n5; *see also* labour, forced
  industrialization of 19
  molasses 224
  prices and tariffs ('sin tax', trade tariffs, export) 19–20, 193, 202

'surplus health' 132; *see also* food supplements
Sweet Medicine (film) 133–5, 162, *164*, 182

Taal (volcano) 209n11
Tactacan-Tumpulan, Doyee 136
Tan, Dr Jaime Galvez ('Dok Jimmy') 1, 7, 48, 75, 82–6, *85*, 102, 125; *see also* First Vita Plus
Taga-Marikina Ako (TMA) 211–25, *212*
taste 197–8
tingi (retail sales of small volumes of commodities) 59–60, 75–7
tirtir (recooked food discards) 67
Tissot, Samuel 15
tourism 128–30
trade, precolonial global 12–14, 25
Traditional and Alternative Medicines Act (1997) 82
transplantation 13
Tuklas Lunas (discovering remedies, medicinal plants research programme) 92, 93

ub-ubo (Kakanaey term for working together) 217
under-nutrition *see* illness and disease, malnutrition
United Nations
    Educational, Scientific and Cultural Organization (UNESCO) 129
    Food and Agriculture Organization (FAO) 24, 30, 203
    United Nations International Children's Emergency Fund (UNICEF) 86, 184
    World Health Organization (WHO) 38, 82, 142
United States of America
    Christianity 150
    Dietary Supplement and Health Education Act (1994, 'Hatch Law') 27, 87, 190
    Environmental Protection Agency 117
    Food and Drug Administration (FDA) 117, 120, 190
    Federal Trade Commission (FTC) 156–7, 192
    Government Accounting Office 117
    Migration to 18, 188
    Philippines, colonial rule of *see* Philippines: colonial rule, American
University of the Philippines 190, 195, 206
usnea (lichens) 113

Van Tulleken, Chris 25
Venhoff, Ester 'Kim' 132–9, *138*, 163
vinegar (*suka*) 65, 195
vitamins, minerals and trace elements *see also* food supplements
    antioxidants 83
    calcium 23, 83–5, 102, 106, 132, 183, 224
    copper 50–1
    folic acid 51
    fortification 22, 25–6, 44, 48–50, 57, 61n3, 186, 191
    glutathione 182–4, 191–2
    history 23
    iodine 47; *see also* illness and disease, iodine deficiency
    iron 23, 46–50, 83, 102, 106, 132–3, 213, 224
    magnesium 144, 224
    phosphorus 85
    potassium 106, 224
    selenium 51
    taurine *99*
    thiamine (tiki-tiki) 23; *see also* illness and disease, beri-beri
    'vitamania' 8, 50; *see also* marketing
    vitamin A 23, 30n2, 46–50, 83–6, 132–3, 144, 149; *see also* illness and disease, vitamin deficiency
    vitamin B1 23, 47, 61n3
    vitamin B2 23

vitamin B6 (pyridoxine) 144
vitamin B12 (cobalamine) 23
vitamin C 23–4, 30n2, 44, 50–1, 102, 106, 110, 132–3, 144, 149, 164, 183–4
vitamin D 23, 47, 50, 110
vitamin G 23
zinc 50–1, 110

witchcraft 6
Werner, David 72
World Instant Noodles Association (WINA) 40–1; *see also* food, ultra-processed, noodles

Zamboanga City 111, 204–5

www.ingramcontent.com/pod-product-compliance
Lightning Source LLC
Chambersburg PA
CBHW050455250125
20677CB00025B/60